IMMIGRANT WORKERS

IMMIGRANT WORKERS

Their Impact on
American Labor Radicalism

GERALD ROSENBLUM

BASIC BOOKS, INC
Publishers
New York

© 1973 by Basic Books, Inc.

Library of Congress Catalog Card Number: 72-89280

SBN: 465-03207-9

Manufactured in the United States of America

73 74 75   10 9 8 7 6 5 4 3 2 1

PREFACE

Although much of the origin of modern sociology in the United States derives from the intensive investigation of immigrant groups in urban America, these concerns have waned with the passing of the immigrant presence in society. Yet, a phenomenon so massive as the movement of some thirty-five million people to America merits, I think, continuing attention in our attempts to understand the evolving character of the society. To attend to this subject, however, requires that an historical cast be given to our research—a cast that sociologists have not always been especially congenial to—though this approach also has a distinguished place in the discipline's lineage.

This book is an attempt to confront as problematic the unusually conservative characteristics of the American labor movement—often referred to as business unionism—that has long intrigued students of political protest and radicalism. I examine the impact of massive late-nineteenth and early-twentieth century immigration on the development of the posture of this movement during the course of vast economic change associated with modernization in the United States. At best, the conclusions must be seen as preliminary; the argument perhaps, and hopefully, provides a new avenue to understanding the subject. Though the nature of the argument is clear enough so that the terms of its refutation are readily apparent, the position is stated in its way not only to provide detractors with a large target but also to permit subsequent, more detailed, probings and refinements in particular times and places.

It is important to emphasize that as a sociological study, the present work attempts to fashion an argument and to bring evidence together for that purpose. Students interested in a sequential account of the events this study seeks to explain are advised to look elsewhere. Present purposes do not involve the beginning-to-end narrative of the period in question. This function has been performed by numerous authors. In other words, the data are old, but, if this book is worth anything, the explanation for them is new and its implications will affect the character of further inquiry.

Preface

It is clear enough that the task of this study is not the accumulation of "fresh" data, but the scrutiny of evidence for the purpose of developing the theoretical point of view that is set out. Needless to say, some new sources (for sociologists) of factual material have been researched in the interest of adequately bridging "knowledge gaps" and comprehensively surveying information that was relevant to the purpose at hand. In the present work, though, the argument is the thing and the evidence has been assessed in the light of this "thing." Any other claim for a book of this length that attempts to weave together three major strands of American history—immigration, labor, and economics—over a span of several decades, would be presumptuous if not preposterous.

The components of the position taken in this book developed from a variety of theoretical writings. My debt here is extensive and I hope that my somewhat compulsive footnoting will provide indication of it. I would like explicitly to thank Wilbert E. Moore for his personal generosity as well as his intellectual guidance while I worked out and developed the argument presented here. Marion J. Levy, Jr., also provided considerable assistance during this early period. Robert A. Lively was most helpful in steering me toward relevant historical materials. Julia Blodgett Curtis has lent the counsel of a labor historian and close friend while monitoring the progress of this project. I am indebted to Robert K. Merton for a series of discussions as a result of which I was able to confront, more clearly, the nature of my task. Thanks are due also to Derek L. Phillips who read and commented on a draft of the lengthy first chapter of this book. Barbara Rosenblum, my wife, shared the burden of much of the final preparation of the manuscript while providing invaluable intellectual insights that have been of profound benefit.

I assume full responsibility, including omissions, deficiencies, and errors in this work. I emphasize this point only because not everyone with whom I have consulted has been in total, or even partial agreement with me.

1973   GERALD ROSENBLUM

CONTENTS

1   The Labor Movement and the Labor Force   1

2   Emigration: The European Push   45

3   Immigration: The American Pull   55

4   Discontinuity, Mobilization, and Social Origins   87

5   Immigration and the Decline of Renovation   121

6   The Immigrant and Business Unionism   143

7   Summary and Conclusions   173

    Index   181

IMMIGRANT WORKERS

1
The Labor Movement and the Labor Force

An almost classic preoccupation among analysts of American society has been the failure of that society to generate a radical working class in pursuit of socialist goals. The present study will deal with one aspect of this broader concern. It will address itself to the somewhat unique posture of organized labor — often designated business unionism — that has come to be a chief characteristic of the American labor movement.

More specifically, the focus here will be on the characteristics of the labor force at the onset of rapid modernization in the United States during the post-Civil War period, especially the 1880's through World War I, and the influence these characteristics had on the shaping of the labor movement. The central consideration will be the major contribution European immigration, in augmenting the American labor force, made in this area. Thus, the problem that will inform this study throughout may be briefly stated as follows: *What were the consequences of the introduction of relatively large numbers of immigrants into American society for the system of industrial relations that came to prevail in this country?*

It will be argued that immigration contributed to the institutionalization of business unionism by (1) muting the strains created by the rapid changes in social structure accompanying modernization, and (2) giving rise to a large segment of the labor force whose exposure to American society tended to be limited primarily to the work setting. The task of the present chapter will be to explore and elaborate theoretical considerations that have a bearing on the American labor movement and to develop the case for the two-pronged argument mentioned.

In examining the problem posed, recruitment and commitment of the blue-collar segment of the industrial labor force during the onset of modernization in the United States will be emphasized in some detail. It is proposed here that the character of a labor movement is, to a large extent, determined by the manner in which workers first confront, and respond to, the strains generated by the inception of rapid modernization. As elaborated below, how this in fact takes place tends to shape subsequent developments in the evolving labor movement.[1] Galenson asserts:

Trade unionism is peculiar to modern industrial society; its rise is attributable to forces activated by industrialization. The growth, structure, and ideology of the labor movement of any country are conditioned by the nature of the industrialization process; that is, by the character of the society in which industry first took root and by the tempo and direction of industrial development. This is not to say that political and cultural factors are not important. On the contrary, they may be decisive in determining the precise lines of trade union growth at a given time. But the dynamic element, in terms of which one may obtain the deepest insight into trade unionism, appears to be the complex events subsumed under the concept of industrialization.[2]

During the course of recruitment to new modes of production in a radically altered social setting, resistances may well be registered by those who resent the new circumstances in which they find themselves. Workers who are committed, or partially committed, to new forms of production, on the other hand, may not eschew disruptive behavior *within* the new system if they feel that the rewards deriving from that system are inequitably distributed. "The process of commitment to an occupational group such as a union has the indirect consequence of involving the transitional worker in the industrial way of life, even if the specific group orientation is one of conflict."[3] It would appear, then, that unions may prove a useful focus of investigation within a modernizing society in assessing commitment to the new forms of production as well as to the specific manner in which these forms are introduced. This then suggests an inquiry into the features of the recruitment of industrial labor.

In examining the history of modern industrial development in American society and the nature of the labor force recruited to occupy the new establishments, one is struck by the coincidence of high levels of immigration during the period when the transition to relatively modernized production was occurring. It is one of the unique features of American modernization that substantial portions of the labor force which helped to carry it through *were not indigenous to American society.* Kuznets and Rubin suggest that: "In few other nations, perhaps in none of major industrial rank, has immigration played so large a role in augmenting population as in the United States."[4] They go on to assert that "immigration was such an important factor both in the intensive growth of the country's economy and its relations with the rest of the world; to visualize the course of events without it is beyond the imagination of the analyst."[5] In short, immigration made a difference in the course of American social change as related to modernization and a specific problem has hence been chosen here from the infinite variety of influences that immigration may have exerted. As Schlesinger states: "In a large sense, all American history has been the product of migratory movements from the Old World."[6] The problem selected here, and stated at the outset, is one of seeking to discover the influence of these "migratory movements" on labor relations in the United States during a crucial phase of its economic development.

Business Unionism

The United States presents a rather singular variation in the nature of its labor unions when compared to other societies that have undergone modernization relatively early and under the aegis of capitalist entrepreneurs. As Gulick and

Bers put it: "The emergence of a 'job conscious' labor movement in the United States was a phenomenon almost unique in labor history."[7] According to these authors, the unique features of the American labor movement may be summed up as follows:

... (1) the renunciation of any broad program of social reorganization designed to improve the status and economic condition of the group involved; (2) the renunciation of political activity in a predominantly "labor" party as a major weapon for the institution of such a program or, at least, for the economic betterment of the group involved; and (3) possibly only a corollary of the first item in this series, apparent contentment with the existing framework of economic institutions and relationships which reserves to another group ("businessmen") the privilege of making many of the crucial decisions for the community as a whole in the vital spheres of output and employment.[8]

Following the work of Hoxie, the designation business unionism has been assigned to the American case. According to this author,

It is essentially trade conscious, rather than class conscious. That is to say, it expresses the viewpoint and interests of the workers in a craft or industry rather than those of the working class as a whole. It aims chiefly at more, here and now, for the organized workers of the craft or industry, in terms mainly of higher wages, shorter hours, and better working conditions, regardless for the most part of the welfare of the workers outside the particular organic group; and regardless of political and social considerations, except insofar as these bear directly upon its own economic ends. It is conservative in the sense that it professes belief in natural rights, and accepts as inevitable, if not just, the existing capitalistic organization and the wage system, as well as the existing property rights and the binding force of the contract. It regards unionism mainly as a bargaining institution and seeks its ends chiefly through collective bargaining, supported by such methods as experience from time to time indicates to be effective in sustaining and increasing its bargaining power.[9]

This type of unionism is basically oriented to the immediate work context, and its members seek improvements as deriving from this context. Wages, hours, and other working conditions within the productive enterprise are the essence of the objectives of business unionism. Such unions, then, place overriding emphasis on the economic aspect of social action.

Business unionism under conditions of capitalist enterprise, as Hoxie has pointed out, is most likely to affect the crafts[10] and, therefore, such unions have appeared in other societies as well as the American. Complex skills, which are often strategic in the process of production (and thereby not easily substituted for), may often be the basis of union formation. Where skills and strategic position in a system of production go hand in hand, a great deal of bargaining leverage may be exerted by those who occupy such roles. "The withdrawal of the services of these relatively few men almost immediately compels, for technological reasons, the complete shutting down or diversion of operations of the plant."[11]

Business unions, then, associated with craft skills, have emerged in other societies than the United States although foreign unions are generally regarded as having a distinctly different form of unionism than the American. Thus, in England:

> ... local grouping by craft was the logical structure for the early unions. They were almost without exception composed of skilled men, who would meet regularly in somewhere like a pub to decide on matters of common interest in their craft. Such matters would have included apprenticeship training, the rate for the job, provident benefits and even unemployment pay — but for their own members only. These men were concerned, fairly enough, first with consolidating their own position and then, as their members travelled around and met similar groups of craftsmen in other districts, with forming loose federations to improve the position of their craft as a whole. They had no interest in letting less skilled members join the union; rather the reverse. For the rationale of the craftsmen's union was to control a scarce and vital element of production — skill. By means of long apprenticeship courses and fixed ratios of apprentices to journeymen, the union limited the number who possessed the skill and thus kept its price up on the labour market. To have let in the less skilled would have meant flooding the market and would thus have reduced the very large differential (much larger than it is today) which the craftsmen in the nineteenth century was paid above the unskilled worker. It is indeed an open question whether craft unionism much raised the standard of the working class generally. For while it served a small group well, it did so in part by denying jobs to other workers who, though debarred from the craft union, might have been quite able to do some of the craftsman's work.[12]

While Hoxie identified craft unions with business unionism, he indicated that industrial unions (whose members are all engaged in work on one or a specified set of related products regardless of occupational role) "tend to be class conscious, socialistic, and theoretical."[13] Nevertheless, he asserted that such were only tendencies, and the goals attached to unions were not necessarily related to type of membership unit (i.e., craft or industrial). Thus, Ross notes that, although the emergence of American industrial unions involved "political action on a somewhat broader front," their goals appeared to remain the same as those of their craft union predecessors.

If primary reliance upon collective bargaining and a belief in "industrial partnership" under capitalism can be regarded as central features of business unionism, then the advent of industrial unions has not brought any essential change. Business unionism is still the dominant strain in the American labor movement.[14]

Stable union organizations that included somewhat less-skilled members emerged in the thirties, well after the United States might safely be characterized as a relatively modernized society. These unions ultimately gave evidence of a membership committed not only to modern productive relationships but also to the specific capitalist mode on which they were based. American unionists are primarily oriented toward gains accruing from the existing work context, not to altering the basic structural features of that context. When such alterations are sought, e.g., when private ownership and control of productive capital is challenged, the political aspect assumes a relatively greater salience in the patterning of union activities.

This is not to say that American unionists attach no importance to the political aspect of action; only that this has, over time, been relegated to a subordinate concern, with primary attention given to the "pure and simple" objectives of wages, hours, and conditions within the work context. Unions, then, are class related but may not necessarily be class conscious, as that term is generally used.

Cyriax and Oakshott's observations on British and American unions provide an example of the differing salience of the political aspect in a European movement. The Labor Party in Britain came into being in large measure through the activities of unionists. Most major unions are affiliated with that party and the fact that they supply an important source of party membership and funds accounts for the large role unionists play in determining party policy. Labor candidates for office frequently run under the direct sponsorship of the unions. Although it is true that many union leaders are antagonistic to party activities,

... the fact still remains that the British unions are "in politics" in a sense in which their United States counterparts are definitely not. Their leaders still subscribe to a large body of Socialist objectives which can only be achieved through political action. They or their predecessors were the signatories of Clause 4 of the 1918 constitution of the Labour Party, which defines the aims of the movement in terms of public ownership of the means of production, distribution and exchange. In America, by contrast, there is no distinct set of political beliefs superimposed on the informal working arrangements between the unions and the Democratic Party. Formally, therefore, the A.F.L.-C.I.O. is not affiliated to any party, and only tends to become involved in actual politics when anti-union legislation is in the air. On such occasions there may be temporary alliances between the unions and a political party; but they will only be temporary.[15]

The likelihood of craft union emergence and the relatively conservative character of their goals indicate that those more favorably positioned during the course of modernization are, on the one hand, most likely to be committed to the general structural features of modern productive enterprise and, on the other, less likely to challenge the prevailing capitalist features of such enterprise within the context of modernization. This is but a specification of a long-standing generalization to the effect that the more highly located the individual relative to scarce values, the less likely will he be to challenge either the values or the structural arrangements relative to approaching them. Hence, commitment may be expected first from those whose accessibility to such values remains or becomes relatively favorable. Those less favorably positioned or whose position in the preexisting context is subverted as a result of changed circumstances are likely, in the latter case, to resist and, in the former case, to demand an altered form of organization as the process continues.

The Danish and Norwegian experiences, as examined by Galenson, are instructive. Danish modernization did not occur rapidly, and large-scale productive organizations were still quite rare by the turn of the century. Unions were mainly of the craft type and primarily oriented to business union objectives.[16]

Though nominally Marxist, Danish socialism was, from the beginning gradualist. It was nurtured in a political milieu devoid of state repression, and derived much of its support from well-situated craftsmen who had achieved substantial economic results through the method of collective bargaining. . . . Dominance by the skilled workers was due in no small measure to the fact that craft unionism was already firmly established when political socialism began to grow. The workers looked upon political action as a means of supplementing union economic power in the daily struggle for better conditions of labor, and not for achieving any social millenium through radical change.[17]

In Norway, however, modernization proceeded quite rapidly, with industrial unions quickly superseding craft types as the dominant worker association.

The ideological history of the Norwegian labor movement is diametrically opposed to that of Denmark. The explosive industrialization of the country, recruitment of industrial workers from small farms without previous experience in steady employment, and the poor working and living conditions they found in the hastily constructed industrial towns, all contributed to the formation of an extreme, radical ideology, matched by few others in Europe.[18]

It appears that, in each case noted, the extension of modernization and large-scale productive organizations resulted in the giving way of exclusive craft unions, generally conservative in orientation, to the more inclusive industrial ones, generally more radical in orientation, and a subsequent formation of a labor party, in large measure oriented to the goals of a working-class constituency. Early dominance of the more conservative craft unions is associated with the less "politicized" nature of the labor movement as a whole. The subsequent industrial recruitment of relatively less-skilled industrial workers, and the emergence of industrial unions, generally alter the picture in varying degrees.

As indicated earlier, this did not occur in the United States. Industrial unions followed the lead of their craft union predecessors in being primarily of the business union type. Again, the focus of the problem here will be to examine this unique feature of the American labor movement when compared to almost all other societies that have undergone modernization relatively early and under the sponsorship of capitalist entrepreneurs.

Levels of Generalization and Social Discontinuity

An apparent disparity of views concerning the modernization of societies arises with reference to the problem under consideration. The following quotation from Levy points up one of the views. Concerning the distinction between relatively nonmodernized and relatively modernized societies, he states:

In terms of social structure highly relevant for problems of international affairs in particular, and social analysis in general, any two cases well on either side of this classification have more in common with one another than any one of them has with a case well on the other. Despite the fact that modern English society clearly developed out of thirteenth-century English society, thirteenth-century English society has more in common with the society of the Trobriand Islanders in more respects relevant both to international affairs and general social analysis than thirteenth-century English society has in common with modern English society.[19]

Feldman and Moore, however, have emphasized the specific qualities or "historical legacies" of individual societies and the influence that these legacies have had on their "trajectory" of change:

Some elements of any preindustrial culture or social system cannot accompany industrialization. These represent impediments or required changes. Yet we can go one step further. The inconsistent elements of preindustrial systems do not simply disappear, lost without trace. Rather, if industrial development does continue, they become attenuated, partially suppressed, partially adapted to changes in the core structure. But by their persistence, they constitute a continuing source of tension, a focus of social problem solving, a challenge to scholars and administrators alike who want the system tidy. The solutions, we suggest, are always partial, and always have further consequences that in turn provide new points of tension.[20]

As hinted at by Levy ("modern English society clearly developed out of thirteenth-century English society") and in a quotation from the authors just cited ("industrial societies share a core set of social structures that together provide a kind of extended operational definition of industrialism"[21]), the difference in the two points of view is more apparent than real and rests on the level of generalization on which the investigator is theorizing. It may be illustrated by paraphrasing the foregoing Levy quotation in two ways. A relatively modernized society, say Japan, is substituted for the Trobriand Islanders:

1. Modern English society has more in common with modern Japanese society in more respects relative to general social analysis than to thirteenth-century Engligh society.
2. Modern English society has more in common with thirteenth-century English society in more respects relative to general social analysis than to thirteenth-century Japanese society.

The first statement has to do with *discontinuities* involved in modernization and is on a more general level. That is to say, it involves alterations in social structure applicable to all societies undergoing modernization regardless of the antecedents specific to each taken individually. The expression "discontinuities" means that certain patterns of action, generally characteristic of relatively nonmodernized societies, will cease to be operative as modernization proceeds. The functions which previous patterns entailed may remain but they are carried out in a different manner. Thus, for example, there occurs, during modernization, a shift of substantial portions of socialization from the family context to formal organizations expressly constituted for such ends.

The second statement has to do with *continuities* involved in modernization and is on a less general level. That is to say, it emphasizes elements carried forward into the relatively modernized setting which are peculiar to the structural antecedents of the society in question. Thus, although Japanese and English society may present similarities with reference to the above-mentioned socialization aspect, they display striking differences when the operations of the two systems are compared in further detail with one another.

The truism that modern English society is the descendant of the same system of an earlier epoch expresses the fact that historical legacies and the tensions generated by their "obsolescence," plus the manner in which such tensions are handled, provide the identifying qualities of any given society for an observer. Higher-level considerations are what provide us with the explanations for the likely emergence of tensions during the course of modernization. They point to the profound structural changes (discontinuities) that any society that undergoes modernization will experience. Lower-level considerations provide us with the detailed information of concrete cases as the changes are confronted and dealt with in terms of the specific system that is subject to them (continuities).

In the present study, we will be concerned with tensions generated by modernization which the members of any society must confront. These general considerations will provide the framework within which the specific American experience will be assessed. The manner in which these strains were dealt with in the United States, and the peculiarities of its historical circumstances which influenced the handling of these problems, will provide the detailed ingredients of the present analysis.

Social Stratification, "Social Class," and Modernization

The present section will consider several of the elements involved in the mobilization to radical action of deprived sectors of the population in the course of modernization. We will address the changing nature of men's legitimate demands as regards the reward hierarchy and the discrepancies that are likely to be experienced between such demands and the prospects for their fulfillment.

Where patterned inequalities exist relative to scarce rewards, the term social stratification is applicable. The discontinuous nature of stratification systems as between relatively modernized societies and relatively nonmodernized ones provides a focal point of strain when any given society undergoes the transition. Since individual access to scarce rewards is, as a society modernizes, increasingly contingent on one's role in large-scale productive organizations, occupation will be the primary indicator through which stratification will be observed.

Weber early recognized the importance of large-scale organizations in modern society in his development of the concept of "bureaucracy."[22] In stressing the administrative functions performed in such settings, he opened up an area of more general relevance, for many of the elements applicable to administrative roles equally pertain to "operating personnel."

The Labor Movement and the Labor Force

The extensive division of labor involved in modern production adduces different criteria for social placement and valuation from those which are typical in relatively nonmodernized productive contexts. The emphases are on rationality (means are selected on the basis of their empirically demonstrable utility in approaching ends), universalistic membership criteria (all with relevant abilities for the purposes at hand may be considered for access), and functional specificity (precisely defined and delimited obligations). By contrast, the relatively nonmodernized case generally emphasizes the nonrational (stress on custom or nonempirical powers), the particularistic (the nature of a person's relationships regardless of their relevance for the role under consideration), and functionally diffuse patterns (vaguely defined obligations).[23]

Such changes are bound to occur during modernization regardless of the auspices under which the process takes place. Again, Weber makes the point with respect to his focus on bureaucracy:

The primary source of superiority of bureaucratic administration lies in the role of technical knowledge which, through the development of modern technology and business methods in the production of goods, has become completely indispensable. In this respect, it makes no difference whether the economic system is organized on a capitalistic or socialistic basis. Indeed, if in the latter case a comparable level of technical efficiency were to be achieved, it would mean a tremendous increase in the importance of specialized bureaucracy.[24]

The concentration of productive roles in large-scale organizations was a major consideration in the work of Marx as well. For him, an important function of such circumstances would be the greater visibility of differential rewards combined with an enhanced potential for communication among those in similar positions. Marx claimed that similarly circumstanced individuals would perceive their common condition and move collectively toward the attainment of common ends.[25] It was one of his major contentions that the closeness of sets of individuals sharing common opportunities would lead to the emergence of differentiated subsystems of action oriented primarily around the allocation of scarce rewards, above and beyond the systems in terms of which they initially came into contact.

This was what Marx conceived of as a "class." It is important that, for him, a class denoted a concrete structure or membership unit characterized by a distinct set of patterns and not merely a set of similarly positioned individuals giving rise to the structure.

The separate individuals form a class only insofar as they have to carry on a common battle against another class; otherwise they are on hostile terms with one another as competitors. On the other hand, the class in its turn achieves an independent existence over against the individuals, so that the latter find the conditions of existence predestined, and hence have their position in life and their personal development assigned to them by their class, become subsumed under it.[26]

Marx's analysis of modernization, carried out amid capitalism, led him to predict a growing economic polarization between a large class of propertyless wage-workers and their employers. Mechanization would produce a skill-stripped, homogeneous set of impoverished laborers in distinct contrast to the growing economic potency of those who concentrated, into ever fewer hands, the means of production. At its most developed degree, capitalism would be done away with when workers, driven by their material circumstances, appropriated productive property, thereby dispensing with the institutions that were the source of their deprivation. The initially economic orientation of the working class would shift, ultimately, to a more political character specifically aimed at government through which capitalist hegemony had been maintained. A political party was the ultimate expression of working-class action.[27] For Marx, then, a class was not a group of similarly circumstanced individuals relative to the economic aspects of stratification, but rather a *social structure* resulting from given conditions of inequality.

Weber, on the other hand, took the concept of class to mean strata or sets of individuals who shared similar economic circumstances. In his usage of the term, class presented a *possible* basis for "communal action" (or the emergence of a "class" in the Marxian sense) which was problematic and not given. Weber's view, together with an apparent aside on Marx, is indicated in this manner:

> Thus every class may be the carrier of any one of the possibly innumerable forms of "class action," but this is not necessarily so. In any case, a class does not in itself constitute a community. To treat "class" conceptually as having the same value as "community" leads to distortion. That men in the same class situation regularly react in mass actions to such tangible situations as economic ones in the direction of those interests that are most adequate to their average number is an important and after all simple fact for the understanding of historical events. Above all, this fact must not lead to that kind of pseudo-scientific operation with the concepts of "class" and "class interests" so frequently found these days, and which has found its most classic expression in the statement of a talented author, that the individual may be in error concerning his interests but that the "class" is "infallible" about its interests.[28]

Weber here appears to be compounding his own usage of the term "class" with that of Marx. Whereas Weber uses the term to mean similar economic circumstances that individuals come to share, Marx uses it as a *structural outcome* of such circumstances. As Marx's statement (above) indicates, separate individuals in the same economic category are not ipso facto a "community." He predicted such an outcome as a result of capitalistic enterprise and termed *the result* a class.[29]

It is with respect to this outcome rather than with conceptual wranglings that Weber's analysis and criticisms are of major sociological relevance. Weber questioned the inevitability of "community" formations and asserted that, if formed, their functions would be variable. Thus, both class formation (in the Marxian sense) and the extent of conflict endemic in such structures were seen as problematic. Weber suggested that perception relative to economic differentials as based on a given order was a crucial intervening factor:

> For however different life chances may be, this fact in itself, according to all experience, by no means gives birth to "class action" (communal action by the members of a class). The fact of being conditioned and the results of the class situation must be distinctly recognizable.[30]

Inequalities alone do not necessarily give rise to communal action. Gross inequalities as to scarce rewards may be a condition for communal action but they are not a sufficient condition. As Moore suggests:

> Polarization . . . is the key indicator of incipient revolution. It is, however, only an indicator and no more causes revolution that [sic] the thermometer causes temperature.[31]

Moore goes on to suggest that a deterioration in circumstances provides a clue.

It is here that an important distinction in social science may be appropriately introduced. It concerns ideal and actual patterns. Ideal patterns that are institutionalized refer to those regarded as "right and proper" by the members of a society. Actual patterns refer to those conditions that do in fact prevail.[32] Complete coincidence between the two is rare, if not impossible. Divergence, however, between the ideal and the actual provides a focal point of strain in any social system, and the greater the divergence the greater the probability that purposive social action will be generated toward bringing the two into closer correspondence.[33]

Patterns having to do with scarce rewards provide excellent substantiation for these remarks. Merton's analysis of deviant behavior is instructive here:

> "Poverty" is not an isolated variable which operates in precisely the same fashion wherever found; it is only one in a complex of identifiably interdependent social and cultural variables. Poverty as such and consequent limitation of opportunity are not enough to produce a conspicuously high rate of criminal behavior. Even the notorious "poverty in the midst of plenty" will not necessarily lead to this result. But when poverty and associated disadvantages in competing for the culture values approved for *all* members of the society are linked with a cultural emphasis on pecuniary success as a dominant goal, high rates of criminal behavior are the normal outcome . . . When we consider the full configuration — poverty, limited opportunity and the assignment of cultural goals — there appears some basis for explaining the higher correlation between poverty and crime in our society than in others where rigidified class structure is coupled with *differential symbols of success*.[34]

The discussion thus far has served to indicate that "class" formation is problematic and depends on a common perception, by a given stratum, of disadvantage relative to some standard. When a deterioration with respect to this standard occurs, concerted actions to "correct" the situation are likely. Again, this is not to say that standards and actualities coincide or are even always closely related. Acceptable limits may be wide of the ideal mark. But an apparent rapid further divergence is likely to call forth concerted action toward the ideals. Merton's discussion of deviancy is of value because he implicitly suggests two types of such action. He notes that a "rigidified class structure" is associated with differentiated ideal patterns appropriate to each stratum. Conversely, a less rigidified class structure, as exemplified in the United States, is accompanied by relatively uniform ideal patterns throughout the stratification hierarchy. Thus Levy indicates:

It might be suggested as a useful hypothesis that societies that have, ideally speaking, open class systems are more likely to have a single ideal class type, whereas those with ideally closed class systems are likely to have a specific ideal class type corresponding to each of the closed class distinctions.[35]

A system of differentiated ideal patterns appropriate to separate strata need not thereby preclude the possibility of "communal action." The not-infrequent occurrence of peasant revolts throughout history provides a useful example. The important feature of many such uprisings was that they were not genuinely revolutionary in nature. They were not directed at altering the basis of inequality as between strata in the society. Rather, they were an affirmation of traditionally expected ideal patterns accruing to a given stratum which were being violated. Thus, in the Japanese case during the feudal period:

More conservative acts of violence have never been witnessed as far as general change is concerned. These revolts were overwhelmingly oriented to redress of specific wrongs viewed as improper given the ideal structures. Even when the peasants had sufficient power at their command to demand and get redress of their grievances, they did not seek to go further and alter the ideal status quo.[36]

The striking feature of these insurrections was that they were not a repudiation of institutions providing inequality but rather of divergences from previously accorded patterns ensuring "appropriate" rewards for occupants of a given stratum as such. Weber sums up the point intended here when, in discussing conflict between subjects and traditional authority holders, he states:

When resistance occurs, it is directed against the person of the chief or of a member of his staff. The accusation is that he has failed to observe the traditional limits of his authority. Opposition is not directed against the system as such.[37]

The mobilization of a stratum into a class (in the Marxian sense), as a result of divergences between ideal prescriptions and actualities, may occur even if the ideals apply differentially throughout the stratification system. These considerations have a related but differing relevance during the onset of modernization.

The discontinuity in social structure that is associated with modernization has been noted. The severity of the departures from a relatively nonmodernized social structure will provide a grievance basis for those who have been previously socialized in the nonmodern setting. Insofar as previously institutionalized expectations are violated, concerted efforts may well be made to reaffirm their legitimacy. Thus, the actualities of modernization diverge from the ideals em-

The Labor Movement and the Labor Force

bodied in a relatively nonmodernized setting.

This period in which members of the society still attest to the viability of traditional institutions, in the face of sharply divergent actualities, may be designated for present purposes as a "transitional stage." It has been claimed that once this stage is under way, it is irreversible and subversive of previously existing social structures.[38] But "holding actions," so to speak, on the part of a labor force whose traditional expectations are no longer being realized, are quite significant. Such actions themselves become a legacy conditioning the direction of the ensuing labor movement after commitment to the new forms of production has been attained.

Referring to the ideal-actual divergences experienced by workers as a "grievance gap," Siegal suggests an ultimate change in "directionality."

Over time, these grievance gaps will change with variations in either the "what is" or the "what should be." Significant shifts in the yardstick of the "what should be" will reshape satisfactions and disatisfactions; marked changes in the "what is" may disturb established norms or redefine new reference points.[39]

Discontent will impart to its protest expression a directional dimension. Protest of the present may look either to the past or to the more or less immediate future as a normative guide. Backward looking protest is defensive. The "what is" is found wanting with reference to the "what has been" and is fought off. Forward looking protest is more aggressive. The "what is" is projected into the "what could be" and is fought for. The former is essentially a conservative or retrogressive response to recent violation of tradition; the latter a reformist or radical expression of the desire to depart from tradition.[40]

Bendix's remarks on the British experience provide an instance of the "backward looking protest" suggested by Siegal.

Industrialization threatened and frequently destroyed the traditionalism of labor. In protesting against this disruption of their way of life large masses of English peasants and workers were aroused to concerted action by an endeavor to reclaim their lost position in society. Under the pressure of great suffering the leaders of the various working-class movements tended to embellish the traditional position of the people with nostalgic references to the "good old days." The contrast with present hardships and the emotional failings of memory inevitably gave a romantic glow to the harsh realities of the past. But this appeal to hallowed traditions only serves to emphasize that the workers' social protest against the effects of industry consciously relied upon images of traditionalism while the forceful creation of a nonagricultural work force gradually undermined the practices which these images idealized.[41]

Such behavior is quite in line with the peasant uprisings discussed above. Workers sought not to undo their subordinate position but to reaffirm the institutions which governed it. The major *difference*, however, lies in the fact that modernization is not a permutation of a traditionalized system of action but a sustained movement away from ideal patterns associated with such a system. From the point of view of the present discussion, the primary function of "communal action" oriented toward the preexisting ideals, though doomed, is that it *mobilizes* those in disadvantaged positions to concerted action and thus provides a more or less organized basis through which altered ideals might be approached.

This is not an empirically uniform process and often involves dualities among those who, within their life span, experience the transition. A key element in this transition is the ultimate commitment to emergent ideals arising along with the actualities of modernization. And one important feature of commitment to a modernized setting is an "open class" system of social stratification. Compared to the differentiated system of ideal patterns as related to scarce rewards in the premodern setting, a uniform system comes to be instituted whereby all are encouraged to vie for valued goals. As Bendix puts it:

It is the mark of all traditional authority-relations that the people are prevented from emulating the qualities of their masters. Yet this emulation is the idea which emerges with the development of industry. Nothing is more characteristic of the entrepreneurs who take the initial lead in this development than the invitation to the people at large to do likewise. In this respect the leadership of the early English entrepreneurs and of the revolutionary vanguard during the years following the Russian Revolution of 1917 have much in common. Both groups elaborated an ideal code of personal conduct which they claimed to exemplify themselves and which they held up to the people as the model that should be followed.[42]

The prospect of improving one's position relative to scarce rewards by upward mobility is a chief characteristic of modernization. The predominance of universalistic criteria of social placement renders this a viable goal for all members of the system and a required feature for the successful operations of a modern society.[43]

Not only does the possibility of altering one's location come to the fore; rising standards of well-being among those in fixed positions as a result of the growing "homogenization" of such standards across the boundaries of strata also become apparent. Hence, one may expect an increase in *ideals* calling for an augmented rate of *upward mobility of men* and an accelerating rate of *downward mobility of scarce rewards.*

It is in the presence of such conditions, then, where the ideals of access to scarce rewards are severely divergent from ongoing actualities, that those who are deprived will exhibit greater deviancy. Thus, in an open class system, Merton argues, greater rates are to be expected from those in the lowest strata.

Despite our persisting open-class ideology, advance toward the success-goal is relatively rare and notably difficult for those armed with little formal education and few economic resources. The dominant pressure leads toward gradual attenuation of legitimate, but by and large ineffectual, strivings and the increasing use of illegitimate, but more or less effective, expedients.[44]

Thus innovation — the rejection of legitimate means in approaching goals which are retained — becomes one manner of dealing with ideal-actual divergences.

A second response of interest here lies in Merton's category of rebellion. Both legitimate means and goals are rejected and an attempt is made to substitute new ones in their place. It is in this category that Merton explicitly recognizes collective activity and the formation of separate subsystems of action.

When the institutionalized system is regarded as the barrier to the satisfaction of legitimate goals, the stage is set for rebellion as an adaptive response. To pass into organized political action, allegiance must not only be withdrawn from the prevailing social structure but must be transferred to new groups possessed of a new myth. The dual function of the myth is to locate the source of large-scale frustrations in the social structure and to portray an alternative structure which would not presumably give rise to frustration of the deserving. It is a charter for action.[45]

Elsewhere, Merton singles this response out as "nonconforming" behavior in contrast to "aberrant" behavior of which the above discussed innovation is one type.[46]

... the nonconformer aims to change the norms he is denying in practice. He wants to replace what he believes to be morally suspect norms with ones having a sound moral basis. The aberrant, in contrast, tries primarily to escape the sanctioning force of existing norms without proposing substitutes for them.[47]

This rejection and replacement pattern Merton discusses only with respect to *both* goals and means. But there are, logically, other possibilities of rejection and replacement. There is a hint of this in Merton's own writing, quoted above, when he suggests that the "institutionalized system is regarded as the barrier to the satisfaction of legitimate goals..." There is the possibility, logically and empirically, of a retention of the goals while norms are deliberately altered to adjust access potentialities. This would still be an analytically separate category from innovation, whose practitioners, while rejecting institutional means and engaging in illicit activities, do not seek to introduce a new normative regimen.

Dubin notes the possibility of active rejection of means while goals are maintained. He suggests, however, that this is what Merton "really means," as it were, by innovation, since "the innovator is actively seeking alternatives for the institutionalized means he rejects."[48] But if one is dealing with norms that are taken to be legitimate in the society at large, Merton's original formulation would still hold. Thus, a normative system characterizing the underworld,[49] to which an individual might turn, would not constitute the "rebellious" activity that is implied here. Such underworld activity (e.g., bootlegging, gambling) may indeed be lucrative precisely because it remains illicit. The legitimation of such activity would amount to a catastrophe for its practitioners.

The consequences accruing to those engaged in rebellious activity are deliberately sought. Institutionalization of new practices as a result of such action may therefore be desired. Dubin, in fact, proposes what is suggested here in his formulation of "institutional invention," which refers to new standards of legitimacy with appropriate behavior patterns following suit, while goals remain unaltered.[50] It is such a pattern that Merton appears, in part, to be suggesting but which Dubin has explicitly elevated to a separate type.

In summary, it has been suggested here that modernization produces a condition whereby all are invited to move upward in the reward hierarchy and that ideal patterns with respect to scarce rewards are unified rather than stratified. Further, many are confronted by the divergence between the actualities of their own experience and the ideals they seek to realize. Thus, more radical types of activity explicitly oriented toward institutional changes have often been "lower class" phenomena while the more conservative spokesmen have been disproportionately represented in the "upper classes."

The data which Lipset has examined relative to political party affiliation illustrates this contention:

More than anything else the party struggle is a conflict among classes, and the most impressive single fact about party support is that in virtually every economically developed country the lower-income groups vote mainly for parties of the left, while the higher-income groups vote mainly for parties of the right.[51]

The leftist parties represent themselves as instruments of social change in the direction of equality; the lower-income groups support them in order to become economically better off, while the higher-income groups oppose them in order to maintain their economic advantages. The statistical facts can be taken as evidence of the importance of class factors in political behavior.[52]

Lipset goes on to point out that the relationship between "class" and party is vitiated by numerous factors within single countries as well as between them. The fact remains, however, that the United States is fairly unique when compared to most Western European countries and it is this difference that is taken here as problematic. Many of the arguments put forward in explanation of this uniqueness will be considered hereafter. The burden here has been to expose the elements of the formation of class as an organized entity relative to the distribution of rewards in a society and the ideals that concern them. The next section proceeds with what are taken to be key elements relevant to such relationships.

Polarization and Radicalism

Marx, as stated, claimed that a polarization of strata in which a relatively homogeneous, skill-deprived set of impoverished individuals confronted an affluent minority would produce concrete structures oriented toward alterations in the given conditions. We have further noted the precipitating function of a nonstratified set of ideal reward patterns. Briefly put, then, the more extreme the inequalities, the greater the probability of "rebellion" on the part of the disadvantaged, provided scarce rewards are legitimately held out to the deprived, whose potential access to them is, at the same time, severely limited.

Marx predicted that the disparity between strata would *widen* as modernization proceeded, thereby giving rise to an increasingly militant class struggle. He appropriately perceived such polarization evident in Europe at the time he wrote. Subsequent events, however, have indicated that it is, in fact, the initial periods of modernization when such bipolar tendencies appear to be most extreme.

In the early stages of industrialization workers are in general relatively unskilled. Moreover, managers and men tend to be drawn from quite different sectors of the social structure. Contrary to common opinion this was markedly true of the early factory system, and the pattern is obviously being repeated in underdeveloped areas. This circumstance throws a somewhat new light on the supposed rigidifying of class structure in industrial economies. For the sector of the population engaged in manufacturing the cleavage between bosses and workers, in terms of skill, wealth, authority, or position in the community, is generally sharpest at early stages of industrial development.[53]

During the course of modernization, the elaboration of occupational gradings, industries, and firms tends to crosscut and obfuscate the initially stark bifurcation between the more and less privileged within nonagricultural production. A diminution of labor solidarity is paralleled by similar differentiations within management.[54] Bendix affirms this early polarization while indicating the strains brought about by discontinuity in social structure and the consequences such conditions give rise to.

Industrialization tends to create a revolutionary potential as a consequence of the problems engendered in the early phase of its development.... The revolutionary threat to an emerging industrial society involves the workers' quest for civic recognition in that society; it involves a struggle between classes over rights of which the workers claim to have been deprived unjustly and which they seek to regain through a political struggle for a more equitable distribution within industrial society.[55]

The argument pursued in this chapter has centered on changing institutions governing the differential distribution of scarce rewards. These changes, it has been suggested, do violence to previous conceptions of equity and tend to call forth a "conservative response" on the part of those most injured by the process. If the discontinuity is severe, concrete structures oriented toward the confirmation of what were considered legitimate expectations are a likely outcome. There is thus created a more or less organized basis through which altered goals might be approached. During the onset of modernization, when an "open class" system has, ideally speaking, been created, the *actual* class system is at the most "closed" level that it is ever likely to be. This strain, a result of the deprived legitimately comparing their position with the privileged, is productive of both innovation and radicalism.

It was pointed out earlier that the operations of labor unions are not devoid of political considerations. The "arena of power," as Moore puts it, may remain localized between employers and their employees as in a strike, or it may shift as "indirect" methods are relied upon in attempts to influence the course of governmental activities. Government has proven an attractive arena for European labor movements in attempts to resolve the strains of unequal distribution of rewards. Ultimately Marx saw the labor movement shift to this arena, as the glaring disparities between the conditions of workers and their employers reached an extreme. The "general social constraint," as he termed it, of legislative enactment would prove a far more viable alternative to scattered tests of strength, as pressing deprivations increased.

In a curious way, one of Marx's major underlying propositions is confirmed by those who find his formulations seriously faulty. The revolutionary potential resident in the stratum of workers, Marx contended, was directly related to the degree of inequality obtaining within the modernizing order. As was observed, the disparities are greatest during the initial decades of modernization, and Marx's extrapolation was at variance with subsequent events in that such disparities appear to diminish over time, as does *labor's revolutionary potential.* Nevertheless, his predictions as to the consequences of grave inequalities appear to hold, though his analysis of the structure of modern capitalism and the course of inequality over time may be questioned.

As has been implied throughout this section, the initial decades of modernization provide clues to the subsequent posture of the labor movement. For the manner in which the strains of equity are here confronted become themselves a legacy conditioning the strategy of the ensuing — although moderated — labor movement. In the next section we turn to a brief consideration of explanations that have been put forward in attempts to account for the unique American experience. The argument presented here is resumed in the section beyond the next.

American Society and Business Unionism

The antecedents of relatively modernized America have been fruitfully pointed to in helping to account for its peculiar ethos. This historical legacy involves the absence of a feudal social structure providing the unique basis of the American "liberal tradition."[56] Early America, as Kurt Mayer has shown, was quite distinguishable from much of Europe by a lack of a hereditary aristocracy and peasantry. Instead, the United States was characterized by a "broad middle class of independent producers" who may have amounted to as much as four-fifths of the (free) people who worked.[57]

This nonfeudal history has proven to be one of the more prominent explanatory tools in assessing America's unique labor movement. As Lipset advances the argument, severe "class cleavages" have failed to develop in America because feudal "carry-overs" of an invidious nature have been absent.

The failure of Canada and the United States to develop a major working-class party, and the relative stability of their democratic systems, may be partially explained by the difficulty of developing a working-class political consciousness where no rigid status groups already existed to create a perception of common interests. On the European continent workers were placed in a common class by the value system of the society, and they absorbed a political "consciousness of kind" from the social structure. Marxists did not have to teach European workers that they formed a class; the ascriptive values of the society did it for them.[58]

The "absence of a base of intense class conflict," this author continues, in Australia and New Zealand, "may be explained, as it can in Canada and the

The Labor Movement and the Labor Force

United States, by the absence of feudal tradition."[59]

In attempting to assess the importance of the absence of a feudal historical legacy on the characteristics of an ensuing labor movement, it is useful to return once again to a consideration of Scandinavia. It has been noted that Denmark's labor movement was considerably more conservative than that of Norway or Sweden. Yet it was Denmark and not the others which had had a feudal social structure and a dependent "agricultural proletariat" even after the formal system of feudal landholding had been done away with. It was primarily from a dependent group of smallholders and landless laborers that the industrial labor force was recruited.[60]

In Norway and Sweden, on the other hand, there had been no landed peasantry or aristocracy. "There were some large farms in the southern portion of the countries, but, even there, the landowners are better described as a yeomanry than as a landed aristocracy."[61] Yet the Norwegian labor movement, as cited earlier in Galenson's work, was characterized by "the formation of an extreme, radical ideology, matched by few others in Europe," while Sweden's, though somewhat less extreme, was markedly left compared with Denmark's.

More paradoxical is the fact that Norwegian and Swedish social structure prior to their modernization bore a striking resemblance to "the broad middle class of independent producers" which characterized the United States.

A greater proportion of the workers attracted to industry in Sweden and Norway came from small farms owned by themselves or by members of their families than was true in Denmark. Their tradition of independence clashed with the requirements of industrial discipline, with important consequences for the labor movement.[62]

Indeed, Galenson suggests that the individualism in Norway was conducive to the extreme radicalism of its labor movement. He finds this value quite similar, in fact, to that evidenced in the United States (where a major Norwegian labor leader had worked for a time and been affiliated with the IWW), and suggests that such values were hospitable to syndicalism which "is essentially an expression of individualism and a revolt against the bureaucracy of both the state and the trade unions. . ."[63]

Whereas in the United States the IWW and other radical labor organizations were short-lived and always fairly limited in size, in Norway there was not only a labor party but the

. . . semisyndicalist movement was soon to gain control of the Labour Party. In 1919 the Norwegian Labour Party was the only one in the West to muster a majority for joining the Third International. By contrast with the developments in the other countries, the splitoff in Norway came on the right wing of the party rather than on the left.[64]

Related to the feudal legacy argument has been the notion that opposition by the privileged of the extension of citizenship rights, especially the franchise, to workers, provides a schism around which militant "class consciousness" may congeal. Perlman has noted that the "free gift of the ballot" came at an early date to American workingmen, before modern industrialism had begun.

In other countries where the labor movement started while the workingmen were still denied the franchise, there was in the last analysis no need for a theory of "surplus value" to convince them that they were a class apart and should therefore be "class conscious." There ran a line like a red thread between the laboring class and other classes.[65]

Swedish labor radicalism is in part accounted for by the protracted struggles of workers in achieving the franchise (thereby providing a confirming instance for the above argument).[66] But what of Norway, where labor radicalism was even more extreme? In that country important extensions of the franchise were obtained in 1884, and, by 1898, universal manhood suffrage had substantially been achieved. The ease with which these changes were brought about was, in fact, related to the absence of an entrenched elite originating from a feudal past. As one writer puts it:

As compared with other European nations, I think that the relative lack of an established upper class, the absence of an upper class with ascriptive claims to govern is the most distinctive characteristic. In many ways it is natural to explain the defeat of the conservative groups in 1884, and the remarkable speed with which they adapted to the new situation as a sign of the weakness of the powers that be.[67]

Further, this "free gift of the ballot" appears to have occurred in Norway prior to the formation of a large industrial labor force. "There was very little industry of any kind in Norway before about 1905" say two observers,[68] and another more moderate view states that "Democratic reforms were ... introduced *pari passu* with the ongoing industrialization, not after the completion of that development."[69] Thus, Norway, which lacked a feudal historical legacy and which experienced early extensions of the franchise relative to modern industrial development, nevertheless exhibited an intensely radical labor movement that matched in vigor practically any other in Western Europe. The uniquely conservative and "unpoliticized" nature of the American labor movement has been attributed to historical antecedents which, in Norway, gave rise to a uniquely radical movement.

It is ironic that the world's first labor party came into being in the United States, a country which has consistently failed to sustain one. Commons offers a further explanation when he attributes this failure to diverse local laws endemic in a federal governmental system and to court obstructionism.

While forces have widened competitive areas to the limits of the nation, a system of government by States has covered these areas by widely divergent laws and administration. At the same time, the courts, blocking the way of a new aggressive class with precedents created to protect a dominant class, have had, in this country, a high authority unknown in other lands. By vetoing the laws which labour in its political struggles has been able to secure, the courts, joined to divergent state policies, have excluded or delayed labour from legislative influence. Consequently the energies of organization are turned to the economic field, and often, in the latter decades, a trade union, by the force of its bargaining power, has exacted over a competitive area wider than any State more drastic regulations than those previously vetoed by the courts or even adopted by the most responsive legislatures. In this way has our Federal and judicial system of government added its pressure on labour and forced it to acquire by trade union action what in other countries has been granted by legislation.[70]

While Ulman agrees that it was easier to secure and keep wages and hours legislation abroad than in the United States, he notes that Commons himself provides the details on numerous legislative gains resulting from labor activity — public schools being a notable example. Further, he argues, if courts overruled some of labor's legislative demands and not others, this "suggests that the source of labor's frustration in the judicial sphere lay not in the existence of certain unique judicial powers but in the principles which governed the manner in which those were exercised."[71] Ulman reasons that, had collective bargaining not proved successful, further and more radical politics might plausibly have ensued. He thus asserts "that the subordination of political activity to collective bargaining was due to the success of the latter as well as to the failures of the former."[72]

But perhaps one of the more striking features of the American labor movement is the relative recency of a large union membership. With some notable exceptions, labor unions down through the New Deal were overwhelmingly craft unions, i.e., skilled worker associations that everywhere proved to be more moderate where they predominated. Collective bargaining "worked" precisely for those whose strategic skills always signified bargaining strength. It worked for those who could make it work, while industrial unions were repeatedly broken by employers who would not countenance the rise of such organizations. Yet a politically oriented wing of the labor movement attracted few adherents among industrial unionists even after truly massive setbacks, as in the steel strike shortly after World War I in which some 300,000 workers participated and were decisively defeated.

A somewhat related argument is contained in Perlman's suggestion of the "resistence power" of capitalists. This author cites the ability of the capitalist group to maintain the going system, to "defend its power against all comers," and to convince opponents that "they alone, the capitalists, know how to operate the complex economic apparatus of modern society upon which the national welfare of all depends."[73] Perlman associates this effective resistance to challenge with a labor movement trend in which tactics are increasingly confined to narrow business union objectives.

Gulick and Bers are highly critical of this attempted explanation. They ask why American workers rejected "broad schemes of social change, whereas in other countries labor movements faced with similar opposition retained their traditional form."[74] They point to Perlman's own description of the German case, where, during the strongest antisocialist resistance, changed worker attitudes did not result. The authors go on to note that, in the latter part of the nineteenth century,

... Austrian workers and their leaders went through the high treason trial of 1870, the wholesale dissolution of their organizations, the enactment of a copy of Bismarck's antisocialist laws under another name, and the imposition of more than seven years of martial law on "Vienna and its surroundings" in an attempt by the "ruling forces" to crush the growing labor movement. Again there was no resultant emergence of a program limited to job-and-wage-conscious unionism.[75]

These authors go on to offer what they feel is the primary explanation for the "job conscious" unionism that has become an institutionalized feature of the American labor movement.

There is in the American experience one colossal datum which has stood above all the rest. It has been the fact of a tremendously growing level of material well-being yielded by the system as a whole. The truth is that whether resulting from the "free air" of competitive enterprise, or from native "know-how" or from the context of fabulously rich resources in which the whole system has been immersed, the American wage earner has experienced over a seventy-five year period a rate of economic betterment which has made him labor aristocrat of the world.[76]

The enormous wealth available in American society, when compared with others, is indeed an indisputable "datum." But beyond this comparative affluence, it is necessary to examine the operations of the system *in question* relative to the allocation of this wealth. It may legitimately be asked: Given the stock of scarce economic rewards accruing to a given system, how have members of that system fared over time in access to these rewards as compared to members of another system relative to the rewards available in their system? Has the American wage earner's "rate of economic betterment," as Gulick and Bers put it, been spectacularly superior when compared with his counterpart elsewhere? The implicit hypothesis contained in the foregoing is, of course, that more rapid income advances are associated with less radical labor activities. Table 1-1 indicates the reverse of what might be expected given the above argument.

TABLE 1-1
Approximate Ratio of Average Real Wage-Rate at End of Period to Its Initial Value

	1860-1913	1913-1939	Cumulative 1860-1939
France	1.6	1.9	3.0
Germany	1.6	1.1	1.8
Sweden	3.0	1.8	5.4
United Kingdom	1.9	1.3	2.5
United States	1.5	1.7	2.6

Source: E. H. Phelps Brown with Sheila V. Hopkins, "The Course of Wage-Rates in Five Countries, 1860-1939," *Oxford Economic Papers,* n.s., Vol. 2 (June 1950), Table V, p. 236. Reprinted with permission.

The Labor Movement and the Labor Force

The first period indicated, 1860-1913, is of special significance and will command most of the attention in subsequent chapters. The authors themselves note with respect to it: "It is surprising, but apparently clear, that real wage-rates rose relatively rather less in the United States than elsewhere down to 1914."[77] Further, the table shows no marked American superiority for the 1913-1939 period or the cumulative 1860-1939 span. The one country that does show an outstanding positive difference is Sweden. It presents the most marked gains overall as well as in the initial period. It nevertheless manifested a quite radical labor movement when compared to the United States.

A more promising lead appears to lie in the discontinuity features of modernization discussed in preceding sections. This has to do, once again, with the severity of departures from the preexisting social structure engendered by modernization. It is suggested that the degree to which previous practices are departed from and the rapidity with which these disruptions occur are likely to result in the *mobilization* of those whose heretofore legitimate demands are no longer being met. A Norwegian historian, Edward Bull, has emphasized this state of affairs in accounting for the extreme nature of his country's labor movement.

He focussed on one central "macro" variable: *the suddenness of the changes brought about by industrialization.* He developed a general proposition and he tried to show in some detail that it fitted the facts: the *slower* the growth of industry and the more of its labor force can be recruited from already established urban communities, the less leftist the reactions of the workers and the less radical their party; the more *sudden* the growth of industry and the more of its labor force has to be recruited from agriculture and fisheries, the more leftist the workers and the more revolutionary their party.[78]

Galenson, who follows this argument in considering Norway, Sweden, and Denmark, notes that the latter country's rate of industrial development was comparatively moderate and that "the average Danish factory is small, reflecting the handicraft character of much of industry." Sweden's rate of change was much more rapid and based more on modern technology, while in Norway "the tempo of industrial development was even more rapid than in Sweden," also utilizing modern technology and being characterized by large-scale productive units and the rapid augmentation of a relatively unskilled labor force complement.[79] Thus, the bipolar tendencies discussed in the preceding section appear to have been more pronounced in Sweden and Norway concomitantly with severe alterations in previous conditions.

The Bull proposition has much to commend it. The discontinuity variable has the scientific virtue of high generality. It is addressed to divergences from *any* preexisting social structure and does not logically preclude one or another *particular historical legacy*. It is linked with the "general level proposition" (the Levy statement, see pp. 6-7) regarding discontinuities. Second, since it does not preclude any particular historical legacy, but implies that it is the divergence from each that must be taken into account in assessing the potential radicalism of an ensuing labor movement, these legacies are of significance and must be individually inspected. Hence, the "lower level proposition" (the Moore-Feldman statement) regarding continuities is of equal importance.

Much of the received doctrine regarding *types* of preceding social structures and conditions is, as has been shown, of little value in accounting for the Norwegian labor movement's radicalism. The Japanese case exemplifies the other side of this coin. Here was a society that underwent rapid modernization out of definitely feudal antecedents, where democratization was slow in spreading, and which, nevertheless, failed to exhibit an early radical labor movement. "For many decades after the Meiji Restoration there was little chance for an effective labor movement, or, for that matter, an effective democracy."[80] Much of the explanation appears to lie in the retention, for a considerable length of time, of traditional features of Japanese society, thereby bridging the hiatus of early modernization despite the characteristic initial polarization. This appears, as Levy notes, to have involved a deliberate policy on the part of Japanese leaders, who thereby insured a remarkable degree of cooperation on the part of early industrial workers.[81] These leaders seemed to be quite aware of what they were doing and knew that such patterns could not be maintained indefinitely.[82] Nevertheless, quasi-feudal controls were transferred into the early industrial enterprises where particularistic loyalties emerged between workers and their employers.[83]

The maintenance, then, of feudallike patterns rather than their drastic overturn partially accounts for the rather quiescent characteristics of the Japanese labor force during the early, and most strain-provoking, periods of modernization. Indeed, this "paternalism" appears to have survived, to some extent, to contemporary times.[84] Scalapino takes note that "although labor condemns paternalism as a cloak for exploitation, the unions under pressure from their members, continue to demand many of its supporting features."[85]

It is important to emphasize, then, as the foregoing remarks have implied, that the rate or speed of modernization is not synonymous with discontinuity, which, however, is seen as a highly probable outcome. The Japanese case offers an example where rapid modernization was in fact carried out while the disruptive potentials engendered by the initial bipolarities were checked as a result of the deliberate maintenance of traditional reciprocities.

The initial influences, then, of modernization appear to be variable and depend not only on the preceding *type* of social structure (as Norway, which lacked a feudal legacy, and Japan, which had one, illustrate) but on how the elements from that structure are brought forward or more or less successfully eliminated. Laissez-faire capitalism as it was carried out in the West was essentially antagonistic to "premodern" carryovers, hence the Bull proposition on rapidity of industrial development and radicalism. Japanese leaders, on the other hand, relying on a degree of centralized authority endemic in the preexisting social structure were, with remarkable sophistication, able to utilize it, for a time, in preventing the explosive disruptions that emerged elsewhere. (The Japanese contrast with the West has frequently been summed up with the reference to the former's "revolution from the top" which permitted a degree of continuity in authority structures.)

But liberal Western entrepreneurs sought to do away with these legacies — and at their own peril. Schumpeter has emphasized the importance of a "protecting strata" of feudal elites whose sense of noblesse oblige may have functioned to maintain a more responsible rule over the deprived. This "symbiotic class," Schumpeter argues, as long as it remained viable, may in fact have helped to ensure capitalist success. But:

... capitalist policies wrought destruction much beyond what was unavoidable. They attacked the artisan in reservations in which he could have survived for an indefinite time. They forced upon the peasant all the blessings of early liberalism — the free and unsheltered holding and all the individualistic rope he needed in order to hang himself.

In breaking down the pre-capitalist framework of society, capitalism thus broke not only barriers that impeded its progress but also flying buttresses that prevented its collapse. That process, impressive in its relentless necessity, was not merely a matter of removing institutional deadwood, but of removing partners of the capitalist stratum, symbiosis with whom was an essential element of the capitalist schema.[86]

The seeming "institutional deadwood" remained quite viable in Japanese society long after modernization was under way. But there was no such "protecting stratum" in Norway and the old institutions fell precipitously as rapid modernization proceeded. Indeed, Engels himself argued that class cleavages would be more unambiguous where a feudal wreckage was not around to distort a perception of competing interests.[87]

The United States, "in the period from 1880 to 1910 . . . underwent the most rapid economic expansion of any industrialized country for a comparable period of time."[88] In this case the sudden and rapid post-Civil War advances were productive of severe discontinuities, a wide polarization of strata, and yet no sustained radical working-class organization. The elements that elsewhere appear to have precipitated labor radicalism, unmediated discontinuities associated with the rapid augmentation of unskilled industrial workers, failed to bring it forth in the United States. In the following section, what is considered here to be the unique character of the American case and a much overlooked key to explanation will be taken up.

Societal Membership and American Modernization

In the previous section some of the more salient explanations regarding the American labor movement were more or less critically examined. The arguments were not thereby disposed of. Rather, it is suggested that the elements they contain are somewhat less than decisive in accounting for the unique American experience.

In proceeding with the present effort, the intent is not to "replace" other accounts but rather to reexamine, sociologically, a crucial feature of American labor history that deserves a prominent place in our explanatory scheme. The limitation of the ensuing discussion to one significant feature of American society is therefore *not* intended as single-factor theorizing but, rather, theorizing *about* a single factor.[89]

Although students of the American labor movement have taken account of the fact that its labor force was significantly swelled by immigrants, surprisingly little attention has been given in recent years to a consideration of the consequences this may have had for that movement. Indeed, although a vast amount of recent social scientific effort has been expended on the problems of modernization, with the United States often providing the model of a highly developed society, not very much account has been taken of how the latter "got that way," despite the so-called "culture boundedness" of American sociologists.[90]

The immigrant was not entirely overlooked in what have come to be our standard treatises on labor history. Commons and his associates take note of the "unequaled variety of races, nationality, and languages thrown together in a single competitive area."[91] It has been held that the resulting ethnic rivalries were a major barrier to "class solidarity," thereby preventing a more militant orientation to industrial relations.[92] This ethnic diversity did not prevent many Jewish immigrants from pursuing radical goals in greater proportion than their numbers in the society would warrant on a random basis.[93] Similarly, Germans had earlier been a quite vocal radical element. Had other ethnic groups been similarly inclined, an ultimate radical alliance might have proven quite difficult and, indeed, there were signs of this difficulty within the nascent radical organizations that an interested observer abroad quickly pointed out.[94] Nevertheless, the basic difficulty — to be taken up presently — was one of mass adherence to such ideologies rather than subsequent fusion among them. The point here, however, exemplified by the Jewish and German cases, is that the various groups were not prevented from espousing radical programs merely because the groups were numerous.

Had the various ethnic members been *initially* more randomly distributed throughout the American social structure than they in fact were, there might have been more difficulty in forming affective bonds among working colleagues. In fact, some employers attempted to "judiciously mix" individuals of various national backgrounds in order to create just such barriers to labor solidarity. One suspects that the barriers to efficient production resulting from antagonisms among work cohorts were at least equal to those discouraging worker cohesiveness.

The more characteristic picture, however, was rather one of ethnic "dominance" within certain occupations and geographic areas as a result of chain migration. Further, such occurrences as the famous Lawrence textile strike indicate that a numerically superior ethnic group (Italians in Lawrence) could cooperate quite effectively with less numerous nationalities.

Lipset and Bendix suggest alternatively that, as a result of ethnic clustering, "If these immigrants felt aggrieved about their position in the New World, their natural form of protest was identification with, and organization as, an ethnic group, rather than an economic-interest group."[95] But Jews, who also had this alternative, found it somewhat less of a "natural form of protest" than other groups. The explanation appears to lie elsewhere.

Galenson has insisted that, among the factors that determine the character of a labor movement, one of great importance is "the social origins of the workers who constitute the original industrial cohorts."[96] A clue, then, may lie in the background of the immigrant, his reason for migrating, and his orientation to American society.

Whereas Russian Jews and German radicals, already mentioned, represented primarily an urban-to-urban move, with political considerations being paramount in their decision to migrate,[97] the great bulk of European immigrants in the late nineteenth and early twentieth centuries were peasants who moved for economic reasons. The former were men who had, as Moore has put it in another context, "industrial traditions" and the latter had not.

Radical leaders who attempted to convert ethnic solidarities into radical action among peasant industrial workers had, Handlin notes, a pronounced lack of success in spite of the manifestly exploited position of the latter. "At most the radicals raised disruptive and confusing issues or split the leadership; they could not arouse the enthusiasm of the masses."[98] Handlin attributes this conservatism to the fact that these people were long inured in their homelands to physical hardships and privation. He suggests that the root cause lay in a kind of peasant docility or submissiveness. Where these people had characteristically eschewed radicalism as peasants in Europe, so they now eschewed it as industrial workers in the United States.[99]

The previous section as well as most of what has been written elsewhere of European labor movements has demonstrated that ex-peasant industrial workers were anything but docile under conditions similar to those in the United States. In Europe workers were ready recruits for radical activities — as the earlier remarks about England exemplify — and, in fact, almost every major country from which peasants came to the United States were themselves ultimately to exhibit labor movements far to the left of the one that came into being here.

It was suggested that the basis of such movements lay precisely in the disruption of the institutional complex which everywhere ensured peasant traditionalism. The rapid modernization and recruitment of an industrial work force was disruptive of previous institutional foundations on which such conservatism was based and called forth protest against the failure of what had "always" been legitimate expectations to be realized. With rapid modernization and industrial growth, the United States exhibited the same discontinuities after the Civil War as occurred elsewhere. At the same time the peasant immigrant, moving from his European plot to an American plant, experienced a personal discontinuity of habitual patterns practically overnight. Yet peasants failed to respond to radical appeals.

Levy, among others, has made much of an important analytic distinction that has been touched upon here, and which will inform the subsequent analysis. It has to do with *sets of individuals* as opposed to *patterns of action* (structures). In speaking of concrete structures or membership units, the reference is thus not to groups of individuals (e.g., chess club members) but to the patterns of action that characterize their participation (e.g., playing chess). A structure then, strictly speaking, does not "do" things; rather its membership does things in terms of the patterns characterizing this unit.

According to the conception advanced here, the patterns of action and those who participate in terms of these patterns are distinguishable. Thus, it is conceivable for a chess club to have been in existence for, say, a century, and to have undergone virtually no change in its relevant patterns while, at the same time, having had one or more *complete turnovers* in its membership.

A society is, similarly, a concrete structure which may be analyzed in the same way. As Levy defines it, a society is

> ... a system of action in operation that (1) involves a plurality of interacting individuals (or group of species) whose actions are primarily oriented to the system concerned and who are recruited at least in part by the sexual reproduction of members of the plurality involved, (2) is at least in theory self-sufficient for the actions of this plurality, and (3) is capable of existing longer than the life span of an individual of the type (or types) involved.[100]

Once again, such analysis distinguishes between patterns and those who operate in terms of them:

> The identity and continuity of a society always involves a set of actors or individuals but it is in the persistence of a system of action in operation in which these individuals participate that the actors can and inevitably are continuously changing. The membership, i.e., the individuals involved, is never constant by definition, for a statement about recruitment of new members is part of the definitions. Furthermore, empirical individuals being mortal as they are, some individuals, given time, are bound to pass out of the picture by death if by no other means. Thus, a society may survive and see a complete change of personnel although, of course, it cannot survive any and all possible changes.[101]

It may be noted, with reference to the matter of recruitment to a society, that the given definition leaves this feature somewhat open. Beyond birth recruitment, new members may also be inducted by extending the boundaries of a society to include them or by the transfer of members from one society into another through individual or group mobility. Whether or not new inductees, in these latter cases, do in fact primarily come to orient themselves to the new system is problematic and uncertain. It will be suggested below that this feature of nonindigenous actors in a system may have significant consequences for the operations of that system.

This issue may be approached by noting Simmel's insight concerning the stranger who (the author states) is the "potential wanderer" who elects to stay and is so perceived by indigenous members.

> He is fixed within a particular spatial group, or within a group whose boundaries are similar to spatial boundaries. But his position in this group is determined

essentially, by the fact that he has not belonged to it from the beginning, that he imports qualities into it, which do not and cannot stem from the group itself.[102]

Simmel goes on to suggest of the stranger that: "He is not radically committed to the unique ingredients and peculiar tendencies of the group, and therefore approaches them with the specific attitude of 'objectivity.'"[103] Simmel's point may be well taken with respect to the immigrant whose initial attachments are often quite minimal. Thus, as Schuetz notes concerning the stranger:

At best he may be willing and able to share the present and the future with the approached group in vivid and immediate experience; under all circumstances, however, he remains excluded from such experiences of its past. Seen from the point of view of the approached group, he is a man without a history.[104]

The relevance of these observations lies in their explicit recognition of the stranger's lack of prior experience with the group he enters. Thus, to return to our immigrant in particular, he was not a "man without a history" but rather a man without an *American* history. In the terms we will use here, he had not been basically socialized.

By *basic socialization* we mean the generalized norms and values characterizing a society that are transmitted to all of its members, making them, as Levy puts it, "capable of adequate performance in . . . [their] several roles throughout life, both as respects skills and attitudes."[105] *Intermediate socialization* may be thought of as the inculcation of specialized patterns of action that takes place in differentiated subsystems within the society which individuals variously enter.[106] Not the least important of these subsystems are the work settings. Thus, with increased modernization, intermediate socialization processes increase as well.

"Genuine members" of a society are those who have undergone basic socialization within it. They are primarily oriented to that society rather than another.[107] If, however, an individual transfers participation from one society to another while maintaining his primary orientation to the former, he may be considered an "expedient member" of the new society.[108] The latter case is well exemplified by the immigrant.

Ordinarily a definite sequence in the process of socialization takes place. Quite simply, basic socialization gives way to intermediate socialization over time with any given age cohort. This means that those moving into specialized structures of action within a society are normally genuine members of that society. The *initial* phases of modernization are likely to pose the most extreme disparities between basic and intermediate socialization. As men move into specialized structures in which previously legitimate expectations fail to be realized, an intense reaction is likely to be manifested. The rapid augmentation of a relatively unskilled industrial labor force during the onset of modernization has characteristically been the center of such disruptions.

Such "strains of discontinuity," it may now be suggested, are lessened to the extent that expedient societal members make up a substantial portion of the personnel involved during this stage. Thus Galenson's previously cited stricture on the "social origins of the workers who constitute the original industrial cohorts" as a determining factor in the character of a labor movement, is uniquely apt in the American case. During the American transition to modernism, some twenty million immigrants entered the populace. They were mostly males of labor force age who were responding to industrial employment opportunities in this country. Although they moved almost at once from a "premodern" setting into a modernizing context, at the lowest skill and remuneration levels, they were poor recruits for radical activity.

This is not to imply that the problem of adjustment was easier for immigrants than for settled Americans. It was, rather, that the former could not demand adherence to expectations deriving from a previous condition that they had never experienced. They could not protest divergences from previously institutionalized practices into which *they had never been socialized.* Further, to the extent that adjustment on the part of the immigrant was difficult or not possible, he had the option of withdrawing entirely from American society.[109]

It will be suggested below that the kind of adjustment made by the majority of immigrants was consistent with modern capitalism and augmented institutions making for the persistence of business unionism even among those occupying relatively unskilled occupational roles. The immigrant's "history" involved a different system of action to which it was possible for him to remain oriented for some time while operating adequately, if minimally, in other contexts.

The Success Theme and Deviancy

The success theme has been a pronounced element almost from the inception of American society and is largely attributable to the background of its founders.

Americans were Englishmen established in a new environment. The New World modified the social order that they established, but it was, in the circumstances, a remarkably orderly society which in many particulars approximated, often quite consciously, that of the mother country.[110]

Lipset observes that the American revolution, on the one hand, laid the basis for doing away with ascribed privilege (its most immediate focus being on colonial rule), while at the same time retaining for the new society a Puritan ethic inherited (through its British settlers) from the mother country in more vital form.

. . . the new United States was particularly fortunate in the religious traditions which it did inherit. Calvanistic Puritanism, which was stronger in the colonies than in the mother country, was not "uncongenial to modernity" as are some of the traditional beliefs inherited by new nations today. A positive orientation toward savings and hard work, and the strong motivation to achieve high positions that derives from this religious tradition, have been seen as causes of the remarkable economic expansion that made possible the legitimation of equalitarian values and democratic government.[111]

Thus, it appears that the success value has been a long-standing feature of American society, one that has been suggested as a characteristic feature of modernization. Further, one of its early outcomes appears to have been a uniformity of ideal patterns having to do with scarce rewards.

Another ideal trait that was wedded to previous ones was individualism, which, in economic affairs, was exemplified by the independent owner-operated enterprise. The elements of success and individualism proved somewhat strain-producing as modernization proceeded. Together, they constituted a duality between what we will later consider as the prerequisites and the requisites of modernization among those societies which entered the process relatively early.

As in the Norwegian case, a reluctance on the part of Americans to assume *employee* roles was rather pronounced. This is, of course, inimical to modernized productive techniques. Into the breach entered several million immigrants whose focus on American society was rather narrowly economic and who, in fact, were willing recruits into the emerging large-scale industrial enterprises. As one author puts it, "It was American industrial development which attracted them in the first place; had they not known that work awaited them in the mines, mills, and factories, they would not even have crossed the Atlantic."[112]

Not only were the recent immigrant arrivals fairly eager to obtain industrial jobs but data which will be presented later provide abundant evidence that their positions within the occupational hierarchy were among the least remunerative. Since immigrant access to dominant success goals and to ideal patterns of material well-being was severely limited as they, in fact, made up a substantial portion of the deprived sector of American society, it is worthwhile to examine the evidence as to their possible deviant adaptation to these conditions.

This evidence, admittedly incomplete but strikingly consistent, indicates important differences in types of criminality when native-born and foreign-born groups are compared. The Immigration Commission study, carried out early in this century, found that gainful crimes included a discernibly higher proportion of native offenses than ones committed by the foreign born. Crimes of personal violence and "offenses against chastity" appear to have comprised a larger portion of foreign-born transgressions.[113] A more recent study, appearing in the early thirties, similarly notes marked differences, with the foreign born exhibiting decidedly lower rates of gainful crimes while crimes of personal violence were fairly similar in proportions as between foreign born and natives.[114]

Van Vechten has shown that when age factors are controlled, the seemingly lower overall crime rate of the foreign born is accounted for by the fact that, as a group, they are more concentrated in the older age categories where criminality is less frequent in any case.[115] Van Vechten's age-adjusted rates, unfortunately, do not separate types of criminality. They do indicate, however, that foreign-born rates are *lower* in the older age brackets and *higher* in the younger age ones than native rates. Since most immigrants arrived in the United States as *adults,* there is reason to believe that their lower crime rates, when compared to natives beyond the age of thirty-five, involve a further element. Van Vechten states:

It is my guess that those who have been brought to this country as small children approximate the behavior of their younger brothers who were born here while those who came as adults more nearly approximate the old-country behavior patterns which involve far less crime than we have in this country.[116]

Similarly, the Immigration Commission report states:

From these records it appears that a clear tendency exists on the part of the second generation to differ from the first, or immigrant generation in the character of its criminality. It also appears that this difference is much more frequently in the direction of the criminality of the American-born of non-immigrant parentage than it is in the opposite direction. This means that the movement of second generation crime is away from crimes peculiar to immigrants and toward those of the American of native parentage. Sometimes this movement has carried second generation criminality even beyond that of the native-born of native parentage.[117]

Other evidence has tended to substantiate the contention that foreign-born adults exhibit types of criminality that are prevalent in the areas from which they came.[118]

Rostow, among many others, has asserted that "each wave of immigration faced a pattern of adjustment to the prevalent values and culture of the nation which was, by and large, accomplished by generational stages."[119] The data summarized here on type, rate, and generational patterns of crime are consistent with this view. Further, though these data are not an independent test of lack of adherence to distinctly American ideal patterns on the part of the migrating generation, they are in striking accord with such a proposition, given the framework of assessment that has been developed in preceding pages.

What is being suggested here is partially self-evident. The adult migrant had undergone basic socialization in another society and thus was oriented to values and norms that constituted another system of action. Of further importance is the relatively attenuated *exposure* to American patterns as a result of the formation of ethnic communities or subsystems which made for the persistence of adherence to other patterns. Wood asserts that an ethnic community's continued viability may preserve low crime rates among its members. However, when "they migrate from their minority-group communities or assimilate the democratic ideology of the American culture such conditions tend to maximize these rates."[120]

The degree of similarity between relatively modernized societies has been pointed out previously (as compared with relatively nonmodernized settings). This is an important focus for assessing the integration of immigrants. E. K. Francis argues that the lower the degree of similarity between the structures of any two societies, the greater the probability that migrants from one to another will form separate ethnic subsystems within the host society. Thus, the movement of peasants from relatively nonmodernized societies into a modernizing setting, as happened in America, results in the likelihood that "immigrants with the same background will tend to re-create a more familiar social situation by forming local communities which, though necessarily urban, nevertheless preserve the solidaristic aspects of the peasant village, resulting in a social subsystem of the urban, solidaristic type."[121] Correlatively, if the parent and host societies are similar ("isomorphic"), migrants may more readily move into the latter's social structure at all levels with a lower probability of ethnic or minority systems being created. "Common understandings of proper behavior and value orientations can be achieved more easily between the alien and his native associates because their social heritages, though different in some respects, are isomorphic with regard to the dominant elements of social organization."[122]

It may be suggested that this latter situation partially explains subsequent radicalism among some groups of immigrants. Common value orientations, it is held here, entail assessment of one's position relative to such values and, according to previous discussion, the likelihood of radical activity among deprived sectors of the population. Second, although ethnic communities were often formed among migrants coming from a more similar setting, they were often, as with Jewish immigrants, a continuation of such communities in the old world. For many of the same reasons that radical manifestations were more likely among these groups, their position upon arrival appeared to be less durable than among other migrants.[123] Finally, as will be pointed out in a later chapter, the migration of such individuals was generally prompted by political considerations and the move conceived, practically from the first, as permanent.

Quite different elements, however, characterized the vast majority of immigrants. As pointed out, these individuals came to maturity within a relatively nonmodernized setting. Second, economic considerations were foremost in their decision to migrate. Finally, the move for a substantial portion of them was not conceived as a permanent one. As will be described later, many immigrants viewed participation in the American labor force as a temporary measure.

In this last regard, Siu's development of a subtype of Simmel's notion of the stranger is of importance. Siu's remarks defining the *sojourner* merit extended quotation. The latter is one who:

. . . spends many years of his life in a foreign country without being assimilated by it. The sojourner is par excellence an ethnocentrist.

. . . The intrinsic purpose of the sojourner is to do a job and do it in the shortest possible time.

Generally speaking, it seems that the time element varies according to individual situations but the job itself is essentially a means to an end. The sojourner may not necessarily like his job and enjoy working at it. It is rather that he is fighting for social status at home.

In his effort to make his job a success, the sojourner stays on long enough to make changes in his life-organization, so that he is no longer the same person; in other words, he has developed a mode of living peculiar to his present situation. He has no desire for full participation in the community life of his adopted land. In other words, his activities tend to be within the limit of his own interest — the job. He tends to think of himself as an outsider and feels content as a spectator in many of the community affairs. If he does take part in certain activities, they are likely to be either matters relating to his job or matters concerning his homeland's social welfare, politics, etc.

Essentially the colony is an instrument to establish or to re-establish some sort of primary-group relationships in the matrix of homeland culture — an effort to create a home away from home. Whatever activities the sojourner may participate in, in the community at large, in private life he tends to live apart from the natives and to share with his countrymen in striving to maintain homeland culture. His best friends are people from his ethnic group, and they entertain one another at their homes. They share their pride and aspirations, hopes and dreams, prejudices and dilemmas and express their opinions about the country of their sojourn.[124]

Siu is here primarily concerned with the foreign-born individual whose job involved an "ethnic specialty" (e.g., the Chinese laundryman), but his analysis may be applied more generally. The job was of similar importance to others. Siu's analysis points up the initial and *persisting* expedient membership of the actor in his host society and applies to a larger element of the foreign born than his interest suggests.

Insofar as late nineteenth- and early twentieth-century immigration was predominantly economic in orientation, such migrants were, to a large extent, "target workers" initially seeking the wherewithal to preserve or enhance a position in the society from which they came. The preponderance of males of labor force age and the rather high return movement, to be noted elsewhere, provides supporting indication that many, and perhaps most, of the new arrivals were sojourners. Herein lies the special "objectivity" of the stranger. Insofar as he directs his focus toward a single aspect in the host society while maintaining primary orientation elsewhere, his behavior may in fact prove highly rational relative to his relevant goals.

The less extensive and intensive the individual's commitment to a full scale industrial social system, the more sharply defined and limited may be his performance and involvement. He may indeed be working for money, and so for the limited range of goods and services that money will buy and that fit his relevant standards.[125]

To the extent that migration was conditioned by economic circumstances that prevailed both within the parent and host societies, such action was highly rational. The expediency which characterized these migrants functioned to provide actors for the less rewarded occupational roles who were, given their relevant standards, "relatively gratified." This often-noted circumstance is crucial when it is recognized that whatever "net gain" the immigrant was likely to perceive at the least-advantaged levels of the American industrial hierarchy was relative to another system in which he was primarily implicated. Thus, the Gulick and Bers remarks on the relative wealth of American society when compared with others were likely to be appreciated precisely by those who experienced both.[126]

Eisenstadt suggests that, characteristically, the migrant attenuates most of his basic attachments to the parent society and shifts his orientation and focus of attention to the various structures of the new.[127] In contrast, he makes note of the fairly distinctive pattern characteristic of the United States.

The Labor Movement and the Labor Force

This lack of basic cultural and social identification and solidarity on the part of the immigrant was more or less reciprocated by the old inhabitants. Although many special propaganda and recruitment services for immigrants existed, their main purpose was to recruit man-power for agriculture and industry. The basic attitude of most of the older inhabitants towards the immigrants was, initially, mainly instrumental. This was more or less in agreement with the immigrants' own orientations, which were also mostly limited to the instrumental field. This juxtaposition of the two sets of motivations gave rise to one of the most important phenomena in the process of immigrant absorption in American — namely, the monopolization of superior economic and social positions by the old inhabitants, and the relation to the immigrants of relatively inferior positions. Thus a complete dispersion of the immigrants among the various strata of social structure could not develop.[128]

This "instrumentalism" of the immigrant was not likely to lead to protest against industrial capitalism operating, as it does, with a fairly open labor market (free labor) mediated by a "cash nexus" (wage labor), thereby providing the sojourner with the conditions by which he might approach his relevant goals.

Consistent with previous remarks about unified ideal patterns relating to relatively modernized stratification systems, T. H. Marshall points out that "class conflict" is contingent on the relatively disadvantaged comparing their position with the relatively advantaged.[129] Coser further asserts that:

Before a social conflict between negatively and positively privileged groups can take place, before hostile attitudes are turned into social action, the negatively privileged group must first develop the awareness that it is, indeed negatively privileged. It must come to believe that it is being denied rights to which it is entitled. It must reject any justification for the existing distribution of rights and privileges. Shifts in the degree of acceptance of a given distribution of power, wealth or status are closely connected with shifts in the selection of reference groups in varying social situations.[130]

As implied, the reference group focus of immigrants on initial contact with the host society remained outside that society and involved what might be termed a "reference system" insofar as the groups in question were operating in terms of another society. A shift in orientation, as implied here, may thus be productive of relative deprivation even if the rewards themselves have not shifted. As indicated, the immigrant tended to be quite insulated from American society and was not socialized into patterns guided by ideals that prevailed in the latter. But he was not unmindful of economic rewards. They were the basis of his initial introduction to American society, his decision to come, and, ultimately, his decision to stay. Permanent residence, however, does not necessarily mean genuine membership. The argument pursued here has been that the formation of minority or ethnic subsystems served to perpetuate expedient membership among the *migrating generation*, if not their children.

The one context that provided exposure and was likely to result in commitment was the one that the immigrant came to enter to begin with, namely, the workplace. In this regard, some remarks by Moore and Feldman on the worker during the course of modernization are pertinent:

In the ideal typical case the individual . . . becomes committed to the system as well as its parts. Although individuals, particularly in transitional situations, may not traverse the entire social territory so encompassed, the industrialized system does traverse it, and the failure of some or many to do so is itself a theoretically significant phenomenon.

. . . Initial exposures to new forms are limited to specific contexts. Thus even when commitment to a specific context occurs, there is no guarantee that overall commitment to an industrial social organization can be achieved more easily.[131]

These remarks apply with altered significance to the immigrant case. It has been implied that the foreign born did not, in fact, "traverse the entire social territory." As modernization proceeded in the United States, this was more likely to occur among native-born individuals whose basic socialization came to more adequately fit their later experiences.

But immigration proceeded apace with modernization in the United States. As suggested, basic socialization ordinarily gives way to intermediate socialization. The immigrant, however, *reversed this process as far as American society was concerned.* He typically initially underwent intermediate socialization with the ultimate likelihood of basic socialization being quite minimal. He was less likely to become a genuine member of American society (or, alternately, committed to the system as well as its parts) if his background was in a relatively nonmodernized society and his move dictated by economic considerations. If he remained, commitment tended to be "arrested" at the one context that he came to enter to begin with — namely, the work setting.

Labor commitment, it was suggested earlier in this chapter, is not necessarily coincident with labor docility. Conflict insofar as it would occur, however, was more likely to be limited in scope to this one "arena" than to broader areas involving general changes in the institutions governing the allocation of scarce rewards. The former, of course, is consonant with business unionism and some indication has already been given of the initial "job consciousness" of the migrant.

Lipset and Bendix have suggested that the "political conservatism" that has characterized the American workman was, in part, due to the fact that a large share of the burdens of deprivation have been borne by those who were "in the society and not of it."[132] Later, one of these authors was to account for the special nature of American unions by pointing to the values which characterized the society of which they were a part:

. . . the narrow self-interested policies traditionally pursued by many American unions would seem to be warranted if the objective of unionism is to secure as much as possible for the members of the given union. This is most likely to be its objective if the union movement reflects the values of achievement and individualism.[133]

There has already been occasion to present the case of Norway, which, if not precisely identical with the United States prior to modernization, nevertheless exhibited much less of the ascriptive features that other European societies retained from a feudal legacy and still generated an extremely radical labor movement. The present argument is therefore more hospitable to the former explanation. It is asserted here that the rather "narrow" form of activity that came to characterize the industrial as well as the craft unions may be partially accounted for by the close association of "job consciousness" on the part of those who made up a substantial portion of the unskilled labor force. Thus it was not only the value system attaching to American society but the structural conditions that enormous immigration gave rise to that provide our focus here. It will be recalled that adherence to these values appeared to have been rather less among the migrating generation than among the native born and it may, following the initial Lipset-Bendix suggestion, be further proposed that genuine members of American society in similarly deprived positions would be more amenable to "broader" changes than their equally unfortunate foreign-born colleagues.

Summary

It seems appropriate now to review briefly the argument presented. The argument actually addresses two aspects of our problem and the remarks will serve to delineate these.

First, the process of discontinuity during the onset of modernization may be addressed. From shortly after the Civil War to about the outbreak of World War I the United States underwent this process. Modernization is a relative concept and it is not suggested that it "began" after the Civil War and "concluded" by 1914. What is being suggested is that the patterns of action associated with American society shifted decisively to those characteristic of relative modernization during this interval. Our focus is on units of production, and instances of such units exhibiting relatively modern patterns may undeniably be found early in the nineteenth century; however, they were exceptional rather than characteristic of America's productive system at that point.

As has been noted, the insistence on viewing patterns of action as distinct from those who operate *in terms* of them is seen as a particularly fruitful means of examining some of the possible strains occurring during what is doubtless one of the most stressful periods that a society is likely to undergo. In proceeding in this manner, the concepts of basic and intermediate socialization have been brought forward. The generalized orientations provided by basic socialization become "operationally defined" in specific contexts as individuals "fan out" to assume differentiated roles. The latter has been referred to as intermediate socialization.

One of the great points of stress during the course of modernization is the disruption of previously expected life sequences during the initial changes and of rather sharp divergences from what have been legitimate expectations on the part of those basically socialized to the relatively nonmodernized state of the system. It is held here that this critical divergence from ideal patterns is likely to result in a mobilization of those who find themselves illicitly threatened by such changes. Values and norms formerly taken for granted in their governance of relationship are, as Feldman and Moore observe, "likely to become overt, precisely because their translation into action patterns reveals the conflict between the new and the traditional practices."[134]

Mobilization, then, is seen as a necessary condition for radicalism. It is maintained that the failure of the American labor movement to exhibit the radical tendencies of its European counterparts is partially accounted for by the failure of its labor force to become mobilized during its period of extreme social discontinuity and polarization of strata, though severe inequality based on "unjust" practices is quite congenial to radicalism.

The guiding proposition with respect to this hiatus is that expedient societal members moving into the new structures will lessen the strains of discontinuity which are likely to be most severe for genuine members who experience contradictions between past ideals and present practices.

Many of those who participated in terms of the new patterns in the United States were, first, eager to enter industrial employment as a means of approaching their own goals elsewhere and, second, not having been socialized to the pre-existing state of the American system, were "objective" in the sense of not carrying with them "preconceptions" of heretofore legitimate standards with which to gauge divergences and protest them. Their own objectives within the system were narrowly economic and easily calculable.

The first part of the argument deals in a "negative" way with immigration. It asserts that it muted or damped down labor force mobilization which is seen as a necessary condition for radicalism. The full formation of a working *class*, in the Marxian sense, was reduced. The second part of the argument asserts a "positive" outcome, i.e., the immigrant's contribution to business unionism. It is argued here that the characteristics of union activity are, in part, a function of the level of commitment exhibited by the labor force.

The immigrant, it is held, reversed the more usual process of socialization. By remaining, in large measure, an expedient member of American society, while becoming committed to one context of that society, the workplace, conflict was more likely to be limited to that one arena and to be oriented around rewards deriving from it, rather than to broader areas involving changes in institutions governing the basis of such allocations.

This "delayed action" of immigrant socialization occurred precisely during the hiatus and polarization characteristic of early modernization. By the time the foreign born had, in large measure passed from the labor force and their native-born children entered it, the structural conduciveness to labor solidarity and radical action on a broad societal front had gone by as well, while the institutions of business unionism had become firmly established.

A larger theoretical problem thus emerges from this study. It is suggested here that primary orientation to a system of action and the values which envelop it may in fact be generative of conflict, while lack of adherence, under certain circumstances, may indeed enhance its stability. The usual notions relating consensus and absence of conflict are therefore brought into question. Dahrendorf asserts that:

> It is hard to see how a social system based on ("almost") universal consensus can allow for structurally generated conflicts. Presumably, conflict always implies some kind of dissensus and disagreement about values.[135]

But if values are defined as desired ends of action and if they are universally adhered to, then conflict may indeed result precisely because of their shared nature.[136] Thus Moore has noted:

> The "relative deprivation" of those *fairly fully incorporated* into the values associated with new modes of social placement and mobility but thereby more envious of full success than their less fortunate compatriots provides the explanatory key to the source of discontent in systems of social inequality.[137]

Dahrendorf has elsewhere very closely approached the point intended here when he stated:

> There can be no conflict, unless this conflict occurs within a context of meaning, i.e., some kind of coherent "system." No conflict is conceivable between French housewives and Chilean chess players, because these groups are not united or perhaps "integrated into," a common frame of reference.[138]

It is precisely this common "frame of reference" (or lack of it) that is expressed in the distinction between genuine and expedient societal members. The clue to the arena of conflict, it has been suggested throughout, is the scope of commitment. Commitment at the work setting is genuine societal membership "writ small." This, of course, is consonant with the narrow focus of business unionism and, it is hoped, goes some small distance in helping to explain its ultimate institutionalization in American society at the industrial as well as the craft union level.

NOTES

1. For a general theoretical statement of this position see Wilbert E. Moore and Arnold S. Feldman, "Society as a Tension Management System," in G. Baker and L. S. Cottrell, *Behavioral Science and Civil Defense*, "Research Group Study No. 16" (Washington: National Academy of Sciences, National Research Council, 1962), pp. 93-105.

2. Walter Galenson, "Scandinavia," in Galenson (ed.), *Comparative Labor Movements* (Englewood Cliffs, N.J.: Prentice-Hall, 1952), p. 105.

3. Arnold S. Feldman and Wilbert E. Moore, "The Society," in Moore and Feldman (eds.), *Labor Commitment and Social Change in Developing Areas* (New York: Social Science Research Council, 1960), p. 70. The concept of commitment developed by these authors "involves both performance and acceptance of the behavior appropriate to an industrial way of life." See, by the same authors, "Commitment of the Industrial Labor Force," in *ibid.*, pp. 1-2.

4. Simon Kuznets and Ernest Rubin, *Immigration and the Foreign Born* (New York: National Bureau of Economic Research, 1954), p. 1.

5. *Ibid.*, p. 44.

6. Arthur M. Schlesinger, "The Significance of Immigration in American History," *American Journal of Sociology*, Vol. 37 (July 1921), p. 72.

7. Charles A. Gulick and Melvin K. Bers, "Insight and Illusion in Perlman's Theory of the Labor Movement," *Industrial and Labor Relations Review*, Vol. 6 (July 1953), p. 528.

8. *Ibid.*, p. 520.

9. Robert F. Hoxie, *Trade Unionism in the United States* (New York: Appleton-Century-Crofts, 1917), pp. 45-46.

10. *Ibid.*, p. 45.

11. John T. Dunlop, "The Development of Labor Organization: A Theoretical Framework," in Richard A. Lester and Joseph Shister (eds.), *Insights into Labor Issues* (New York: The Macmillan Co., 1948), p. 179.

12. George Cyriax and Robert Oakshott, *The Bargainers: A Survey of Modern British Trade Unionism* (New York: Frederick A. Praeger and London: Faber and Faber Ltd., 1960), p. 45. Quoted with permission.

13. Hoxie, *op. cit.*, p. 88.

14. Arthur M. Ross, "The Natural History of the Strike," in Arthur Kornhauser, Robert Dubin, and Arthur M. Ross (eds.), *Industrial Conflict* (New York: McGraw-Hill Book Co., Inc., 1954), p. 32.

15. Cyriax and Oakshott, *op. cit.*, pp. 212-213 (quoted with permission). Part of this quotation also appears in Seymour M. Lipset, *The First New Nation: The United States in Historical and Comparative Perspective* (New York: Basic Books, Inc., 1963), p. 173, n. 8.

16. Galenson, *op. cit.*, pp. 123-125.

17. *Ibid.*, p. 149.

18. *Ibid.*

19. Marion J. Levy, Jr., *Modernization and the Structure of Societies: A Setting for International Affairs* (Princeton: Princeton University Press, 1966), Vol. 1, p. 5.

20. Arnold S. Feldman and Wilbert E. Moore, "Industrialization and Industrialism: Convergence and Differentiation," *Transactions of the Fifth World Congress of Sociology*, Washington (September 1962), Vol. 2, pp. 157-158.

21. *Ibid.*, p. 156.

22. Max Weber, *The Theory of Social and Economic Organization*, trans. A. M. Henderson and Talcott Parsons (New York: Oxford University Press, 1947), pp. 329-336.

23. Marion J. Levy, Jr., "Some Sources of the Vulnerability of the Structures of Relatively Non-Industrialized Societies to those of Highly Industrialized Societies," in Bert F. Hoselitz (ed.), *The Progress of Underdeveloped Areas* (Chicago: University of Chicago Press, 1952), pp. 116-122.

24. Weber, *op. cit.*, pp. 137-138.

25. Karl Marx and Friedrich Engels, "Manifesto of the Communist Party," in Lewis S. Feuer (ed.), *Basic Writings on Politics and Philosophy: Karl Marx and Friedrich Engels* (Garden City: Anchor Books, Doubleday & Co., Inc., 1959), p. 16.

26. Karl Marx and Friedrich Engels, *The German Ideology* (New York: International Publishers, 1947), pp. 48-49.

27. Marx and Engels, "Manifesto . . . ," p. 16. See also Ralf Dahrendorf, *Class and Class Conflict in Industrial Society* (Stanford: Stanford University Press, 1959), pp. 16-17.

28. Max Weber, *From Max Weber: Essays in Sociology*, H. H. Gerth and C. Wright Mills (eds.) (New York: Oxford University Press, 1946), pp. 184-185.

29. Marx does confuse the issue by often speaking of class in the Weberian sense. But it is fairly clear that he recognizes a distinction between common position and "community," considering one a prelude to the other, as the following remark further indicates: "Economic conditions had first transformed the mass of people of the country into workers. The combination of capital has created for this mass a common situation, common interests. This mass is thus already a class as against capital, but not yet for itself. In the struggle, of which we have noted only a few phases, this mass becomes united, and constitutes itself as a class

for itself." Karl Marx, *The Poverty of Philosophy* (Moscow: Foreign Languages Publishing House, n.d.), p. 166.

30. Weber, *Essays* . . . , p. 184.

31. Wilbert E. Moore, "Predicting Discontinuities in Social Change," *American Sociological Review*, Vol. 29 (June 1964), p. 338.

32. See Marion J. Levy, Jr., *The Structure of Society* (Princeton: Princeton University Press, 1952), pp. 123-214.

33. Wilbert E. Moore, *Social Change* (Englewood Cliffs, N.J.: Prentice-Hall, 1963), p. 20.

34. Robert K. Merton, *Social Theory and Social Structure* (rev. ed.; New York: The Free Press, 1957), p. 147.

35. Marion J. Levy, Jr., "Some Social Obstacles to 'Capital Formation' in 'Underdeveloped Areas'," in Moses Abramovitz (ed.), *Capital Formation and Economic Growth* (Princeton: Princeton University Press, 1955), p. 474.

36. Levy, *Modernization* . . . , Vol. 2, p. 487, n. 15.

37. Weber, *Theory* . . . , p. 342.

38. Levy, "Some Sources of Vulnerability . . . ," pp. 124-125.

39. Abraham J. Siegal, "Method and Substance in Theorizing About Worker Protest," in National Bureau of Economic Research, *Aspects of Labor Economics* (Princeton: Princeton University Press, 1962), p. 22.

40. *Ibid.*, p. 24.

41. Reinhard Bendix, *Work and Authority in Industry: Ideologies of Management in the Course of Industrialization* (New York: John Wiley & Sons, Inc., 1956), p. 46.

42. *Ibid.*, pp. 439-440.

43. Levy, *Structure* . . . , p. 178.

44. Merton, *op. cit.*, pp. 145-146.

45. *Ibid.*, p. 156.

46. Robert K. Merton, "Social Problems and Sociological Theory," in Merton and Robert A. Nisbet (eds.), *Contemporary Social Problems: An Introduction to the Sociology of Deviant Behavior and Social Disorganization* (New York: Harcourt Brace Jovanovich, Inc., 1961), pp. 725-727.

47. *Ibid.*, p. 726.

48. Robert Dubin, "Deviant Behavior and Social Structure," *American Sociological Review*, Vol. 24 (April 1959), p. 147.

49. Edwin H. Sutherland, *The Professional Thief* (Chicago: University of Chicago Press, 1937).

50. Dubin, *op. cit.*, pp. 150-151.

51. Seymour Lipset, *Political Man: The Social Bases of Politics* (Garden City: Doubleday & Co., Inc., 1960), pp. 223-224.

52. *Ibid.*, p. 229.

53. Wilbert E. Moore, "Occupational Structure and Industrial Conflict," in Kornhauser, *et al., op. cit.*, p. 226.

54. *Ibid.*, pp. 227-230.

55. Bendix, *op. cit.*, p. 437.

56. Louis Hartz, *The Liberal Tradition in America: An Interpretation of American Political Thought Since the Revolution* (New York: Harcourt Brace Jovanovich, Inc., 1955).

57. Kurt Mayer, "Recent Changes in the Class Structure of the United States," *Transactions of the Third World Congress of Sociology*, Amsterdam (September 1956), Vol. 3, p. 69.

58. Lipset, *The First* . . . , p. 290.

59. *Ibid.*

60. Galenson, *op. cit.*, p. 109.

61. *Ibid.*, p. 110.

62. *Ibid.*

63. *Ibid.*, p. 151.

64. Stein Rokkan and Henry Valen, "Parties, Elections and Political Behavior in the Northern Countries: A Review of Recent Research," in Otto Stammer (ed.), *Politische Forschung: Schriften des Instituts für Politische Wissenschaft* (Cologne: Wesdeutscher Verlag, 1960), p. 108.

65. Selig Perlman, *The Theory of the Labor Movement* (New York: Augustus M. Kelley, 1949), p. 167. See also Lipset, *The First . . .* , p. 340.

66. Galenson, *op. cit.*, p. 152.

67. Ulf Torgersen, "The Structure of Urban Parties in Norway During the First Period of Extended Suffrage 1884-1898," in Erik Allardt and Yrjo Littunen (eds.), "Cleavages, Ideologies and Party Systems: Contributions to Comparative Political Sociology," *Transactions of the Westermarch Society,* Vol. 10 (1964), p. 393.

68. Rokkan and Valen, *op. cit.*, p. 107.

69. Torgersen, *op. cit.*, p. 398.

70. John R. Commons, *et al., The History of Labor in the United States* (New York: The Macmillan Co., 1918-1935), Vol. 1, p. 9. © 1918 by The Macmillan Company, © 1946 renewed by John A. Commons. Quoted with permission of The Macmillan Company.

71. Lloyd Ulman, *The Rise of the National Trade Union: The Development and Significance of Its Structure, Governing Institutions and Economic Policies* (Cambridge: Harvard University Press, 1955), p. 578.

72. *Ibid.*

73. Perlman, *op. cit.*, pp. 4-5.

74. Gulick and Bers, *op. cit.*, p. 526.

75. *Ibid.*, p. 528.

76. *Ibid.*

77. E. H. Phelps Brown with Sheila V. Hopkins. "The Course of Wage-Rates in Five Countries, 1860-1939," *Oxford Economic Papers,* n.s., Vol. 2 (June 1950), p. 236.

78. Rokkan and Valen, *op. cit.*, p. 110. This quote also appears in Lipset, "Political Cleavages in 'Developed' and 'Emerging' Polities," in Allardt and Littunen, *op. cit.*, p. 31. As elsewhere in the present work, Lipset's writing has generated ideas (sometimes critical) and led me to important sources in the literature that have been valuable when pursued.

79. Galenson, *op. cit.*, pp. 106-107. Lipset concurs with the view that rapid modernization and militant labor movements are positively related. Besides taking note of Galenson's work, cited here, he provides material on other countries which supports this proposition and states that: "Wherever industrialization occurred *rapidly*, introducing sharp *discontinuities* between the pre-industrial and industrial situation, more rather than less extremist working-class movements emerged." See *Political . . .* , p. 68.

80. Robert A. Scalapino, "Japan," in Walter Galenson (ed.), *Labor and Economic Development* (New York: John Wiley & Sons, Inc., 1959), p. 141.

81. Levy, "Some Social Obstacles . . . ," p. 468.

82. Reinhard Bendix, *Nation-Building and Citizenship: Studies of Our Changing Social Order* (New York: John Wiley & Sons, Inc., 1964), pp. 200-202.

83. Scalapino, *op. cit.*, p. 98.

84. James C. Abegglen, *The Japanese Factory: Aspects of Its Social Organization* (New York: The Free Press, 1958). For a critical assessment of the degree to which these patterns are presently operative in Japanese industry, see Robert M. Marsh and Hiroshi Mannari, "Lifetime Commitment in Japan: Roles, Norms, and Values," *American Journal of Sociology,* Vol. 76 (March 1971), pp. 795-812.

85. Scalapino, *op. cit.*, p. 135.

86. Joseph A. Schumpeter, *Capitalism, Socialism, and Democracy* (3d ed.; New York: Harper & Row, 1950), p. 139.

87. Friedrich Engels, "The Labor Movement in the United States," in Feuer, *op. cit.*, p. 491.

88. Bendix, *Work and Authority in Industry*, p. 254.

89. Concerning this matter of "theorizing about a single factor," see the remarks of Hartz, *op. cit.*, pp. 20-23.
90. Lipset's *The First New Nation* is an important exception.
91. Commons, *et al., op. cit.*, Vol. 1, p. 9.
92. Henry Pelling, *American Labor* (Chicago, University of Chicago Press, 1960), p. 221.
93. On the relatively high foreign-born Jewish proportion of radical and labor leaders, for example, see Pitirim A. Sorokin, "Leaders of Labor and Radical Movements in the United States and Foreign Countries," *American Journal of Sociology*, Vol. 33 (November 1927), pp. 390-391.
94. See letter by Friedrich Engels to Friedrich A. Sorge, December 2, 1893, in Feuer, *op. cit.*, p. 458.
95. Seymour Martin Lipset and Reinhard Bendix, *Social Mobility in Industrial Society* (Berkeley: University of California Press, 1959), p. 105.
96. Galenson, *op. cit.*, p. 109.
97. This was, incidentally, true of only a small fraction of the large German immigration but this fraction proved quite influential in the early labor movement. See Marcus Lee Hansen, *The Immigrant in American History* (New York: Harper & Row, 1964) pp. 87-89, 134-135.
98. Oscar Handlin, *The Uprooted: The Epic Story of the Great Migrations that Made the American People* (New York: Grosset & Dunlap, 1951), p. 196.
99. *Ibid.* See especially Chapter 8.
100. Levy, *The Structure . . .*, p. 113.
101. *Ibid.*, pp. 116-117.
102. Georg Simmel, "The Stranger," in Kurt H. Wolff, *The Sociology of Georg Simmel* (New York: The Free Press, 1950), p. 402.
103. *Ibid.*, p. 404.
104. Alfred Schuetz, "The Stranger: An Essay in Social Psychology," *American Journal of Sociology*, Vol. 49 (May 1944), p. 502.
105. This is the definition that Levy gives to socialization *per se* in *The Structure . . .*, p. 189. It seems quite useful to split the concept in the manner suggested here.
106. This concept draws from Levy's notion of intermediacy as expressed with reference to cognitive orientations. See *ibid.*, pp. 171-172. The basic-intermediate socialization distinction should not be thought of as analogous to the distinction between child and adult socialization although the articulation between the two may be highly relevant for theory-building. Both refer to the process of inculcation of patterns of action. The basic-intermediate concepts are addressed to *what* is socialized (i.e., the general culture on the one hand and subcultures on the other); the child-adult concepts, to *who* is socialized. The literature, for example, on social class differences in child-rearing indicates that much intermediate socialization occurs during the early years of one's life. In all events, exactly what the basic-intermediate, child-adult "mix" is remains an open, and empirical, question around which useful theory may be constructed.
107. *Ibid.*, p. 123.
108. *Ibid.*, p. 126.
109. Stanley Lieberson, "A Societal Theory of Race and Ethnic Relations," *American Sociological Review*, Vol. 26 (December 1961), p. 905.
110. Rowland Berthoff, "The American Social Order: A Conservative Hypothesis," *American Historical Review*, Vol. 65 (April 1960), p. 503.
111. Lipset, *The First . . .*, p. 94.
112. Maldwyn A. Jones, *American Immigration* (Chicago: University of Chicago Press, 1960), p. 216.
113. U.S. Immigration Commission, *Report of the Immigration Commission*, Vol. 36: *Immigration and Crime* (Washington, D.C.: Government Printing Office, 1911), p. 13.
114. Alida C. Bowler, "Recent Statistics on Crime and the Foreign Born," in National

Commission on Law Observance and Enforcement, *Report on Crime and the Foreign Born* (Washington: U.S. Government Printing Office, 1931), pp. 83-96.

115. L. L. Van Vechten, "The Criminality of the Foreign Born," *Journal of Criminal Law and Criminology*, Vol. 32 (July-August 1941), p. 142.

116. *Ibid.,* p. 143.

117. U.S. Immigration Commission, *loc. cit.*, p. 14.

118. See Thorsten Sellin, *Culture Conflict and Crime* (New York: Social Science Research Council, 1938), pp. 98-99.

119. W. W. Rostow, "The National Style," in Elting Morison (ed.), *The American Style: Essays in Value and Performance* (New York: Harper & Row, 1958), p. 253.

120. Arthur Lewis Wood, "Minority-Group Culture and Cultural Integration," *Journal of Criminal Law and Criminology*, Vol. 37 (March-April 1947), p. 510.

121. E. K. Francis, "Variables in the Formation of So-Called 'Minority Groups,'" *American Journal of Sociology*, Vol. 60 (July 1954), p. 10.

122. *Ibid.*

123. Thus Sklare notes of Jewish immigrants: "In contrast to other groups, social mobility in the Jewish community frequently begins with the first rather than the second generation." Marshall Sklare, *Conservative Judaism: An American Religious Movement* (New York: The Free Press, 1955), p. 48. See also Nathan Glazer, *American Judaism* (Chicago: University of Chicago Press, 1957), pp. 80-82.

124. Paul C. P. Siu, "The Sojourner," *American Journal of Sociology*, Vol. 58 (July 1952), pp. 34-37. Copyright © 1952 by the University of Chicago. Quoted with permission.

125. Arnold S. Feldman and Wilbert E. Moore, "The Market," in Moore and Feldman, *op. cit.*, p. 52.

126. These authors note that immigration must be taken into account when they state that: "In the thirty-year period 1885-1914, over twenty million persons representing diverse backgrounds and a previous experience of relative poverty entered the United States." Gulick and Bers, *op. cit.*, p. 529.

127. S. S. Eisenstadt, *The Absorption of Immigrants: A Comparative Study Based Mainly on the Jewish Community in Palestine and the State of Israel* (London: Routledge & Kegan Paul Ltd., 1954), p. 5.

128. *Ibid.*, p. 244.

129. T. H. Marshall, *Class, Citizenship, and Social Development* (Garden City: Doubleday & Co., Inc., 1964), p. 168.

130. Lewis A. Coser, *The Functions of Social Conflict* (New York: The Free Press, 1956), p. 37.

131. Feldman and Moore, "The Society," in Moore and Feldman, *op. cit.*, p. 65.

132. Lipset and Bendix, *op. cit.*, pp. 104-105.

133. Lipset, *The First . . .* , p 182.

134. Feldman and Moore, *loc. cit.*, p. 63.

135. Ralf Dahrendorf, "Out of Utopia: Toward a Reorientation of Sociological Analysis," *American Journal of Sociology*, Vol. 64 (September 1958), p. 120.

136. Irving Horowitz appears to be suggesting something similar to what is here offered when he states that: "There is a distinction to be made between types and levels of conflict, especially between conflict *over* the basis of consensus, and those conflicts arising *within* the consensual apparatus." "Consensus, Conflict and Cooperation: A Sociological Inventory," *Social Forces*, Vol. 41 (December 1962), p. 183.

137. Moore, *Social . . .* , p. 84. Emphasis added.

138. Dahrendorf, *Class . . .* , p. 164.

2
Emigration: The European Push

The following pages provide a brief account of international migration during the nineteenth and early twentieth centuries. We begin by examining the broad picture of intercontinental migration and move to a consideration of the changing European origins of migrants and the conditions that prompted their move. The aim here is to establish the economic character of much of the movement, the significance of which will be explored in subsequent chapters.

Intercontinental Migration

One of the more important factors surrounding the massive migrations of the nineteenth and early twentieth centuries was the relative lack of restriction imposed on such movement in either the countries of origin or of destination. The interval between 1815 and the early 1920's has been referred to as the "period of free immigration," where the decision to move was primarily a personal one and the move itself mainly one of independent individuals or family units.[1] In the United States it was only after World War I that substantial legal means were imposed to curtail the hitherto almost free flow of immigration[2] while, on the other side of the Atlantic, "the desire of the European countries themselves to promote industrialization, gave rise to national policies directed at discouraging or even prohibiting the outward movement."[3]

During the "free period" of migration an unprecedented flow of people crossed the Atlantic. In a rather intensive analysis of available data on international migration, investigators for the National Bureau of Economic Research found that:

The statistics of European intercontinental emigration and the immigration statistics of overseas countries show about the same totals. For the years 1820-1924 the latter figure is about 55 ½ millions, while the total recorded emigration from Europe for 1846-1924 amounts to 50 millions. When one remembers that immigration as a rule is more completely recorded than emigration, these totals indicate that no important series of figures are missing.[4]

It has further been estimated that this European movement accounted for approximately 96 percent of total intercontinental migration in the world.[5] This massive European movement was not a constant stream over time. If one looks at a curve of emigration covering the period in question, distinct "waves" can be discerned, each one higher than its predecessor until the final peak, then numbering in the millions, was reached in the early part of this century.[6]

Although the data for the whole period being considered are not entirely precise, they do indicate that the overwhelming majority of European migrants came to the Western world. Carr-Saunders asserts that, for the period 1821-1932, "America as a whole ... attracted well over 90 percent of those who went overseas from Europe."[7]

Finally, with respect to *country* of destination, "It appears that the United States has absorbed about 60 percent of the total overseas emigration from Europe."[8] Of migrants coming to American countries, the United States received the largest, although a progressively decreasing, proportion of the total. This is indicated in Table 2-1 showing five peak periods of migration.

TABLE 2-1

Average Annual Immigration of Aliens

Period	Into All American Countries (Thousands)	Into the United States (Thousands)	Percentage to United States
1851-1855	397	343	86
1871-1875	410	308	75
1881-1885	652	516	79
1906-1910	1,482	949	64
1921-1924	844	426	51

Source: Taken from Walter F. Wilcox (ed.), *International Migrations* (New York: National Bureau of Economic Research, Inc., 1929-1931), Vol. I, p. 82. Reprinted with permission.

In absolute figures, some 36 million people migrated to the United States between 1820 and 1924. As with total intercontinental migration, the overwhelming majority (87.6 percent) came from Europe.[9]

Thus far data have been presented on numbers who went from one place to another but not on those who returned. The evidence here is even more fragmentary than gross migration statistics show, but such that is available suggests that return movements were also relatively large.[10] In this matter the United States was no exception. A substantial minority, approximately 30 percent, of those who migrated to this country later left. Further, it appears that this return movement increased proportionately over time. Significantly greater return movements occurred during later periods than in the early years of the nineteenth century.[11]

In summary, the overseas movement of people was primarily one of individuals making independent decisions, in steadily increasing numbers, the overwhelming majority of whom were Europeans. Of these, the greatest proportion

Emigration: The European Push

moved to the Western hemisphere, with the largest numbers coming to the United States. Finally, estimates of the entire "free period" suggest that a substantial and increasing minority returned.

The main burden of the present chapter is to examine briefly the origins of the migrant and the conditions in his setting which partially account for the enormous movement we have been reviewing. We turn, then, to the European situation.

Shifting European Origins

An important feature of the century of European migration being considered is that the proportions emigrating from different areas of Europe altered over time. There were radical shifts indicating that the majority of those coming to the United States in the early part of the period were of different national origins from the majority coming in the late nineteenth and early twentieth centuries. The main concern will be with the latter-day immigrants to this country, but, in accounting for the shifts in national emigration, we go far in accounting for the entire movement of the period.

The direction of the shift in European origins was one which moved progressively from the north and west of the continent to the south and east. The early 1880's may be taken as an approximate reference point for the appearance of this shift and, by the turn of the century, the major areas of origin had clearly reversed themselves. This may be summarized as follows:

The years 1820-40 showed a growth in British, German and French emigration; during 1846-55 came the first crest in British (or Irish) emigration. At the same time oversea emigration from other northwestern European nations began to be of importance. The second crest of British and German emigration fell in the decade 1881-1890. Simultaneously, emigration from the Scandinavian countries, from France and from Switzerland reached their crests, and emigration from southeastern Europe became of importance. Until the War emigration from Italy, Austria-Hungary, Russia, Portugal, Spain, Poland, and Finland increased; while emigration from northwestern Europe diminished.[12]

Jerome's highly significant work demonstrates the overwhelming importance that economic conditions in the United States had on rates of emigration from Europe. Rates of departure evidenced a direct relation to American business cycles, rising during boom times and falling during slack periods.[13] But, though this relationship is an important one, it helps little in explaining long-term increases in the volume of migration.[14] Further, Jerome's analysis does little to help us explain the changes in composition of migrants, i.e., the supersession of the so-called "new" (Southern and Eastern European) migrants over the "old" (Northern and Western European). To do this, it is necessary to examine, briefly, changing conditions *within Europe*. By accounting for the shift one goes far to account for the predisposition to migrate generally as it existed throughout this period, conditioned, albeit, by perceived opportunities elsewhere.

Local Conditions

In examining the European situation one discovers that the successive waves of migrants closely corresponded to marked population changes resulting from the influence of modern industrialism as it spread eastward and southward across the continent from England. Greater reliability in food supplies and, later, improved medical techniques were accompanied by reductions in the death rate, while declines in the birthrate lagged, producing rapidly growing populations.[15]

This lag between decreasing death rates and birthrates produced marked differentials in population increases in Europe which reflected the introduction and spread of modern industrialism. Thus, early in the century it was Northern and Western Europe which evidenced rapid population growth, while in the latter half of the century growth had slowed there (due to offsetting subsequent declines in the birthrate) but was accelerating in the Southern and Eastern portions of the continent.[16]

Although population expansions alone do not explain emigration, a significant correlation has been found between such increases and emigration twenty to twenty-five years later when these increases are felt in the labor market.[17]

But the large population increases experienced throughout Europe as a result of this "demographic transition" do not tell the whole story. As Moore has noted, in considering population density as a measure of "overpopulation," it neglects, among other things, the social structural "middle terms."

> The regions of Europe that have prospects for stable or declining populations and that have achieved high productivity per capita in agriculture, are by no means thinly settled. In fact, Northwestern Europe is not only the most densely populated part of the continent . . . but is one of the most thickly settled areas of the world.[18]

It was indeed in these areas that modern production and its attendant consequences, including the subsequent decline in birthrates, first appeared. Paradoxically, it was the *initial* incursions of modern technology that gave rise to the emigration impetus. As the influence of modernism spread eastward and southward, the most readily assimilable life-sustaining features of the process gave rise to the dramatic mortality changes that are being noted here. The rapid population growth that ensued created a deteriorating economic situation that could not, during the early periods, be ameliorated within the confines of the existing institutions of hitherto relatively nonmodernized societies. "Emigration [thus] followed the spread of modern economic development from its centers in Northwestern Europe to the peripheries of the continent."[19] Once modern economic technology became dominant, however, creating local opportunities, migration levels tended to fall. "Even though these opportunities may not [have equaled] the more distant ones this differential [was] counterbalanced by the undesirable necessity of adjusting to the alien customs and frequently the alien language of an overseas country."[20]

Emigration: The European Push

It was, then, the rural population of Europe, especially the peasantry, first exposed to modern influences that created severe social structural dislocations, who were motivated to migrate.[21] The character of the shifting origins of European migrants indicates the overriding importance of the economic aspect in the migration process. The great "waves" of migration within the Atlantic community in the late nineteenth and early twentieth centuries were primarily an international (and intercontinental) rural to urban movement, made up largely of peasants whose economic position was threatened by changes taking place in European social structure.

There were exceptions to this economic characterization of European migration. Among these were Armenians,[22] Syrians,[23] some Poles (to be touched on below), and Jews from Eastern Europe. In all these cases the political aspect superseded others in considerations attending migration. The Jewish population of Eastern Europe constituted, by far, the numerically most significant exception to the general features that have been discussed and we take up this case briefly.

One author, Hersch, points to the economic aspect as affecting Jewish emigration. He suggests that Jewish concentration in urban occupations led to a deteriorating economic situation with increasing competition from non-Jews moving into similar fields of activity.[24] But here underlying political considerations may be seen to operate. Hersch notes the increasing intensity of anti-Semitism as others competed in the urban job market. Further, the occupational differences between Jews and other European immigrants[25] were themselves a function of long-maintained legal sanctions imposed on the European Jewish population. The following remarks concerning Russian Jews would indicate that the political aspect was of inestimably greater importance in the decision to move than with Eastern Europeans generally.

On the one hand, for the sake of economic interests the czarist government had to make concessions and grant rights of residence in all of Russia to certain Jews, rich merchants, manufacturers of the first and second guilds (a kind of commercial franchise), individuals with academic training, qualified artisans; on the other hand, it expelled Jews from the villages even in the Pale of Settlement, instituted quotas in the universities, and high schools, and interfered with the economic Jewish institutions of mutual and self-help and with Jewish communal and charity institutions. Add to this the fact that in 1871 there was a pogrom in Odessa, in 1881 and 1882 a whole series of pogroms with many dead and wounded, in 1903 the Kishinev pogrom, and in 1905, during the October Revolution, over five hundred pogroms in five hundred places: it becomes clear why emigration from Russia continued and increased.[26]

Approximately 1.5 million Jews entered this country between 1899 and 1914, and 1.8 million in the period of 1899-1924.[27] Relative to their numbers in Europe, they exhibited among the highest recorded rates of emigration. They also represented among the highest recorded rates of *net* migration at 94.8 per hundred, a striking difference from the Russian net figure of 49.5 per hundred or the Polish figure of 60.3 for the years 1908-1924.[28] Given the conditions noted, it is evident that the minority position of the Jewish population of Eastern Europe played a distinctive role in determining their decision to move and their understandable reluctance to return.

Jewish immigrants differed substantially from many of the other "new" immigrants in ways that affected their orientation to American society upon arrival, and their participation in the labor movement within it. The space is taken here to note this and other relatively small exceptions to the overall character of the "new" migrants so that future discussion will be duly qualified.

This overall character is summed up by Zubrzycki:

> The very great majority of emigrants from Eastern Europe from the beginning of the mass migratory movements in the 'eighties down to the advent of the Great Depression of the 'thirties of this century were of peasant origin. If we disregard a relatively small proportion of political emigrés who left the Russian part of Poland after the Revolution of 1905 or the Slovak and Ukrainian Separatists exiled from Austria-Hungary the only other element of non-peasant origin in the large current of East European migration were the Jews. It seems therefore that the masses of non-Jewish migrants from Eastern Europe were relatively homogeneous and in addition to the linguistic and racial affinity had a common rural background. They contributed to the earlier streams of North European and contemporary Latin migration in search of better economic opportunities.[29]

In noting the fundamentally economic character of Eastern European emigration, Zubrzycki indicates three factors as helping to explain the outflow: (1) relatively little industrial development, thus providing little employment as an alternative for the agriculturalist; (2) land scarcity and small holdings, partially the result of traditional land-tenure systems; (3) the impact of a market economy on peasant self-sufficiency, resulting in severe dislocations both to the agriculturalist and various others dependent on an agrarian-based, relatively closed economy.[30] These Eastern European conditions are an exemplification of what had taken — and was taking — place throughout Europe.

In Russia, landless agricultural laborers and peasants with landholdings too small for an adequate livelihood were the dominant source of emigrants.[31] The growth in the Russian peasant population without commensurate growth in available land led to minute subdivision of holdings or complete landlessness, resulting in a surplus agricultural labor force subject to low wages. Traditional agricultural techniques, producing low yields, further intensified the situation of scarcity. This together with the fact that industrial employment opportunities were rather meager (more than 85 percent of the Russian population was estimated as rural in 1907) made the economic situation of the agriculturalist most tenuous.[32]

Some areas of divided Poland exhibited similar characteristics. In the Austrian part of Poland (Galicia), the average size of a peasant's holding had been decreasing steadily, while the number of persons deriving their livelihood from the land was rising. "The typical peasant holding at the beginning of the twentieth century was from 1 to 5 hectares, an area insufficient to maintain its owner without resort to seasonal employment elsewhere, and there were about 200,000 holdings of 1 hectare or less."[33]

The Russian sector of Poland was affected by similar trends. Those migrating were primarily from the rural areas.[34] Some politically inspired emigration took place in this sector, however, as a result of governmental persecution of adherents to the Uniate religion.[35]

In Prussian Poland, the political aspect was the dominant factor in emigration which resulted from the German intention of doing away with distinctly Polish social patterns and, in effect, extending German society throughout this area. Many Poles were forcibly dispossessed of their land and replaced by Germans.[36] These migrants resembled those of the dominant movement, though, in that most Polish emigrés were agriculturalists and rural dwellers.

The Austro-Hungarian territories displayed the general trends that have been noted. Migrants were largely peasants with small, uneconomic holdings or a landless rural proletariat subject to low wages.[37] The Immigration Commission cites low wages, low crop yields and inefficient agricultural techniques, land scarcity, and few employment alternatives in industry as reasons for emigration from these areas around the turn of the century.[38]

In looking to Southern Europe, it is evident that much the same conditions were operative as exemplified by the most important emigration country in this sector of Europe, Italy. The major areas of emigration within Italy, when the movement approached its largest proportions, were in the southern and predominantly agricultural parts of the country.[39] Agricultural workers dominated the outflow[40] and a later decrease in farm laborers appears to have been the result of reclassifying them according to employment experience during previous seasonal migration.[41] In south Italy the familiar pattern of excessive parcellation of land among smallholders, lack of improved productive techniques, and an agricultural labor force subject to low wages and levels of living combined to create an impetus toward overseas alternatives.[42]

Conclusion

It appears, then, that population increases relative to the "middle terms" of agrarian social structure resulted in a situation of severe economic scarcity across Europe at different times throughout the nineteenth century. The focus here will be on the latter part of this period, the era of the "new" migration, and therefore it has been in those more recent areas of heavier migration where major attention has been concentrated.

Throughout the period, the modernization of transport facilities was one of the major factors facilitating the increasing volume of transatlantic migration. Vessels under sail coming into New York, for example, accounted for 96.4 percent of the total in 1856 but only 3.2 percent in 1873.[43] These increases in modern shipping had the further effect of dramatically reducing the cost of passage.[44]

A further function of increased international communications is related to the importance of awareness of alternatives on the part of the potential industrial recruit in conditioning his decision to effect a change.[45] With local industry unable to absorb the labor available and with agricultural conditions deteriorating, improved means of communication brought both new information and a viable means of bringing about a personal amelioration of conditions.

Thus, as modernism moved southward and eastward from its origins, it produced successive population increases in the regions in its path. This in turn gave rise to an expansion in the labor force that was beyond the absorptive capacities of local agriculture or industry. By the end of the nineteenth century Southern and Eastern Europe were the prime areas of emigration and, abetted by modern transport facilities, these sectors helped generate the highest volume of intercontinental migration in European history.

NOTES

1. Oscar Handlin and Mary F. Handlin, "The United States," in *The Positive Contribution by Immigrants* (Paris: UNESCO, 1955), pp. 17-18. See also Marcus Lee Hansen, *The Immigrant in American History* (New York: Harper & Row, 1964), Chapter 1, "Migrations Old and New."

2. Carl Wittke, "Immigration Policy Prior to World War I," *Annals of the American Academy of Political and Social Science,* Vol. 262 (March 1949), pp. 5-14.

3. Paul Wiers, "International Implications of American Immigration Policy," *ibid.,* pp. 42-43.

4. Walter F. Wilcox (ed.), *International Migrations* (New York: National Bureau of Economic Research, Inc., 1929-31), Vol. I, p. 82.

5. A. M. Carr-Saunders, *World Population: Past Growth and Present Trends* (Oxford: Clarendon Press, 1936), pp. 49-50. See Wilcox, *op. cit.*, pp. 140-166, for a discussion of Asian migration statistics which somewhat contradicts Carr-Saunders' remark that there were "no records at all for the movements of Chinese . . ." See also United Nations, *The Determinants and Consequences of Population Trends* (New York: United Nations, 1953), p. 105.

6. Wilcox, *op. cit.*, Diagram 5, p. 183.

7. Carr-Saunders, *op. cit.*, pp. 54-55 and Figure 9, p. 49.

8. United Nations, *op. cit.*, p. 102.

9. Wilcox, *op. cit.*, Table 4, p. 178.

10. For an examination of available data from all relevant countries, see *ibid.*, pp. 196-207.

11. Walter F. Wilcox, "Immigration into the United States," in *ibid.*, Vol. II, p. 89. This will be taken up in greater detail in Chapter 4.

12. Wilcox, *op. cit.*, Vol. I, p. 189. Davie places the initial point of shift, when substantial numbers of Eastern and Southern European migrants began coming to the United States, as 1882. See Maurice R. Davie, *World Immigration: With Special Reference to the United States* (New York: The Macmillan Co., 1939), p. 96.

13. Harry Jerome, *Migration and Business Cycles* (New York: National Bureau of Economic Research, Inc., 1926), Chapter 8, "The Influence of Economic Conditions in the Countries of Emigration."

14. United Nations, *op. cit.*, p. 16.

15. See Dudley Kirk, "Demographic Trends in Europe," *Annals of the American Academy of Political and Social Science,* Vol. 262 (March 1949), p. 47.

Emigration: The European Push

16. See Donald R. Taft and Richard Robbins, *International Migrations: The Immigrant in the Modern World* (New York: The Ronald Press Co., 1955), p. 57.

17. H. Ravnholt, "A Quantitative Concept of International Mobility of Population and Its Application to Certain European Countries in the Period 1851-1935," in Congrès International de la Population, *Théorie Générale de la Population*, Vol. I (Paris: Hermann et Cie, 1938), pp. 224-229.

18. Wilbert E. Moore, *Economic Demography of Eastern and Southern Europe* (Geneva: League of Nations, 1945), p. 57.

19. Dudley Kirk, *Europe's Population in the Interwar Years* (Geneva: League of Nations, 1946), p. 81.

20. *Ibid.*, p. 81.

21. For a general discussion of this point see Oscar Handlin, *The Uprooted: The Epic Story of the Great Migrations that Made the American People* (New York: Grosset & Dunlap, 1951), Chapter 1, "Peasant Origins."

22. Davie, *op. cit.*, pp. 174-176.

23. *Ibid.*, pp. 176-177.

24. Liebmann Hersch, "International Migration of the Jews," in Wilcox, *op. cit.*, Vol. II, p. 516.

25. *Ibid.*, Table 212, p. 490.

26. Jacob Letschinsky, "Jewish Migrations, 1840-1956," in Louis Finklestein, *The Jews: Their History, Culture, and Religion*, Vol. II (3d ed.; New York: Harper & Row, 1960), pp. 1550-1551. Concerning Russian Jews see also V. V. Obolensky-Ossinsky, "Emigration from and Immigration into Russia," in Wilcox, *op. cit.*, Vol. II, pp. 524-544.

27. Hersch, *op. cit.*, Table 200, p. 474.

28. *Ibid.*, Table 203, p. 477.

29. J. Zubrzycki, "Patterns of Peasant Migration with Special Reference to Eastern Europe," *R.E.M.P. Bulletin*, Vol. IV (October/December, 1956), p. 74.

30. *Ibid.*, pp. 74-75.

31. Obolensky-Ossinsky, *op. cit.*, pp. 550-551. Exclusive of Jewish migrants.

32. U.S. Immigration Commission, *Report of the Immigration Commission*, Vol. IV, *Emigration Conditions in Europe* (Washington, D.C.: Government Printing Office, 1911), pp. 265-271.

33. J. Zubrzycki, "Emigration from Poland in the Nineteenth and Twentieth Centuries," *Population Studies*, Vol. VI (March 1953), p. 253.

34. Obolensky-Ossinsky, *op. cit.*, pp. 534-535.

35. Zubrzycki, "Emigration . . . ," p. 252.

36. *Ibid.*, pp. 255-257.

37. See Felix Klezl, "Austria," in Wilcox, *op. cit.*, Vol. II, pp. 390-410.

38. U.S. Immigration Commission, *op. cit.*, pp. 362-368.

39. Anna Maria Ratti, "Italian Migration Movements, 1876 to 1926," in Wilcox, *op. cit.*, Vol. II, pp. 447-448.

40. *Ibid.*, Table 191, p. 456.

41. Robert F. Foerster, *The Italian Emigration of Our Times* (Cambridge: Harvard University Press, 1919), pp. 39-40.

42. For an extended discussion of south Italy's agricultural system and its emigration consequences, see *ibid.*, pp. 64-105. See also U.S. Immigration Commission, *op. cit.*, pp. 153-160.

43. Wilcox, *op. cit.*, Vol. I, p. 86, n. 1.

44. H. A. Citroen, *European Emigration Overseas Past and Future* (The Hague: Martinus Nijhoff, 1951), p. 61.

45. On this general issue see Wilbert E. Moore, *Industrialization and Labor: Social Aspects of Economic Development* (Ithaca: Cornell University Press, 1951), pp. 15-19.

3

Immigration: The American Pull

In the preceding chapter it was suggested that the decision of millions of Europeans to migrate was prompted by continental social changes, the importance of the economic aspect being overriding. The aim of this chapter is, in part, to indicate why the United States provided a viable choice in the array of alternatives open to the emigrant. The discussion will center, then, on American economic development and its consequent steady expansion of employment opportunities, or what has often been referred to as the "pull" feature in the migration process.

The main burden here goes well beyond this. We will be looking primarily at the migration process from the point of view of American society and asking what part immigration played during a crucial period of social change. The period in question spans, roughly, the thirty-five to forty years from the early 1880's through World War I. This may be thought of as a transition period during which the United States passed from the upper limits of a relatively nonmodernized society to one that was relatively modernized. It may be asked, then, what position the immigrant assumed in this massive context of structural change that attracted him in the first place. A consideration of the consequences both of his position in American society and his orientations toward that position, consequences of major relevance to the overall process, will be reserved for following chapters.

We begin with a general consideration of economic development. This is followed by turning more directly to the American experience with the transformation of production. Finally, the composition of the labor force in American industry is taken up, the emphasis, of course, being placed on the position of the foreign born in it.

The Process of Economic Development

Three concepts of prime significance for social change that are embedded in most discussions of economic development may be discerned. Together they can be taken as a *scale* of economic development.[1] At the "lower" end of the scale may be placed the concept of *economic growth*. This concept will refer to increases in output of goods and services per capita, that is to say, productivity.[2] The second concept, occupying an "intermediate" point on the scale, is *industrialization*.

This concept will be taken to mean increases in the proportion of the labor force engaged full time in nonagricultural productive activities.[3] The third and "topmost" position on the scale is *modernization*. This concept will denote increases in the number of tools used and the employment of inanimate sources of energy to multiply the effect of human effort for productive purposes.[4]

As implied in these distinctions, economic growth is not limited to more recent periods after the "industrial revolution." There have, in fact, been earlier periods in human history when increases in output were realized:

Among the instances of growth prior to 1750, that in Western Europe between 1000 and 1300 is one of the best known. Much of the evidence concerning it is archeological. The extension of arable land can be seen in connection with the large number of new villages founded during this period of growth. City walls record the enlargement of towns to embrace urban population; and the rise of cities is also an indication of the growth of income, since the cities produced goods demanded by a rising standard of living. An increase in product per capita cannot be calculated from any statistics, but the existence of such an increase can be inferred quite soundly from the new forms of consumption. There was extensive building of churches, castles, and bridges in the twelfth century, and increased use of spices, silks, and other luxuries.[5]

It appears, then, that substantial extensions in agriculture resulted in significant growth for the development of nonagricultural production (i.e., industrialization, following the definition given above). Without markedly changed patterns in production, however, a mere proliferation of traditional handicrafts and artisanry tends to have limits set by subsequent increases in population over the long run.[6] Thus, industrialization can never proceed very far under such conditions, and agriculture maintains its dominance relative to shares of the labor force as well as total production.

Although the above quotation indicates that economic growth *can* lead to industrialization, there is no reason why the relationship should be necessary. It always involves decisions as to whether surpluses should be channeled back into existing forms of production or *alternative* forms.[7]

On the other hand — stepping up in the scale — industrialization, when it occurs, is indicative of the *necessary* (although not sufficient) condition of prior economic growth. In short, without surpluses accruing to existing primary forms of production (particularly agriculture), industrialization cannot proceed. When we have discovered that the latter has, in fact, taken place, we may safely conclude that surpluses have been achieved which surpass the subsistence requirements of the population. Although the former remarks referred to the "premodern" period (i.e., pre-1750) of human history the same principles apply to contemporary, densely populated, "underdeveloped" countries:

In the older and more crowded countries the main question is how to pull out of the vicious circle in which low productivity in the dominant industry — agriculture — means low real-capital formation (either in commodities or in the capacity of the working population) and hence a low base either for a technological revolution in agriculture or for productive employment of the idle labor force. The problem here is not what to do with a given substantial surplus arising in the primary industries, but rather how to bring the economy to a point where adequate real surplus will flow into the proper channels to provide a widening base for sustained economic growth.[8]

Moving yet further along the scale, for the limits on industrialization to be transcended modern productive techniques must be brought into play. "It is always the essence of modernization that the use of machinery and power so multiplies the effort of the people engaged in production that the members of the unit in terms of which production takes place can never hope to consume directly all or even most of the products they produce."[9] Such a condition has rather important social structural implications. For present purposes it is sufficient to indicate that the process can never proceed very far without specialization of productive activities also taking place. Thus the locus of nonagricultural production shifts away from the agricultural context to systems devoted more exclusively to such production (and hence there occurs a rise in nonagricultural labor).[10] This rise is further abetted through substitution for agriculturally derived products of more efficient "functional equivalents" made possible by modern productive techniques. Finally, given the general increases in per capita income as a result of greater productivity, the demand for agricultural products, relatively speaking, falls and appears to "level off" sooner than for nonagricultural products. Stated another way, a shift in demand will occur with increased per capita income such that the proportion expended on agricultural products will drop, however much it may rise absolutely.[11] Together, these factors provide the minimal grounds for the proposition that when we move to the suggested scale's topmost position, modernization, both industrialization and economic growth will have occurred as well.

Briefly, then, for industrialization to occur in any substantial degree, productivity for subsistence must rise to a level that permits individuals to engage in productive activities other than providing directly for their own physical survival. Indeed, during earlier times spoken of, increases in agricultural productivity often resulted in increases in industrial production as that term is used here. But, for an "industrial revolution" to come about, an "agricultural revolution" must also occur. In speaking of modernization and its implied technological innovations, we refer not only to the nonagricultural sectors of the economy but to the entire productive capacity in a society, not the least important of which is agriculture. Thus, changes that result in a proliferation of tools and inanimate sources of energy to multiply human effort on an increasing scale permit the overwhelming amount of human labor in a society to be devoted to industrial production under conditions of sustained economic growth.[12]

The Changing Structure of American Production

We now turn more directly to the American experience of the general process outlined in the foregoing section. By way of introduction, we quote at length from a summary of these events by a student of the process.

The growth of this country's national product per head — the best simple measure of economic growth that we have — has averaged about 1¾ per cent a year over the last 120 years [1839-1959] after adjustment for price changes, and has shown remarkable steadiness if periods of at least 40 years' duration are considered. This trend under which real income per head doubles every 40 years and increases almost sixfold every century, is far above the growth rate experienced by the United States in its earlier history; has hardly if ever been equaled for as long a stretch of time in any other country or period; and has been the vehicle which has propelled the United States to its present eminence in the world as the country with the largest aggregate output, the most advanced technology and the highest standard of living; and as the main source of foreign capital for less developed areas.[13]

Goldsmith goes on to divide this long stretch of history into three forty-year subperiods:

The first of them, from 1839 to 1879, can be regarded as the formative period of modern America, politically and economically. The second subperiod, stretching from 1879 to 1919, witnessed the creation of the country's industrial and financial system as we still know it notwithstanding all the extensive and intensive changes that have since taken place. The last subperiod, extending from 1919 to the present, circumscribes fairly accurately the period of economic preeminence of the United States, a position characterized by a share in total world production of not less than one fourth; the highest standard of technology and of consumer welfare found anywhere in the world; and the role as the chief supplier of capital and technical assistance to less developed countries.[14]

It is, in fact, to this second subperiod, as delineated by the writer, and in which "the creation of the country's industrial and financial system as we still know it" occurred, that the present study is addressed. This was also the era in which the highest levels of immigration in American history were attained; the phenomenon will be discussed in the latter portion of this chapter. In the present section the shifting balance between agriculture and industry is considered.

Prior to the 120-year period considered by Goldsmith, American economic growth was considerably slower than subsequently. It appears that significant changes in the growth rate might not have occurred until about 1800 or, in any event, as Goldsmith suggests, not very long before 1839, and that this "reflects both the transition of the United States from a predominantly agricultural to a more and more industrial country and the advent of the railroads."[15] The data on labor force distribution, although far from precise for this early period, indicate little change between the years 1820-1840, with those engaged in agriculture remaining at about 70 percent.[16] Subsequent shifts, however, were quite pronounced, and this, together with other evidence to be noted below, indicates that introduction of modern productive techniques occurred not long before 1840.

As noted briefly at the outset of this chapter, one of the more important concomitants of modernization is that the level of specialization increases substantially with respect to the production of goods and services; i.e., goods and services that are forthcoming in a society are increasingly the result of operations of separate units oriented around producing one or a specified limited number of them. To the extent that this occurs, the level of self-sufficiency of productive units falls; that is, the degree to which members of such units consume what they produce and produce what they consume is diminished. Finally, the growth and centralization of markets and the proliferation of a generalized medium of exchange, together with increases in transport facilities to move products physically to consumers, are inextricably linked with the foregoing.[17]

Although the American farm unit may not have been completely self-sufficient in the early nineteenth century,[18] one thing clearly stands out: it became progressively *less* so over time. While farms were relatively isolated from potential sources of demand for their products, little change occurred in agricultural production. The impetus toward modernization in agriculture was related to a growing transportation network which increased long-distance communications and extended the market.

The farmer finally had access to the means with which to move surpluses long distances relatively cheaply. Equally important, farmers themselves became accessible to the sale of improved agricultural implements that were rapidly being developed.[19] During the period 1820 to 1860, then, the foundations were laid for the modernization of American agriculture.

This revolution in agricultural technology got under way in the 1830's. A generation earlier the cotton gin had made possible extensive cotton culture. Now it was the invention of the mechanical implements for the farm — the reaper, the mower, the seed drill, the steel plow, the threshing machine — that made farming possible on an extensive scale, particularly in the prairie regions of the midwest where old style farming practices had proved impracticable. As farming became a large scale operation, it became at the same time a commercial enterprise and the process resulted in an agricultural revolution.[20]

Kuznets concludes that the rise in product per agricultural worker during this period might have been 20 to 30 percent.[21]

The increase of specialization accompanying modernized production and increases in markets has been noted. It was fairly clear that the farm unit in America had, by 1860, become more purely a unit of agricultural production, and this proved a continuing trend.[22] In one area, for example:

The coincidence in time and place between the decay of household industries and the rise of the market is striking. The reports of agricultural fairs show that the exhibits of home-made textiles fell off rapidly between 1820 and 1830 in counties where industrial growth and urban concentration were progressing most rapidly .... It seems safe to conclude that by 1860, although the use of homespun fabrics still continued, their further production in farmers' families in southern New England had come to an end.[23]

With such increasing specialization and the concomitant necessity for acquiring goods and services no longer produced within the farm unit, a "money economy" proceeded apace. This perhaps may best be indicated by the real (adjusting for price changes) money supply per capita in the United States. It increased from 5.8 dollars in 1799 to 31 dollars in 1859. By 1919, the figure stood at 155.2 dollars per capita.[24]

Finally, the relatively large-scale production of new farm implements indicates further specialization away from the farm of those functions formerly performed either on it or by local artisans, as well, it might be added, as indicating the spread of agricultural modernization. Thus, tens of thousands of plows were being manufactured in plants located in Massachusetts and Pittsburgh even before mid-century.[25]

Much of the farm equipment that now characterizes American agriculture first appeared, although in less sophisticated form and without benefit of inanimate sources of power, before the Civil War. By 1860, according to one writer, the basis of mechanized farming had been established. "The agriculture of the twentieth century is more highly advanced in its reliance upon artificial power and more common use of steel, but it is based upon the machinery introduced, perfected, and brought into common use in the nineteenth century."[26]

Thus, during the remainder of the nineteenth century and through World War I, agricultural production increased at a fairly rapid pace, and a large part of this growth was doubtless due to the spread and refinement of techniques already developed. These advances were reflected in the growing productivity of farm labor. Reviewing farm production figures, Shannon indicates that, for twenty-seven different agricultural commodities, the required labor using late nineteenth-century methods fell 47.7 percent when compared with early-century hand methods.[27]

What was considered an adequate outlay for farm equipment rose spectacularly during the century,[28] and the volume of farm power equipment, which of course was wedded to earlier advances, increased 4.77 times between 1870 and 1920. Per-worker output in 1920 was almost twice what it had been in 1870.[29]

Much of the initial agricultural growth in the United States was the result of extensions of cultivation in a fairly empty country with millions of acres being increasingly brought into production under conditions that pressed for machinery to work relatively large holdings. By the end of the nineteenth century, the most fertile of the lands were settled and, by World War I, further extensions in settlement had, by and large, been completed. Work opportunities by the 1880's lay not on the farm but in urban-industrial employments.[30]

Despite the enormous gains made in agriculture during this period of extension of land cultivation and of mechanization, they were less rapid than those in the nonagricultural sectors and evidenced a continuing downward trend with respect to share in the national product as well as labor force involved. The gains in agriculture provided the basis which permitted a parallel — even more spectacular — growth in industry.

The well-known proposition of Adam Smith that the division of labor is dependent on the extent of the market[31] is to some degree exemplified in the development of American agriculture. But it was of similar importance to industrial growth in the United States. Weber characterizes capitalistic "shop industry" as a productive unit operated by an entrepreneur, utilizing free labor in specialized and coordinated work making use of fixed capital and capitalistic accounting. "Where labor discipline within the shop is combined with technical specialization and co-ordination and the application of nonhuman sources of power, we are face to face with the modern factory."[32] Weber recognized as a prerequisite for the emergence of such facilities "mass demand, and also steady demand — that is, a certain organization of the market."[33]

In the development of a large internal market the United States was peculiarly favored because, by constitutional mandate, a national market of vast size, and free of internal barriers, was encouraged. This favored conditions conducive to regional specialization and large-scale production.[34] Market conditions for factory emergence were thus present early in American history.

The presence of such market conditions was to prove attractive to an emerging body of entrepreneurs, some of whom were migrating from the economically advanced sectors of Europe with values already "adjusted to capitalist needs and goals."[35] These businessmen were therefore sensitive to production innovations making their appearance in Europe, particularly England. "Independence enabled our industrial pioneers to procure from Great Britain and to use freely the great mechanical inventions of the eighteenth century, that under the old colonial system might have been monopolized by the mother country."[36]

European migrants with industrial experience were a major source of transfer of ideas quickly seized upon by resident entrepreneurs eager to employ their resources in new and more efficient methods of production.[37] Further, the successively rising levels of immigration provided investors abroad as well as at home with favorable conditions to extend funds to American industry.[38] The United States, then, was a "latecomer" to the process of modernization and derived the benefits of that status by being able to draw on the experience of predecessors, most especially England.

The technological transfers from Europe were not merely duplicated by local entrepreneurs, however. Great changes and adaptations took place in the American setting which were to have far-reaching consequences. Clark, in fact, makes clear that "no feature of this apprenticeship of our manufacturers to those of the Old World was more characteristic than the originality of the learned." He emphasizes that this was not a period of "mere passive borrowing" but rather that foreign inventions "were speedily transformed into the machinery of a truly native system of production."[39]

Noting the extensive borrowing of techniques from England, Rezneck asserts a rise in "industrial consciousness" in the United States and suggests that, as early as 1830, "American technology and industrial organization were . . . comparable to those of England."[40] Sawyer emphasizes that a distinctive "American system" had evolved by 1850 that proved quite impressive to British observers. The rather high capital intensity of American productive techniques exhibited perhaps one most significant feature in certain areas, namely, the principle of interchangeable parts, first applied by Eli Whitney to the manufacture of arms. Sawyer sums up this development as follows:

> Centering in southern New England and in the light metal-working industries, notably in firearms, clocks, watches, locks, and tools of various kinds, and then spreading into neighboring states and a broadening range of industries, there came into being the basic elements and patterns of modern mass manufacturing; that is, the principles and practices of quantity manufacture of standardized products characterized by interchangeable parts and the use of a growing array of machine tools and specialized jigs and fixtures, along with power, to substitute simplified and, so far as possible, mechanized operations for the craftsman's arts. Hand in hand with the technical advances went parallel developments in the organization of productive effort and in the new methods necessary to market standardized quantity products.[41]

British observers were impressed with the degree of mechanization in American manufacturing,[42] and Burn, considering British impressions, indicates that the technical influence began to feed back over the Atlantic to Britain after mid-century. This "reversal" is striking indication of independent American elaboration after first relying extensively on European ideas, particularly those of the British.[43]

American industrial production distinguished itself early in the nineteenth century from its European counterparts by the establishment of a pattern of high capital intensity in its operations. Conditions in the United States making for greater willingness to invest in machinery on the part of early entrepreneurs had to do with the higher cost of American labor and the inelasticity of its supply.[44] Habakuk develops this argument to explain the sequence of American industrial development. He suggests that the abundant alternative possibility of highly remunerative farming and relatively low immigration rates in the earlier part of the nineteenth century created a rather high premium on labor in industry and an inducement for entrepreneurs to adopt the more capital-intensive of available production alternatives. Further, the price of skilled labor appeared to be less in the United States than in England, while the cost of unskilled appeared to be higher. Since skilled labor is required in the building of complicated machines for manufacturing purposes that will use less — though unskilled — labor, Habakuk suggests that the cost of *manufacture plus use* of the capital-intensive techniques required relatively more skilled-to-unskilled labor than more labor-intensive techniques.

> Where this was so, the fact that unskilled labour, in relation to skilled labour, was dearer in America than in England gave the American an inducement to make a more capital-intensive choice of technique. There is also the additional point that the type of labour which was relatively dearest performed the simple, unskilled operations which were, from a technical point of view, most easily mechanized.[45]

Labor-saving techniques, the author continues, were quite likely to be adopted earlier in the United States than elsewhere.

Immigration: The American Pull

In the early decades of the century the principal effect of labour-scarcity in America was probably to induce American manufacturers to adopt labour-saving methods invented in other countries earlier and more extensively than they were adopted in their country of origin. The number of autonomous inventions was greater in the older industrial countries. But where their principal advantage was that they were labour-saving, they were more quickly adopted in the U.S.A. and labour-scarcity then induced further improvements, each additional improvement being perhaps small in relation to the original invention. And already in the early nineteenth century there were a number of important American inventions induced directly by the search for labour-saving methods and these became increasingly common as time went on.[46]

These developments, as noted, occurred early in the nineteenth century; yet they indicate even at that point a relatively high degree of modernization in non-agricultural production in the United States. The availability and wage differentials of different grades of labor were to change by the time industry became dominant; still a pattern had been set with respect to technology, and accumulated knowledge concerning such methods was quite extensive by the end of the nineteenth century.

Although the nature of production was altering, the United States was still, during the pre-Civil War period, primarily agricultural. This situation was to be reversed by the end of the nineteenth and beginning of the twentieth century. As in agriculture, the foundations of modern production in industry had already been laid. Cumulative developments were quite rapid after the Civil War. Not the least important of such changes was the rapid growth in the extent of the market ("mass demand") which permitted the expansion of industrial production and which depended fundamentally on the construction of an adequate and reliable transportation network, brought to effect most spectacularly by the railroads.

It was in the latter part of the century that the creation of a national transport system was accomplished. The consequent specialization thus permitted between areas, within areas and within enterprises, was of course crucial to the modernization of industry. Increases in productivity, as indicated, depend on being able to move products to consumers. After the Civil War it was the railroad that provided such means. "Beginning in the 1870's, the railroads became nearly synonymous with domestic transportation for the next sixty years."[47] Railroad mileage more than tripled between 1860 and 1880 to over 90,000 miles. Between 1880 and 1920 it very nearly tripled again, totaling about 260,000 miles by the latter date, very nearly its peak in this country. If anything, mileage diminished after the thirties.[48]

By the end of the century, then, the transport network of the United States was fairly complete and the accruing advantages of market extension were impressive. The "mass demand" effected by making most of the country accessible by rail was accentuated by a growing population which increased from almost 40 million, in 1870, to over 76 million, by the turn of the century. As Clark observes:

IMMIGRANT WORKERS

In many respects the development of manufactures in the United States during the last half of the nineteenth century was parallel with that of Europe. But conditions in our country differed from typical conditions across the Atlantic in two important ways. In the first place we continued to make goods almost entirely for home consumption at a time when other large manufacturing nations were producing for export markets. Our people formed the largest consuming unit in the world — measured by population, purchasing power and standard of living — and one that was rapidly expanding; so that we had little inducement to seek foreign customers.[49]

During the period after the Civil War, a continuing rapid rise in American productivity was evidenced. Commodity output increased some 54 percent between 1869 and 1899, while population increased only 24 percent, and number of gainful workers increased 27 percent. Output per capita and output per worker rose 24 and 21 percent respectively throughout this period.[50] This was also the interval in which the shares of the various commodity-producing sectors shifted decisively in favor of nonagricultural production. The average decade rate of change in value added between 1869 and 1899 was 32 percent for agriculture, 99 percent for mining, 80 percent for manufacturing, and 36 to 45 percent for construction.[51]

These value-added differentials are reflected in sector shares calculated by Gallman. In 1869 agriculture accounted for 53 percent of total commodity output while manufacturing accounted for 33 percent. By the turn of the century agriculture and manufacturing had exactly reversed their respective shares (33 and 53 percent in 1899).[52] The nonagricultural sector (including mining and construction) was clearly the dominant area of commodity output by 1900.

One summary measure of nonagricultural modernization, the fixed capital utilized in productive enterprises, is given by Gallman. Of the total fixed capital in the commodity-producing sectors between 1839 and 1899,

Manufacturing output shared in the growth of investment. Indeed, the proportion of total output of fixed investment goods accounted for by manufactured producers' durables increased from 1/10 to about 3/10.[53]

Kuznets presents data extending into the twentieth century for all production sectors (Gallman's data are confined to commodity-producing sectors). Kuznets' data indicate, in terms of all members of the labor force, that reproducible capital (1929 values) more than doubled between 1879 and 1919 ($2.3 thousand to $5.2 thousand per labor force member).[54] In terms of overall production, then, modernization was proceeding quite rapidly in the decades centering around the turn of the century. Commenting on sector shares, Kuznets notes:

The conspicuous trends in the distribution of fixed capital are the decline in the share of agriculture, and the rise in those of mining and manufacturing and of the tax exempt sectors (the latter includes governments and non-profit institutions such as churches, educational bodies, etc.). These trends are observed whether or not we include land, although they are more conspicuous for fixed capital excluding land.[55]

It appears fairly clear that the production of goods and services was becoming increasingly modernized and that nonagricultural sectors were utilizing a greater share of the total capital available. Much of the overall increase, of course, involved use of power equipment. The power aspect can be roughly gauged from Table 3-1. It indicates that when the power aspect is viewed in isolation, increases were fairly substantial in the industrial sector of nonagricultural production. As indicated by the designations in the table, strict consistency between periods was not possible due to the information at hand. Jerome's data do indicate a trend that is both substantial within consistent series and at least indicative over the total period.

TABLE 3-1
Horsepower per Wage Earner in Manufacturing

Census Year (Hand, Neighborhood, and Factory Industries)	Wage Earners (Thousands)	Total hp (Thousands)	hp per Wage Earner
1869	2,028	2,314	1.14
1879	2,772	3,560	1.28
1889	4,171	5,857	1.40
1899	5,209	10,670	2.05
(Factories with $500 or more product)			
1899	4,713	9,942	2.11
1904	5,468	13,488	2.47
1909	6,615	18,675	2.82
1914	7,036	22,437	3.19
1919	9,096	29,505	3.24

Source: Harry Jerome, *Mechanization in Industry* (New York: National Bureau of Economic Research, Inc., 1934); adapted from Table 15, p. 217. Reprinted with permission.

In industry, then, the general direction of innovations was toward labor-saving, capital intensive alternatives characterized by increasing increments of power. Similar changes were occurring in agriculture which were, in fact, a prerequisite for industrialization as that term has been used here. As Kuznets notes:

The decline in the relative weight of agriculture in the labor force in this country — an inter-industry shift — was due to the rise in the net product per worker in agriculture — an intra-industry change that was not inferior to the rise in net product per worker in the rest of the economy. It was the increased productivity in agriculture, combined with the persistent structure of human wants, that produced a situation in which needs for agricultural products were satisfied with a smaller proportion of the total labor force in agriculture. And this labor force was lured away from agriculture partly by higher returns in non-farm industries which were made possible because under conditions of overall increases in productivity, wants of consumers were directed toward products of non-agricultural industries.[56]

Table 3-2 indicates the "inter-industry shift" referred to by Kuznets.

TABLE 3-2
Percent Gainfully Occupied—Persons Ten Years Old or Over

Census Year	Agricultural Pursuits	Nonagricultural Pursuits
1820	71.81	28.19
1830	70.52	29.48
1840	69.63	31.37
1850	63.68	36.32
1860	58.94	41.06
1870	53.00	47.00
1880	49.36	50.64
1890	42.62	57.38
1900	37.53	62.47
1910	31.02	68.98
1920	26.98	73.02
1930	21.45	78.55

Source: U.S. Bureau of the Census, *Statistical Abstract of the United States: 1950* (Washington, D.C.: Government Printing Office, 1950), p. 172.

It has been maintained that, with increasing modernization of production, a shift occurs in the activities of the labor force such that the proportion employed in agriculture decreases steadily. The term "industrialization" has been applied to this shift and it presents a gross but important indication of a changing occupational structure. The figures presented here for the United States indicate that the balance changed in favor of industrial production in the decades centering around the turn of the century and that, by World War I, the employment distribution was decisively industrial.

It was noted earlier that these decades also saw the creation of the type of productive operations that have characterized American society ever since. It was during this period that the United States took the lead in certain of the highly strategic areas of production. In 1880, American coal and pig iron production trailed Britain's and just equaled the latter's crude steel output. By 1913, the United States had surpassed Britain, Germany, France, and Belgium-Luxembourg combined in production of coal and crude steel and nearly equaled their total of pig iron (35 million tons to 31.9 for the United States).[57] In terms of total manufacturing production, the United States trailed the United Kingdom in 1870 but by 1913 equaled the total production of the latter, plus Germany and France.[58]

This, then, was the period of the organization of the American industrial complex. It is proposed now to pursue this topic in terms of labor force components. As indicated, the distribution of labor force in the various sectors provides the central measure of industrialization that will be used here. This, however, will be only part of the following discussion and such changes have already been indicated quite briefly. What is further intended is to discuss the foreign born relative to the labor force and the manner in which each factor was related to the emerging productive structures during this important transitional period.

The Changing Occupational Structure and the Labor Force

The present section brings together the occupational and labor force correlates of the "pull" features discussed. The enormous economic expansion provided a continuing place within American productive enterprises for immigrant arrivals. The nature of this expansion, however, determined both where and at what level a new arrival might enter employment. A separate section is devoted to this discussion, although in many respects it extends the foregoing remarks. The division is intended to bring the central theme of this study into more distinct focus. It begins by discussing the overall employment picture and ends by reviewing the part immigration played in it.

Labor Demand. The positive injunction for social mobility, it was indicated earlier, is necessary for a modernizing society, as rapid alterations in social structure produce new roles that must be filled if the system is to remain viable. This latter point on role differentiation represents the "demand side" of the picture. Herein lies the major explanation for observed rapid rates of social movement within relatively modernized societies. For not only are boundaries between strata fairly permeable, but a continuing reallocation of personnel among and within such strata is a necessary condition for the operations of such systems.[59]

In the previous section a simple but important measure of a major shift in the American occupational structure was presented. This dichotomous classification, indicating a marked shift from agricultural to nonagricultural pursuits, masks changes occurring within each of these categories. Closer scrutiny of the nonagricultural category may begin by citing a well-known statement by Colin Clark, who suggests that, "A wide, simple and far-reaching generalization in this field is to the effect that, as time goes on and communities become more economically advanced, the numbers engaged in agriculture tend to decline relative to the numbers in manufacture, which in their turn decline relative to the numbers in services."[60] Although this generalization may not entirely hold for societies that have recently embarked on modernization, it does appear to stand up well for the relative "early-comers"[61] and the data on the United States fit Clark's formulation well, as Edwards' remarks make clear:

From 1870 to 1910 manufacturing and mechanical industries were next in importance to agriculture as a field of employment of gainful labor, and in 1920 and in 1930 these industries outstripped agriculture in this respect. Their relative importance, however, was somewhat less in 1930 than in 1920, but was, nevertheless, far above that of agriculture.

In 1870, over 75 per cent of the Nation's labor force was engaged in the production of physical goods, that is, in agriculture, forestry and fishing, extraction of minerals, and manufacturing and mechanical industries. The trend since 1870, however, has been plainly away from production of physical goods and toward pursuits in transportation, communication, and trade; service pursuits; and clerical pursuits. With the advance in scientific and technological improvements — particularly with the rapid advance in the mechanization of industry — a smaller and smaller proportion of the Nation's labor force was needed to produce food and goods, and a larger and larger proportion found employment in distribution and service (public service, professional service, and domestic and personal service).[62]

The decades around the turn of the century were those in which the peaks were reached in proportion of gainful workers in manufacturing and mining. In 1870, the proportion of gainful workers in agriculture was some two and one-half times that in manufacturing (53.0 percent as against 20.5 percent). By 1910 agriculture had declined significantly, while the manufacturing sector nearly equaled its proportions (31.0 percent to 28.5 percent) and by 1920 agriculture for the first time trailed manufacturing which was now the leading sector (27.0 percent to 30.3 percent). This was the peak period for manufacturing, which subsequently declined (along with agriculture) in favor of service pursuits.[63]

In the foregoing discussion of industry and agriculture, the extent of the market was discussed relative to division of labor between areas and within areas of production. It was maintained that the factory system itself depended on "mass demand" and was characterized by coordinated activities of a number of individuals utilizing tools and inanimate sources of power. The typical unit of production under such circumstances becomes a system of interrelated activities carried out by separate individuals rather than the single artisan or group of artisans individually manufacturing a completed product. One important implication of such conditions is that the *scale* of productive units increases.

The elaborate specialization of productive tasks discussed with reference to mechanical technology is in large degree possible only within a single organization and, indeed, in a single plant. Although very considerable specialization between plants and companies occurs, this is much more in the nature of transfer of raw materials and component parts than of semi-finished goods as such. Part of the reason is also social: the greater ease of regulating specialized activities through supervision and the authority of the employer than through the mechanism of the market for goods. In other words, a great deal of specialization is actually internal to large productive enterprise and is likely to be somewhat proportional to the size of the enterprise.[64]

The figures in Table 3-3 document the increasing scale of manufacturing operations in the United States:

TABLE 3-3
Growth of Manufacturing Establishments

	1859	1899	1904	1914	1919
Average product	$13,429	$54,969	$68,433	$76,993	$215,157
Average wage earners	9.34	20.49	25.30	24.64	31.36

Source: Harold U. Faulkner, *The Decline of Laissez Faire* (New York: Holt, Rinehart & Winston, Inc., 1951), p. 155. Reprinted with permission.

Although important developments in nonagricultural production occurred prior to the Civil War, it appears only fairly late in the nineteenth century that such technologies became extensively applied. The transformation of handicraft manufacturing to the factory system occurred largely in the latter half of that century and became the continuing basis for expansion.[65] By 1919, 2.2 percent of manufacturing establishments in the United States employed over 251 workers each but accounted for 53.5 percent of all wage earners in such enterprises. Further, "approximately one twenty-eighth of all establishments employed 56.9 percent of all wage earners and produced 67.8 percent of the total value of products during that year."[66]

The foregoing remarks imply yet another significant change in the structure of employment that is summed up by Jaffe and Stewart:

> With modern technology a relatively small number of large establishments produce goods manufactured or processed by means of division of labor. This in turn means that the individual has to offer his services for hire to someone else who controls the means of production. Such a situation does not often occur among pre-industrialized peoples, among whom the means of production tend to be owned and controlled by the individual or his family or tribal group.[67]

Thus, Lebergott's estimates indicate an overwhelming shift in the proportion of the labor force which works for others as indicated in Table 3-4:

TABLE 3-4
Employment Status of the American Labor Force

Labor Force	1800	1860	1910	1957
Total	100%	100%	100%	100%
Self-employed	57	37	22	14
Slaves	31	23		
Employees	12	40	78	86

Source: Stanley Lebergott, "The Pattern of Employment Since 1800," in Seymour E. Harris (ed.), *American Economic History* (New York: McGraw-Hill Book Co., 1961), p. 292. Reprinted with permission.

Consistent with previous discussion, this author indicates that increasing wage earner proportions were, in large measure, a function of employment in factories of increasing size.

Finally, reference may be made once again to the skill distribution of the labor force during the course of modernization. As was noted in the first chapter, it is during the initial inception of modern industrialism that the most severe bipolar tendencies are evidenced. Previous skills tend to be either "fractionated" into simplified tasks or obliterated entirely by new techniques. New skills arise, especially in the form of managerial roles required by larger-scale operations, and it is at this point that the widest gulf appears to exist between those who are the product handlers and those who coordinate their activities. Over time, the least skilled positions in the labor force tend to contract and a general upgrading is to be expected,[68] but the initial and most stressful period is one in which a relatively less-skilled portion of the industrial labor force is at its peak. This appeared to occur in the United States in the decades just before and after the turn of the century.

Labor Force Composition. Approximately 38 million immigrants entered the United States in the 120-year period 1820-1940. The peak periods of this enormous influx, as indicated in Table 3-5, were in the years immediately preceding and following the turn of the century. Between 1881 and 1915, some 22 million individuals entered from abroad.

TABLE 3-5

United States Immigration: 1820 to 1940

Period	Number
1820-1830	151,824
1831-1840	599,125
1841-1850	1,713,251
1851-1860	2,598,214
1861-1870	2,314,824
1871-1880	2,812,191
1881-1890	5,246,613
1891-1900	3,687,564
1901-1905	3,833,076
1906-1910	4,962,310
1911-1915	4,459,831
1916-1920	1,275,980
1921-1925	2,638,913
1926-1930	1,468,296
1931-1935	220,209
1936-1940	308,222

Source: U.S. Bureau of the Census, *Statistical Abstract of the United States: 1950* (Washington, D.C.: Government Printing Office, 1950), p. 97.

Immigration: The American Pull

The origins of these migrants shifted discernibly during the course of this enormous flow. Beginning in the 1880's, the streams originating in Southern and Eastern Europe rose dramatically. By the turn of the century, during the highest levels of immigration ever reached (before or since), the substantial majority were coming from these areas (see Table 3-6). Between the years 1896 and 1915, three countries, Russia, Austria, and Italy, accounted for over 60 percent of the arrivals.[69]

TABLE 3-6
Areas of Origin of Immigrants to the United States

Dates	Northern and Western Europe	Other Europe	All Other
1910-1919	17.5%	62.1%	20.3%
1900-1909	22.1	71.0	6.9
1890-1899	49.4	47.5	3.1
1880-1889	72.5	16.0	11.6
1870-1879	75.8	6.3	17.9
1860-1869	82.5	8.6	8.9
1850-1859	90.3	2.8	6.9
1840-1849	95.6	0.3	4.1
1830-1839	77.5	1.1	21.5
1820-1829	74.7	2.6	22.7

Source: U.S. Bureau of the Census, *Immigrants and Their Children: 1920*, "Census Monographs VII," by Niles Carpenter (Washington, D.C.: Government Printing Office, 1927), p. 62.

It has been maintained that the economic aspect was of overriding importance in the great movement that is being considered. In this regard, it is of prime significance to note that these movements were consistently geared to business cycles in this country. As discussed in Chapter 2, Jerome finds a discernible positive relationship between business cycles and migration. His evidence indicates that this relationship was weaker before the Civil War but grew in the latter part of the century. An intensive analysis of the 1890-1914 interval discloses an exceptionally close association between prior changes in production and employment and migration flows.[70]

Thomas similarly finds a closer association between these elements after the Civil War and asserts that the "pull" factor was more salient then, while the "Malthusian push" was the prominent explanatory feature in the earlier period.[71]

The aim here has not been to disentangle the relative weights of the "push" and "pull" factors in transatlantic migration but to indicate their mutual relevance. Although the relationship between business cycles and migration during the latter part of the nineteenth and early part of the twentieth centuries is of great significance for later analysis, the evidence is here referred to in order to corroborate the economic character of the movement rather than to suggest that the "pull" influence was more pronounced during this period than earlier. This interval, when the closest relationship between business cycles and foreign influxes is discerned, occurs during the decisive shift in labor force participation to industrial employee roles in large-scale enterprises. The classical economically rational response of European migrants to business conditions here, of necessity, had to be predicated on opportunities within such a context. Indicators of business cycles are a greater reflection of the total economic performance of a more modernized society than they are of one less modernized. It is therefore suggested that the earlier weaker relationship observed between business cycles and migration was partially a function of the type of society that existed at that time and, of itself, may not necessarily imply a lower "pull" salience. The earlier period was one in which the probability of acquiring cheap land for individual farming provided a greater employment consideration than later. (About a third of the foreign born were farmers in 1850 compared to 11 percent in 1890.) And this in a society where much less of the total output "moved through the market." Thus, an individual's decision to migrate during the later period was much more contingent on the "state of the market" than earlier, where the ease of acquiring a sufficient tract of land may have exerted a large economic attraction, but one that was independent of business fluctuations.

A fair summary of the two sides of the coin is provided by Kuznets:

While the over-all volume of immigration responded to the short-, and sometimes, longer-, term economic changes in this country — rather than the push in the countries of origin — distinguishing the latter reveals that the "push" exercised considerable influence on the *secular* changes in origin of American immigration. The shift from Great Britain and Ireland to Germany and the Scandinavian countries, and then to Italy and Eastern Europe, follows the trail of the industrial revolution in Europe. It at least suggests that immigration into the United States (and, at a far second remove, into other countries in the Western Hemisphere) provided a welcome alternative to population groups displaced by revolutionary changes in agriculture and industry; and thus facilitated in no small measure the course of industrialization in the European countries. This migration may thus be viewed as an adjustment of population to resources that affected a substantial part of the world, that in its magnitude and the extent to which it could adapt itself to purely economic needs has few parallels in history. Indeed it is matched only by the vast and free *internal* migration that occurred in the process of economic growth of such larger land-mass units as the United States and Russia.[72]

Further proof of the economic character of immigration during the period in question is indicated by the age and sex distributions of the migrants (see Table 3-7). They were such as to make for a relatively high propensity to participate in the labor force. Throughout this period, males exceeded females substantially. Between 1879 and 1918 the male percentage of gross immigration never fell below 60 and rose to 68.7 and 68.0 in the intervals 1899-1908 and 1904-1913 respectively. These were the two peak decades of United States immigration. In fact, the proportion of males tended to rise whenever the rate of change in gross immigration rose. "Since the male immigrants had by far the highest rate of participation in the labor force, this movement of the proportion of males is further support of the view that fluctuations in the rate of immigration were an economic response to varying opportunities for work in this country."[73]

TABLE 3-7
Percentage of Immigrants by Age

Year	Under 15	15-40	Over 40
1880	19.1	71.6	9.3
1890	19.0	69.2	11.8
1900	15.5	73.8	10.7
1910	14.9	74.7	10.4
1920	18.4	66.8	14.8

Source: Walter F. Wilcox, "Immigration into the United States," in Walter F. Wilcox (ed.), *International Migrations* (New York: National Bureau of Economic Research, Inc., 1931), Vol. II, Table 33, p. 114. Reprinted with permission.

The high labor force participation rate suggested by the age and sex distribution of immigrants is borne out by the fact that, though the cumulative contribution of net immigration to population increase between 1870 and 1910 was over one-seventh, contributions to the labor force amounted to one-fifth.[74] Among the foreign born ten years of age or older in 1910, 60.3 percent were engaged in gainful occupations. The corresponding percentages of native-born whites of foreign or mixed parentage and native-born whites of native parentage were 50.4 and 48.4 respectively. The figures are perhaps more revealing in the case of males alone. Taking the groups in the same order, the corresponding percentages are 90.0, 76.5, and 78.5.[75]

Tables 3-8 and 3-9 indicate the extent of foreign-born white (FBW) employment as compared with native white workers of native parentage (NWNP) and native white workers of foreign or mixed parentage (NWFMP).[76] The first table indicates that, although accounting for only a fourth of all white male gainful workers, the foreign born comprised more than half of those engaged in mining and well over a third employed in manufacturing and domestic and personal services. The second table confirms that the foreign born as a group were concentrated in the industrial sector of the labor force. Indeed, more than half of the foreign-born workers were engaged in mining and manufacturing alone as compared to about a third of the total group of gainful workers.

Table 3-10 reveals that, in certain rather important areas of production, the foreign born might have been of even greater proportional significance than the totals suggest.

IMMIGRANT WORKERS

TABLE 3-8
Percentage of Distribution by Occupation of White Male Gainful Workers Ten Years of Age or Over, 1910

General Division of Occupations	NWNP	NWFMP	FBW
Agriculture, forestry, animal husbandry	73.55	14.81	11.63
Extraction of minerals	34.07	14.55	51.38
Manufacturing and mechanical industry	42.16	21.79	36.05
Transportation	49.75	19.93	30.33
Trade	52.71	24.14	23.15
Public services (n.e.c.)	50.63	25.96	23.41
Professional services	64.42	19.87	15.71
Domestic and personal services	39.27	21.65	39.08
Clerical occupations	55.66	32.58	11.76
Total	55.58	19.78	24.65

Source: U.S. Bureau of the Census, *Immigrants and Their Children: 1920,* "Census Monographs VII," by Niles Carpenter (Washington, D.C.: Government Printing Office, 1927), computed from Table 124, p. 274.

TABLE 3-9
Percentage of Distribution by Occupation within Three White Male Gainful Worker Groupings Ten Years of Age or Over, 1910

General Division of Occupations	Total	NWNP	NWFMP	FBW
Agriculture, forestry, animal husbandry	33.4	44.2	25.9	15.8
Extraction of minerals	3.4	2.1	2.5	7.0
Manufacturing and mechanical industry	30.8	23.3	33.0	45.0
Transportation	8.5	7.6	8.5	10.4
Trade	11.3	10.7	13.8	10.6
Public services (n.e.c.)	1.6	1.4	2.1	1.5
Professional services	3.4	4.0	3.5	2.2
Domestic and personal services	3.5	2.4	3.8	5.5
Clerical occupations	4.2	4.2	6.9	2.0

Source: U.S. Bureau of the Census, *Immigrants and Their Children: 1920,* "Census Monographs VII," by Niles Carpenter (Washington, D.C.: Government Printing Office, 1927), computed from Table 123, p. 272.

Immigration: The American Pull

TABLE 3-10
Percentage of Foreign-Born White Male Workers in Selected Industries, 1910

Coal mines	48.3	Tanneries	52.9
Copper mines	65.4	Breweries	49.2
Iron mines	66.8	Piano and organ factories	43.2
Quarries	45.2	Brass mills	45.8
Lime, cement, and gypsum factories	40.0	Blast furnaces and steel rolling mills	51.0
Marble and stone yards	44.2	Mills	48.3
Clothing factories (suits, coats, cloaks, and overalls)	75.9	Silk mills	46.5
Clothing factories (except suits, coats, cloaks, and overalls)	75.2	Textile, dyeing, finishing, and printing mills	48.7
Hat factories (wool and felt)	42.4	Woolen and worsted mills	50.2
Bakeries	50.5	Rubber factories	40.3
Slaughter and packing houses	45.8	Construction and maintenance of streets, roads, sewers, and bridges	46.0
Car and railroad shops	45.6		

Source: Ross Eckler and Jack Zlotnick, "Immigration and the Labor Force," *Annals of the American Academy of Political and Social Science,* Vol. 262 (March 1949), Table 5, p. 100. Reprinted with permission.

In 1908, an intensive investigation of immigrants in industry was begun by the Immigration Commission. The commission examined immigrant participation in industrial activities between the Rocky Mountains and the Atlantic Seaboard but devoted its greatest attention to the eastern states, where immigrant settlement was quite heavy. Information gathered as to 181,330 foreign-born male manufacturing and mining employees revealed that but 15.3 percent had been engaged in manufacturing before arrival while 53.9 percent were engaged in farming and farm labor. These data also indicated that, with important exceptions, migrants coming from Northwestern Europe had larger proportions with previous manufacturing experience (the most notable exception being the Irish) than the now-dominant streams from Southeastern Europe, who were predominantly agriculturalists (Jewish migrants being the most important exception here).[77]

The commission tended to draw conclusions from these skill differences that were biased against the "new" immigrants. The impression was given that the character of the "old" immigration had not altered since the period when those expatriates represented the dominant stream of migrants. If the skill ratios of the "old" migrants are taken from this earlier period (1871-1882), differentials between the two groups are seen to be quite small.[78] The "old" groups, at the time the commission collected its data, were coming from relatively more modernized societies than the "new." They were moving into a structurally more isomorphic situation when their home societies were compared with the United States as opposed to Southeastern European.[79]

The dominant element overall, then, was one of individuals with relatively little industrial experience. Commission data indicate that migrants were often recruited into large-scale productive enterprises characterized by high capital investment, such as iron and steel manufacture and various branches of mining. Even slaughtering and meat-packing, although less capital intensive, had undergone a high degree of rationalization and subdivision of work processes.[80] Commenting on the relatively large influx of those without prior industrial experience, the commission stated that: "As a consequence their employment in the mines and manufacturing plants of the country has been made possible only by the invention of mechanical devices and processes which have eliminated the skill and experience formerly recognized in a large number of occupations." It went on to assert of the newer mechanized mining techniques that:

Such work can readily be done, after a few days' apprenticeship, by recent immigrants who, before immigrating to the United States, had never seen a coal mine. The same situation is found in cotton factories, where unskilled and inexperienced immigrants can, after a brief training, operate the automatic looms and weavers and mule spinners. In the glass factories, also, which are engaged in the manufacture of bottles and window and plate glass, untrained immigrants, through the assistance of improved machinery, turn out the same products which in the past years required the services of the highly trained glass blowers. In the iron and steel plants and other branches of manufacturing similar inventions have made it possible to operate the plants with a much smaller proportion of skilled and specialized employees than was formerly the case. It is this condition of industrial affairs as already stated, which has made it possible to give employment to the untrained, inexperienced, non-English-speaking, immigrant of recent arrival in the United States.[81]

Habakuk notes that whereas an earlier scarcity of labor stimulated a capital intensive bias in American industry, under late-nineteenth-century conditions a more elastic labor supply permitted a more extensive application of this trend:

The principal effect of immigration was not on the manufacturer's choice of technique but on his ability to give effect to his choice . . . Immigration encouraged the American industrialists to buy additional machines, and they naturally bought the most economic machines, but machines which would have been the most economic even in the absence of heavy immigration. Indeed it might be said that the U.S.A. was lucky in this respect. After mid-century, the labor supply available to American industry became less inelastic; heavy immigration damped down wage rates; so that profits were high in the U.S.A. and therefore investment more rapid, at a time when technical progress everywhere was considerable.[82]

Similarly, the Immigration Commission stated:

It may be said, therefore, that industrial expansion was the original reason for the employment of races of recent immigration, but that after the availability of this labor became known further industrial expansion was stimulated by the fact of this availability, the original cause thus becoming largely an effect of the conditions it had created.[83]

Immigration: The American Pull

Thus, of those who had been in agricultural labor in Europe, not more than 10 percent entered agricultural pursuits in the United States around the turn of the century. Further, of the smaller proportion of immigrants coming with skilled-trade experience, few could pursue their previous expertise. For example, of sixteen such trades, taken as a whole, only 23.7 percent of their practitioners took up their former occupation. It appears that the high level of modernization achieved in the United States not only made it easier for those without industrial experience to enter such employment, but often required those with previous skills in a less modernized setting to change occupation on arrival.[84]

Previous figures have shown the disproportionate contribution of the foreign born in the industrial sector (with manufacturing and mining being the two leading categories) of gainful employment. The immediately preceding discussion further indicated that immigrants in substantial numbers entered the less-skilled occupations. A scale of occupational stratification was not developed for census purposes until 1910. But this first year of its use followed a high-water mark of immigration to the United States. Table 3-11 indicates that the foreign born were considerably overrepresented at the lower end of the occupational hierarchy. They constituted nearly half of the laborers and over a third of the operatives, although they made up only a quarter of the total white male gainful workers, ten years of age or over.

TABLE 3-11

Percentage of Foreign Born among White Male Gainful Workers Ten Years of Age or Over, 1910

Occupation	Percentage
Total	24.7
Professional, technical, and kindred workers	15.6
Farmers and farm managers	12.8
Managers, officials, and proprietors, except farm	26.4
Clerical and kindred workers	10.9
Salesworkers	18.0
Craftsmen, foremen, and kindred workers	29.6
Operatives and kindred workers	38.0
Service workers, including private household	36.8
Farm laborers and foremen	8.4
Laborers, except farm and mine	45.0

Source: E. P. Hutchinson, *Immigrants and Their Children: 1850-1950* (New York: John Wiley & Sons, Inc., 1956), Table 38, p. 202. [It seemed advisable to recompute percentage figures from the measure of "relative concentration" offered by Hutchinson in order to remain consistent with the format of other related tabulations that have been presented.] Reprinted with permission.

In the blue-collar portion of the gainfully employed generally, and in the less-skilled categories particularly, the foreign born are represented in numbers that exceed their proportion of total gainfully employed. Immigrants, then, assumed those occupational roles in modernizing America that were within the industrial sector and also at the lower reward levels of that sector. The ranking immediately above corresponds roughly to income gradations.[85] In general, the lower the remunerative level of industrial occupations, the greater the proportion of foreign-born workers at that level.

In this regard, data gathered by the Immigration Commission in 1908 are of interest. With regard to weekly earnings, for example, commission information on some 220,000 male workers showed that white native-born employees whose fathers were also native born earned an average of $14.37. Those native-born workers whose fathers were foreign born averaged $13.91. The foreign-born workers averaged $11.92. Within the foreign-born group, the "new" immigrants generally earned less than the "old."[86]

The income differentials between "new" and "old" immigrants (as well, it may be added, as between foreign born and native born) has frequently been explained by the well-known characterization of later arrivals "pushing" previous residents up in the occupational hierarchy. It was implied earlier, however, that a more appropriate view of mobility is achieved from the perspective of the "demand side." Seen from this vantage point, the explanation was not that recent migrants propelled previous arrivals upward but rather that both were responding to opportunities created by expanding industry in which the later groups were at a disadvantage in competing for the more remunerative occupations. One of the reasons for this state of affairs has already been pointed out when it was noted that the numerical minority coming from Northwestern Europe were moving from societies that were more isomorphic to the United States than those of Southeastern Europe. It was shown, however, that Northwestern Europeans were not significantly more skill-endowed than the Southeasterners when the former's highest migration movement is examined some three decades earlier. The "older" migrants at the later date, then, were more readily able to move into the higher-paying occupational roles when compared with both Southeastern Europeans and their own countrymen several decades before them.

But this only explains a small segment of the differentials noted. A further factor of high significance is that "new" immigrants had been, at the time the Immigration Commission comparisons were made, in this country a shorter period of time, as a group, than the "old." They were, by definition, the more recent arrivals. Kuznets notes the important contribution of recently arrived immigrants to the labor force:

The newly arrived foreign born were, in general, in age and sex classes that participated more heavily in the labor market than the older resident foreign born. Therefore, those in the country less than ten years might have constituted close to half of the foreign born labor force in 1890 and 1910. At the same dates, all foreign born gainfully engaged were well above 20 per cent of the total labor force in the United States. This means that in 1890 and 1910, over 10 per cent of the total labor force of this country were adults who had been in the country for 10 years or less.[87]

Thus the "old" immigrants who themselves had earlier constituted a large and inexperienced labor force element, were, by the later period, through longer residence, a more experienced group within the industrial setting than their "new" colleagues, even if the former had not done such work in their homelands. Indeed, the Immigration Commission tabulations themselves bear out these remarks. Of some 290,000 foreign-born (male and female) mining and manufacturing employees in 1908, 63.1 percent had been in this country under 10 years and 40 percent under 5 years. In general "old" immigrants had been here longer than "new." Figures presented for "old" immigrants include those for the English, 31.5 percent of whom had been in the country 10 years or less and 19.5 percent 5 years or less. For Germans, the respective percentages are 25.1 and 14.4. The corresponding figures for the Irish are 20.1 percent and 10.4 percent, and for the Swedes, 28.9 percent and 12.7 percent. Figures for "new" immigrant groups include Russian Jews, of whom 76.5 percent had been in the United States 10 years or less, 48.9 percent 5 years or less. For southern Italians the corresponding figures are 87.8 percent and 52.9 percent. For Poles the figures were 76.9 percent and 49.1 percent, while the corresponding percentages for Slovaks were 72 and 40.5.[88]

To the more recent arrivals, then, fell the lot of the less-skilled and lower-paid occupational roles. It appears that the abundant additions of labor at this level operated to retard wage increases by providing a supply large enough for employers to bid down the wage rate.[89] Lebergott, however, finds that wage fluctuations were of little influence in determining immigration rates, since wages in this country were far above European and Asian alternatives in any event. Instead, he finds a close association between immigration and *job opportunities*.[90]

It is not unreasonable to conclude that if wage differentials between Europe and the United States were large, they were even larger between the industrial sector of the latter and the agricultural sector of the former, from which most European migrants came, than they were between the agricultural and industrial sectors *within* the United States. Hence the net advantage to European migrants was relatively greater than to native Americans given length of work sufficient to overcome the (decreasing) cost of travel.

Of related interest is Thomas' suggestion on an inverse relation between internal and external migration such that after the war, when foreign-born entrants dropped substantially, internal movement increased.[91] Interestingly enough, this *internal* movement is seen as a partial explanation for a retardation of wage levels between 1919 and 1926, after initial increases during the war years.[92] Thus, nativists of the period notwithstanding, it appears that structural conditions within the industrial sector, requiring heavy influxes of unskilled labor at a higher wage than for farm work, nevertheless produce a short-term wage-retarding "pull" on rural population, foreign *or* native, who are relatively inexperienced at industrial pursuits.

It was argued earlier that two important features characterizing the early stages of rapid modernization are marked discontinuity with previous practices and severe polarization of strata. The earlier sections of this chapter pointed to the rapid changes in post-Civil War production in the United States. Kuznets, while readily admitting a lack of data on the subject, provides some pertinent conjectures on trends in income inequalities during this period generally, and for the United States specifically.

It seems most plausible to assume that in earlier periods of industrialization, even when the nonagricultural population was still relatively small in the total, its income distribution was more unequal than that of the agricultural population. This would be particularly so during the periods when industrialization and urbanization were proceeding apace and the urban population was being swelled, and rapidly, by immigrants — either from the country's agricultural areas or from abroad. Under these conditions, the urban population would run the full gamut from low income positions of recent entrants to the economic peaks of the established top-income groups. The urban income inequalities might be assumed to be far wider than those for the agricultural population which was organized in relatively small individual enterprises (large-scale units were rarer then than now).[93]

Kuznets thus proceeds to suggest that there occurs an initial *widening* of income inequalities during the early shifts from agriculture to industry. There are two reasons for this outcome: First, there exists a general per capita income differential between the agricultural and industrial sectors favoring the latter and, second, the above-mentioned greater income inequality *within* the industrial sector as compared to that within the agricultural sector may be noted. The indications are that the agricultural-industrial income differential is a persisting one, thereby leading Kuznets to the conclusion that "the major offset to the widening of income inequality associated with the shift from agriculture and the countryside to industry and the city must have been a rise in the share of the lower groups within the nonagricultural sector of the population."[94]

These remarks corroborate earlier statements on the initial polarization of strata. Of further importance to the problem under consideration here is Kuznets' estimate of the period of income widening for the United States, for this also involves the most unequal income phase of the industrial sector. The author suggests that the widening of income inequality in the United States occurred between 1840 and 1890, *but especially after 1870.* He further indicates that a narrowing of income inequality may not have begun until the beginning of World War I.[95] This period of greatest income inequality occurs, of course, precisely during the peak influx of immigrants to the United States and, as the initial quotation above implies, is not unrelated to Kuznets' reasoning.

We have indicated earlier that the structure of nonagricultural production during the course of modernization is a major clue to these inequalities. The changing occupational distribution, involving a general upgrading as the least skilled and least remunerative categories shrink (and the middle widens), is an important explanatory link.

It was pointed out earlier, citing Thomas, that internal migration appeared to be inversely related to external, and thus the former might well have been more substantial earlier than it was had the latter been less so. Immigrants, then, entered the American scene at the most polarized structural phase of its modernization, a phase that would have been the most unequal without their presence. Although it is possible that immigrant entry may have retarded wage increases further than native migration would have, it was nevertheless the foreign born themselves who bore a disproportionate burden of lower income, while quite possibly (following Habakuk's argument on cheap labor stimulating investment) making this phase of high inequalities less protracted than it otherwise might have been.

Conclusion

The preceding pages have contained an attempt to document the sequence of American productive modernization. It has been asserted that the period in which the transition to relative modernization was decisively achieved lay in the post-Civil War years, especially from the 1880's through World War I. Prior to this time — indeed quite early in American history — spectacular productive innovations had been accomplished in a variety of pursuits. The general application of these techniques, however, came in the latter part of the nineteenth century and it was during this period that the institutions characteristic of modernization were extensively realized.

The aim in what has preceded, as well as that in subsequent discussion, is to relate a number of general aspects of modernization (i.e., those which *any* society undergoing these changes will evidence) to the specific American experience. Two of these aspects are paramount. One has to do with the radical structural discontinuity as between a relatively modernized and a relatively nonmodernized society. The other is what might be referred to as severe structural polarization during the early phases of modernization.

In the first chapter an explicit distinction was made between social structure, or patterns of action, and those who "populate" the structure, or operate in terms of such patterns. It was argued that individuals moving into a milieu of rapid social change, who were not members of the system in question *prior* to such change, present a significant factor in assessing the resolution of tensions which the many changes bring about. Relevant data have been assembled here indicating that immigrants came to the United States in vast numbers during a period of rapid social change associated with modernization. Since our concern is with the labor movement in this country, data were presented indicating that immigration of this period was economically oriented such that those entering the United States were most likely to seek employment. Further, such employment was overwhelmingly in the industrial sector, most especially in those areas characterized by large-scale and capital-intensive processes requiring heavy increments of relatively unskilled labor. The countrywide figures presented, striking as they are, may nevertheless understate the immigrant labor contribution to such enterprises, which were heavily concentrated in the East where most migrants of this period were located.

Finally, during the polarizing inception of modernization, it was primarily the foreign born who disproportionately bore the burden of the less-advantaged levels of the industrial occupational hierarchy. The vast influxes of immigrants, it was pointed out, meant that possibly half the foreign born in the labor force were quite recent arrivals. Since the evidence also suggests that late arrivals generally entered the lower end of the occupational hierarchy, it is reasonable to impute a far higher proportion of newcomers the further down the scale one moves. Thus, those occupational categories with the greatest concentration of immigrants were also likely to have the highest proportions of newly arrived.

Therefore, an attempt has been made to "locate" that strain-producing interval during which American social structure underwent fundamental and severe changes while, at the same time, indicating that a substantial portion of those who participated in the process were "strangers" to American society. The following chapter will be addressed primarily to the problem of discontinuity and the strains manifested therefrom as they related to America's developing labor movement.

NOTES

1. For a similar, but not identical, treatment of this subject see Wilbert E. Moore, *The Impact of Industry* (Englewood Cliffs, N.J.: Prentice-Hall, 1965), pp. 4-7.
2. Simon Kuznets, *Six Lectures on Economic Growth* (New York: The Free Press, 1959), pp. 13-14.
3. The term "full time," calls attention to the fact that much nonagricultural labor is connected with agriculture in the early stages of industrialization in that farmers and their families produce a variety of goods and services that cannot be classified as "agricultural." When such shifts in labor force occur there results the concomitant of specialization as farm work becomes more purely agricultural. See Simon Kuznets, "Toward a Theory of Economic Growth," in Robert Lekachman, *National Policy for Economic Welfare at Home and Abroad* (Garden City: Doubleday & Co., 1955), p. 34.
4. Marion J. Levy, Jr., *Modernization and the Structure of Societies* (Princeton: Princeton University Press, 1966), Vol. I, pp. 9-15.
5. Frederick C. Lane, "Comment," in Lekachman, *op. cit.,* p. 91.
6. See W. W. Rostow, "Industrialization and Economic Growth," in *Contributions to the First International Conference of Economic History* (Paris: Mouton & Co., 1960), pp. 19-22.
7. Simon Kuznets, "Problems in Comparisons of Economic Trends," in Kuznets, Wilbert E. Moore, and Joseph J. Spengler (eds.), *Economic Growth: Brazil, India, Japan* (Durham: Duke University Press, 1955), p. 18.
8. *Ibid.,* p. 18.
9. Levy, *op. cit.*, p. 238.
10. See Kuznets' discussion in Lekachman, *op. cit.,* pp. 33-36.
11. Simon Kuznets, "Consumption, Industrialization and Urbanization," in Bert F. Hoselitz and Wilbert E. Moore (eds.), *Industrialization and Society* (Paris: Mouton & Co., 1963), p. 99. See also Kuznets' remarks in his *Six . . .* , p. 48.
12. The "model case" assumes, of course, a relatively closed society. It is conceivable for agriculture within a given society not to modernize substantially while marked industrialization occurs, subsistence requirements being met by trade with other societies. In this case the scale may still be applicable, but to a larger unit of analysis including more than one society.

13. Raymond W. Goldsmith, "Statement on National Product and Income: Long-Term Trends," in U.S. Congress, *Employment, Growth and Price Levels: Hearings Before the Joint Economic Committee, Congress of the United States* (Washington, D.C.: Government Printing Office, 1959), p. 267.

14. *Ibid.*, p. 269.

15. *Ibid.*, p. 278.

16. See P. K. Whelpton, "Occupational Groups in the United States, 1820-1920," *Journal of the American Statistical Association,* Vol. 21 (September 1926), p. 340.

17. This paragraph draws on Levy, *op. cit.,* pp. 243-265.

18. Louis Hacker has vigorously maintained that, as far back as colonial times, the American farm unit was not as self-sufficient as some have suggested. See his *The Triumph of American Capitalism* (New York: Columbia University Press, 1940), pp. 118-119.

19. Paul W. Gates, *The Farmer's Age: Agriculture, 1815-1860* (New York: Holt, Rinehart & Winston, 1960), p. 280.

20. John W. Oliver, *History of American Technology* (New York: Ronald Press Co., 1956), p. 222. See also Gates, *op. cit.*, pp. 279-293 for a general discussion of various farm implements introduced before 1860.

21. Simon Kuznets, "Long-Term Changes in the National Income of the United States of America Since 1870," in Kuznets (ed.), *Income and Wealth of the United States: Trends and Structure,* "Income and Wealth Series II" (Cambridge: Bowes & Bowes, 1952), pp. 232-235.

22. Everett E. Edwards, "American Agriculture – The First 300 Years," in U.S. Department of Agriculture, *The Yearbook of Agriculture: 1940* (Washington, D.C.: Government Printing Office, 1940), p. 207.

23. Percy W. Bidwell, "The Agricultural Revolution in New England," *American Historical Review,* Vol. 36 (July 1921), p. 694.

24. J. G. Gurley and E. E. Shaw, "Money," in Seymour E. Harris (ed.), *American Economic History* (New York: McGraw-Hill Book Co., 1961), Table 1, p. 205.

25. Oliver, *op. cit.*, p. 224.

26. Clarence H. Danhof, "Agriculture," in Harold F. Williamson (ed.), *The Growth of the American Economy* (2d ed.; Englewood Cliffs, N.J.: Prentice-Hall, 1951), p. 140.

27. Fred A. Shannon, *The Farmer's Last Frontier: Agriculture, 1860-1897* (New York: Farrar & Rinehart, Inc., 1945), p. 144. See also Martin R. Cooper, Glen T. Barton, and Albert P. Brodell, *Progress of Farm Mechanization,* "U.S. Department of Agriculture Miscellaneous Publication No. 630" (Washington, D.C.: Government Printing Office, 1947), Table 1, p. 3. For a detailed survey of farm implements relative to labor requirements with special emphasis on wheat production see Leo Rogin, *The Introduction of Farm Machinery in Its Relation to the Productivity of Labor in the Agriculture of the United States During the Nineteenth Century* (Berkeley University of California Press, 1931).

28. Danhoff, *op. cit.*, p. 150.

29. Cooper, *et al., op. cit.*, Table 4, p. 71.

30. Fred A. Shannon, "A Post Mortem on the Labor-Safety-Valve Theory," *Agricultural History,* Vol. 19 (January 1945), pp. 31-37.

31. Adam Smith, *An Inquiry into the Nature and Causes of the Wealth of Nations* (New York: Random House, 1937), pp. 17-21.

32. Max Weber, *General Economic History,* trans. Frank H. Knight (New York: Collier Books, 1961), p. 133.

33. *Ibid.*, p. 129.

34. Stuart Bruchey, *The Roots of American Economic Growth: 1607-1861, An Essay in Social Causation* (New York: Harper & Row, 1965), pp. 96-97.

35. Thomas C. Cochran, "The Entrepreneur in American Capital Formation," in Moses Abromovitz (ed.), *Capital Formation and Economic Growth* (Princeton: Princeton University Press, 1955), p. 341.

36. Victor S. Clark, *History of Manufactures in the United States* (New York: McGraw-

Hill Book Co., 1929), Vol. I, p. 234.

37. *Ibid.*, pp. 260-262. Berthoff notes the special contribution of British skilled craftsmen who brought the ideas and often, such as in the case of Samuel Slater, the detailed plans of European manufacture. Such movements, often accomplished against British legal restrictions, provided an important basis of our technological "borrowing." See Rowland T. Berthoff, *British Immigrants in Industrial America* (Cambridge: Harvard University Press, 1953), pp. 30-77.

38. For a discussion of the British "migration of capital" see Brinley Thomas, *Migration and Economic Growth: A Study of Great Britain and the Atlantic Economy* (Cambridge: Cambridge University Press, 1954), pp. 96-102.

39. Clark, *op. cit.*, p. 262.

40. Samuel Reznick, "The Rise and Early Development of Industrial Consciousness in the United States, 1760-1830," *Journal of Economic and Business History,* Vol. 4 (August 1932), p. 784.

41. John Sawyer, "The Social Basis of the American System of Manufacturing," *Journal of Economic History*, Vol. 14, No. 4 (1954), pp. 369-370.

42. See *ibid.*, pp. 372-374.

43. D. L. Burn, "The Genesis of American Engineering Competition," *Economic History: A Supplement of the Economic Journal*, Vol. 2 (January 1931), pp. 292-311.

44. See Clark's remarks on this point, in *op. cit.*, pp. 292-311.

45. H. J. Habakuk, *American and British Technology in the Nineteenth Century: The Search for Labour-Saving Inventions* (Cambridge: Cambridge University Press, 1962), p. 25.

46. *Ibid.*, p. 50.

47. Morton Peck, "Transportation in the American Economy," in Harris, *op. cit.*, p. 343.

48. U.S. Bureau of the Census, *Historical Statistics of the United States: Colonial Times to 1957* (Washington, D.C.: Government Printing Office, 1960), pp. 427, 429.

49. Clark, *op. cit.*, Vol. II, p. 2.

50. Robert E. Gallman, "Commodity Output 1839-1899," in William N. Parker (ed.), *Trends in the American Economy in the Nineteenth Century* (Princeton: Princeton University Press, 1960), Table 1, p. 16.

51. *Ibid.*, Table 3, p. 24.

52. *Ibid.*, Table 4, p. 26.

53. *Ibid.*, p. 42. See also Table 10, p. 36.

54. Kuznets, "Long-Term . . . ," Table 11, p. 78.

55. *Ibid.*, p. 119.

56. *Ibid.*, p. 130.

57. Lance E. Davis, R. T. Jonathan Hughes, and Duncan M. McDougall, *American Economic History* (Homewood, Ill.: Richard D. Irwin, 1961), pp. 266-267.

58. League of Nations, *Industrialization and Foreign Trade* (Geneva: League of Nations, 1945), Table 1, p. 13.

59. Wilbert E. Moore, "Changes in Occupational Structures," in Neil J. Smelser and Seymour M. Lipset (eds.), *Social Structure and Social Mobility in Economic Development* (Chicago: Aldine Press, 1966), pp. 194-212.

60. Colin Clark, *The Conditions of Economic Progress* (3d ed.; New York: St. Martin's Press, 1957), p. 492.

61. Moore, *The Impact of Industry,* p. 64.

62. U.S. Bureau of the Census, *Sixteenth Census of the United States: 1940, Comparative Occupation Statistics for the United States, 1870-1940,* by Alba M. Edwards (Washington, D.C.: Government Printing Office, 1943), p. 101.

63. *Ibid.*

64. Wilbert E. Moore, "Occupational Structure and Industrial Conflict," in Arthur Kornhauser, Robert Dubin, and Arthur Ross (eds.), *Industrial Conflict* (New York: McGraw-Hill Book Co., 1954), p. 224.

65. U.S. Bureau of the Census, *The Integration of Industrial Operation*, "Census Monographs III," by Willard L. Thorp (Washington, D.C.: Government Printing Office, 1924), p. 14.
66. *Ibid.*, pp. 76-78.
67. A. J. Jaffe and Charles D. Stewart, *Manpower Resources and Utilization: Principles of Working Force Analysis* (New York: John Wiley & Sons, Inc., 1951), pp. 25-26.
68. See Moore, *loc. cit.*, p. 223.
69. Walter F. Wilcox (ed.), *International Migrations* (New York: National Bureau of Economic Research, Inc., 1929), Vol. I, p. 179.
70. Harry Jerome, *Migration and Business Cycles* (New York: National Bureau of Economic Research, Inc., 1926), pp. 77-122.
71. Brinley Thomas, *op. cit.*, pp. 93-94.
72. Simon Kuznets, "Long-Term . . . ," pp. 198-199.
73. *Ibid.*, p. 204. See Table 45, p. 202.
74. Simon Kuznets and Ernest Rubin, *Immigration and the Foreign Born*, "Occasional Paper 46" (New York: National Bureau of Economic Research, Inc., 1954), p. 44.
75. U.S. Bureau of the Census, *Immigrants and Their Children: 1920*, "Census Monographs VII," by Niles Carpenter (Washington, D.C.: Government Printing Office, 1927), Table 121, p. 269, and Table 122, p. 270.
76. Comparisons are confined to white workers in order to remain consistent with other sources of information drawn upon and because the employment experiences that nonwhite workers, largely black, have historically been subject to in the United States are of such a profoundly different character as to render their consideration beyond the scope of the present study.
77. U.S. Immigration Commission, *Report of the Immigration Commision*, Vol. 19, *Summary Report on Immigrants in Manufacturing and Mining* (Washington, D.C.: Government Printing Office, 1911), pp. 17-34; Table 17, p. 95. See Louis Bloch's tabulation of these figures in his "Occupations of Immigrants Before and After Coming to the United States," *Publications of the American Statistical Association*, Vol. 17 (June 1921), Table 7, p. 762.
78. Commission data show that, during the period 1899-1909, 22 percent of the "old" arrivals were skilled laborers or professionals compared with 14 percent of the "new." At the other extreme, 23.8 percent of the "old" were farm laborers or common laborers compared with 51.1 percent of the "new." U.S. Immigration Commission, *Report of the Immigration Commission*, Vol. 1, *Abstract* (Washington, D.C.: Government Printing Office, 1911), Table 7, p. 174. Paul Douglas, using the period of "old" immigrant dominance as the basis of comparison found "that 1.7 percent of the total number of immigrants with occupation from countries representative of the old immigration were professional, whereas only 0.5 percent of the new immigrants were of this class. Skilled workers comprised 22.9 percent of the immigrants from the countries from Northwestern Europe; 18.1 percent of those from Southeastern. Here the difference though real is not decisive. Two-ninths of the earlier immigrants with occupations from the countries which we believe to be ethnically and industrially similar to ours were skilled; two-elevenths of those that we regard as absolutely alien to us are skilled." "Is the New Immigration More Unskilled Than the Old," *Publications of the American Statistical Association*, Vol. 16 (June 1919), p. 400. If the comparison is made on the basis of *total* immigration without regard to those having an occupation (mostly dependents), the proportion of skilled among the "new" groups is greater than the "old" who had a greater proportion of those with no occupation.
79. For a vigorous general criticism of the Immigration Commission's work see Oscar Handlin, *Race and Nationality in American Life* (Garden City: Doubleday & Co., Inc., 1957), pp. 74-110.
80. See note 77. An important exception is clothing manufacture, which had high proportions of foreign born but was characterized by small-shop operations. It is significant to note that Jewish migrants dominated this field at the time and that they exhibited a high

level of previous experience, which is consistent with their more urban European origins.

81. U.S. Immigration Commission, *Abstract,* p. 495.
82. Habakuk, *op. cit.*, p. 131.
83. U.S. Immigration Commission, *loc. cit.,* p. 494.
84. Bloch, *op. cit.*, p. 752.
85. U.S. Bureau of the Census, *Comparative . . .* , Table 24, p. 181.
86. U.S. Immigration Commission, *Summary Report on Immigrants in Manufacturing and Mining,* Table 29, p. 111. For extensive coverage of income see pp. 103-127. It is important not to overlook the fact that, though immigrants fared poorly relative to native whites, native-born black workers, who at this point (1908) in time constituted a relatively small percentage of northern manufacturing employees, earned less than either of the other groups ($10.66). See note 76.
87. Kuznets and Rubin, *op. cit.*, pp. 42-43.
88. U.S. Immigration Commission, *loc. cit.,* Table 11, p. 80.
89. Paul H. Douglas, *Real Wages in the United States: 1890-1926* (Boston: Houghton Mifflin Co., 1930), pp. 179, 565. See also Table 59, p. 177. Albert Rees, *Real Wages in Manufacturing: 1890-1914* (Princeton: Princeton University Press, 1961), p. 126. Stanley Lebergott, *Manpower in Economic Growth: The American Record Since 1800* (New York: McGraw-Hill Book Co., 1964), p. 162.
90. *Ibid.*, p. 47.
91. Thomas, *op. cit.*, p. 179.
92. Douglas, *Real . . .* , p. 179.
93. Simon Kuznets, "Economic Growth and Income Inequality," *American Economic Review*, Vol. 45 (March 1955), p. 16.
94. *Ibid.*, p. 17.
95. *Ibid.*, p. 19.

4

Discontinuity, Mobilization, and Social Origins

The issue to be dealt with in this chapter involves the alterations in patterns of action (social structure) in the course of modernization and the nature of the response to such alterations. In Chapter 1 it was stated that the most general distinction that can be made regarding the structure of societies is that having to do with relative modernization and relative nonmodernization. The attendant alterations in patterns of action that occur when any given society moves from one side of this continuum to the other are so extensive as to be described as revolutionary, in that they present a radically different set of circumstances when compared to what existed prior to such change. Modernization, then, is potentially one of the most severe strain-producing changes that may occur within any given society. It was also pointed out that, from the point of view of any particular society, the specific strains that result are partly a function of the preexisting social structure peculiar to it. These strains, however, amount to an empirical instance of the general structural transformations to be expected of any society undergoing modernization. The specific nonmodernized "state of the system," though, will determine the greater or lesser "ease" with which the hiatus is overcome, though this in all events will be productive of tensions. The manner in which these tensions are managed, and the resultant new ones created by such action, are indicative of the individual society's "path" of modernization within the general limits suggested earlier.

When discussing such changes, the reference is to regularized activities that come to be altered. The manner in which such activities are viewed by many contemporary sociologists; how they are governed and the implications for society of their change should, therefore, be addressed.

The discussion in Chapter 1 brought forward an important way of viewing social action, namely, that it is value- (or goal-) oriented and that it is governed by norms. The first aspect has to do with *ends*, that is, a desirable state of affairs toward which action is directed. The second has to do with the limits set on actors in approaching these ends. These limits involve various "internal" checks, such as guilt or shame, when their bounds are trespassed, and satisfaction or pride when what is considered appropriate action is adhered to. Similarly, "external" checks, generally referred to as sanctions, such as disapproval of others or physical punishment directed at violators, and material rewards or public approval enjoyed by those who remain within the limits, function to ensure adherence.[1]

Values and norms are not independent of one another. "Values," Moore states, "provide the rationale for particular norms, or rules of organization and conduct."[2] A minimum of basic dominant values (i.e., shared by most if not all actors and having priority over other values) is generally posited as a requisite feature of societal persistence. Without some basic values, disintegrative disruptions are likely as individuals pursue ends that may prove contradictory to one another. Second, it is held that appropriate behavior in pursuit of concrete (or intermediate) goals, guided by values (or ultimate goals), must be fairly well inculcated in the majority of actors. Conformity resting primarily on sanctions would assume a body of "enforcers" so large as to be impracticable for the operations of a society and adherence on the part of these latter individuals would perforce assume commitment in any event. Hence, the "internal" aspect, an outcome of socialization, is seen as a second feature of societal persistence.[3]

Implied in the notion of the requisite of shared values is the further element of their consistency. That is, the shared values may not severely contradict one another, although the fact that they are multiple does inevitably involve a degree of mutual incompatibility and hence some strain. The possibility of severe contradictions, however, is raised most notably when a society undergoes modernization. It is to this issue that the present chapter is primarily devoted — i.e., to the structural dualities related to value inconsistency during the course of societal modernization.

Countervailing Tendencies during Modernization

It has already been noted that strains during the process of modernization are a function of the confrontation of the preexisting social structure with a radically different set of circumstances. That such strains are quite likely may be deduced from one feature that is fairly characteristic of relatively nonmodernized societies, namely, a traditional orientation to the "state of the system." This means a subscription to the maintenance of existing patterns of action as time-honored and inviolable. "The ordinary expectation for the members of all relatively nonmodernized societies has been that their children would live in roughly the same kind of world as the parents."[4] If, as has been asserted, the inception of modernization so subverts a preexisting social structure as to be appropriately termed revolutionary in its implications, then a "counterrevolutionary" potential of varying intensity is generated. The nostalgic references to the "good old days" on the part of British workers, cited earlier, exemplified what is indicated here. Modernization is dysfunctional for the established system at the same time as institutionalization of the patterns associated with the former is not assured. This poses a serious challenge to the persistence of a society as an ongoing unit.

It was suggested in Chapter 1 that the greater the degree of divergence between ideal and actual patterns, the greater the probability of purposive social action being initiated to bring the two into closer correspondence. This proposition addresses itself to intermediate goal states as governed by generalized values. It suggests that perceptions on the part of actors in a social system are likely to be directed toward alterations in concrete activity as evidenced by divergences from institutionally expected behavior on the part of others and an increasing inability to operate satisfactorily in terms of such patterns on their own part. Action oriented to the new values becomes institutionalized insofar as the values come to be extensively shared and dominant (i.e., have priority), hence "downgrading" previous standards of the desirable. This downgrading makes for a continuing, if decreasing, source of strain between old and new.[5]

The immediate remarks refer to the problem of lack of consensus during the process of modernization. They suggest that the discontinuous changes that are initiated produce dualities of commitment and that segments of the population, especially those whose relative position comes to be threatened by the new forms, are likely to become mobilized as the degree of discontinuity becomes more severe. It is further indicated that such action is likely to be of a renovating nature, i.e., oriented toward a restoration of a previous condition or state of affairs.[6] Finally, and of crucial importance for the present discussion, it is asserted that such mobilization occurs primarily among those who have been socialized to the relatively nonmodernized state of the specific system. Thus, the core of such a movement is to be expected from among those who are both genuine members of the society and committed to a given structural arrangement (both being outcomes of socialization) and therefore demand that legitimate expectations be adhered to.

The attenuation of previous orientations, then, is seen as crucial if structural changes are to be carried through, for new modes of action must assume priority over former ones. Adult socialization has been recognized as an important and, given the attention that the Freudian emphasis on early socialization has received, an overlooked aspect of this transition.[7]

Adult socialization has frequently been noted as being of high significance in relatively modernized societies and involves much of what has been termed "intermediate" socialization. There is some reason to believe that past emphasis on early socialization may not be entirely misplaced, because it may well be of comparatively greater importance when considering relatively nonmodernized societies, where the formative years are perhaps "more" formative than in the modernized case. On the one hand the already-mentioned orientation to a fairly predictable future may be contrasted with the modern condition of "a future neither adult nor young envisages."[8] Further, the concrete structural contexts in which the bulk of socialization is carried out vary considerably between the two settings. Socialization of both the basic and intermediate variety occurs almost wholly in terms of the family in the premodern case[9] while, in the modern setting, most of the intermediate and much of the basic socialization takes place in other contexts, such as schools.

Related to the contextual features of socialization is the further factor that the greater proportion of total socialization is likely to be completed much earlier in the nonmodern setting than in the modern. First, problems of cognition are less extensive in the former and even where socialization may be of long duration, such as in apprenticeship training, it most probably will begin at an earlier age than in the latter case. Second, beyond the greater expectation that children will experience roughly the same patterns as their parents, they are likely to know in greater detail what the patterns of adults are. Much adult activity in nonmodern settings and — of especial relevance here — much occupational activity is carried out through the family, while such action normally occurs in distinctly separate structures in the modern setting. Thus, adult occupational roles are more highly visible to youngsters in the nonmodern environment, while the modern is characterized by separation of home and work.[10] Referring to relatively nonmodern societies, Brim notes the

> ... continuity over time of the significant others with whom one is involved. The earliest groups of significant persons remain on the scene through much of one's life. Parents may live on through one's middle years; friendships may persist through much of the life span; one marries into a homogamous group whose expectations are similar to those of prior reference figures. All of this enables socialization to be developmental in nature, that is, to occur in a regular progression from infancy through old age, and for anticipatory socialization for later-life roles to be more effective.[11]

In brief, the individual presents more of a "closed system" at a relatively younger age in the nonmodern setting than he does in the modern. A pattern of assumptions of a much more explicit nature is built into his attitude set, such that severe alterations in objective conditions present more of a disruption in his total expectational configuration than that of the actor fairly well attuned to change and unanticipated circumstances. Adult socialization, though essential to the transitional process being considered, is more likely to encounter resistances during this crucial period of change as a result of traditional expectations attached to rather well-defined goal states. The high potential for disruptive behavior arises from the lack of congruence of previously socialized and legitimate expectations with actual conditions of present experience.[12]

The American Experience

Value Dominance—Individualism vs. Pecuniary Success. In this first subsection, we consider the theoretical basis for locating a major feature of discontinuity during the process of modernization in American society. It involves the growing cleavage between two major American value premises: individualism and success.

Individualism may be defined as the maximization of decision on the basis of the actor's own criteria and judgment. Emphasis is placed here on maximizing *decentralization* of control in the social system.[13] Where individualism is a dominant generalized value, the potential of heterodox decisions is vastly increased. Further, "a high and general positive evaluation of individualism is a practical guarantee that, for better or for worse, things will be radically different within two or three decades."[14]

Discontinuity, Mobilization, and Social Origins

It has been argued that, for "early comers" to modernization, such decentralization was prerequisite (i.e., a necessary condition or state of affairs that must obtain prior to the emergence of a particular type of unit) to the process. Hence, the greater the decisional decentralization with respect to step-by-step innovations of heretofore unrealized productive techniques, the greater the probability of more effective capital formation from among the array of alternatives.[15]

Conversely, modernization for latecomers occurs in an altered context in which technological developments have already reached a high degree of sophistication no longer requiring the step-by-step innovations necessary at an earlier period. A backlog of knowledge already exists and modern technology may be introduced more or less intact from elsewhere. The problems, however, of large outlays of resources for capital formation, and the attendant necessities of planning, are now beyond the scope of single entrepreneurs. Thus, whereas decentralization is seen as a prerequisite for early modernizers, centralization is posited as a preliminary for latecomers.

Something further is suggested by the above remarks with regard to the requisite (necessary condition or state of affairs that must obtain if a particular type of unit is to persist) features of relatively modernized societies. Advanced technology and the productive advantages of a high degree of division of labor in such societies brings forth concrete units of increasing size and interdependency.

The industrially developed countries may have *fewer* enterprises per 1,000 population than those initiating development . . . . One can conclude with some certainty that industrially developed countries do not require more enterprises per capita than do newly industrializing countries. Increases in production would appear to come more from the growth of individual enterprises through higher worker productivity and larger plant sizes than from growth in the number of enterprises.[16]

Thus it appears that highly modernized societies require a high level of *centralization* as evidenced in part by a lower relative number of productive units of larger relative scale. Further, the greater interdependency of the various subsystems within a highly modernized society may be expected to lead to greater control over those actors making decisions within such units in structures primarily oriented around the allocation of power and responsibility, namely, governments.[17]

If, as has been suggested, decentralization was a necessary basis from which modernization proceeded among early comers, and centralization is a necessary condition for the persistence of high levels of modernization, then a key element of *discontinuity* is indicated for this group of societies.

It is suggested here that this was one of the significant strains engendered in American society during its transition to relative modernization.[18] Related to these strains is the strong American emphasis on success already alluded to in the first chapter. It may be suggested that the ascendency of this value is essentially antithetical to that of individualism insofar as the first is hospitable to modernization which, as noted, creates conditions in which patterns associated with the latter are increasingly difficult to maintain. There thus occurred in the United States a transfer in value premises from individualism to pecuniary success and this chapter is addressed to that aspect of the strains involved during the transition.

Ideal-Actual Divergence — Self-Employment vs. Employeeship. It has already been pointed out that, unlike much of Europe (Norway being a notable exception), the relatively nonmodernized American social structure contained a broad stratum of independent producers. Again, this historical legacy influenced the character of the strains engendered during modernization.

The difference between a peasant mass and a scattering of farmers is one of the historic differences between the social structure of Europe and America, and is of signal consequence for the character of the middle classes on both continents. There they begin as a narrow stratum of free farmers. Throughout the whole of United States history, the farmer is the numerical ballast of the independent middle class.[19]

Whereas an espousal of individualism on the part of European entrepreneurs had to contend with preexisting feudal institutions that were inimical to it, individualism was the dominant pattern practically from the beginning in the United States. These were the traditions that themselves later would be the focus of a renovating response.

The ideal patterns most profoundly associated with an individualistic value orientation in early America were those associated with the owner-operator, the small businessman who worked his own enterprise.

The extreme individualism of American business betrays a rural influence . . . The farmer maintained that any man of enterprise could take up and become an independent producer; that those who preferred to work for others did so because they lacked enterprise. Now many of the early manufacturers were also farmers or had been farmers before they became manufacturers. Like the farmer they employed only a few men; and these men, when business in the mill was slack, worked on the farms. These manufacturers maintained that any man of enterprise could save money, borrow what more he needed and start in manufacturing. His business was his by right of creation, to run as he pleased.[20]

Access to independent enterprise in the early years was fairly open, as evidenced by the high proportion of self-employed noted earlier. Mills comments on this while also indicating that such patterns were quite traditionalized:

The wide distribution of small property made freedom of a very literal sort seem, for a short time, an eternal principle. The relation of one man to another was a relation not of command and obedience but of man-to-man bargaining. Any one man's decisions, with reference to every other man, were decisions of freedom and of equality; no one man dominated the calculations affecting a market.[21]

Discontinuity, Mobilization, and Social Origins

Since productive property was generally no more than their owners could themselves manage, differences between them were quite small. Although there were some wealthy merchants and large landowners, the major glaring exception to this pattern was the South and slavery.[22] Outside of the South, in the regions where modern industrialism was to appear earliest, the small property owner was the ideal and in large measure the actuality. Where one was not an independent producer, the objective situation encouraged him that he could be.

The ideal of universal small property held those without property in collective check while it lured them on as individuals. They would fight alongside those who already had it, joining with them in destroying holdovers from the previous epoch which hampered the way up for the small owner.[23]

Such orientations were closely associated with a revitalized Puritan ethic among colonists who, though Protestantism had been legally established in England, felt hampered by those in authority and sought a return to more fundamental conceptions associated with the Reformation. "The Protestant Reformation was fundamentally a religious revolt against authority — easily transferred to the political or economic — in the name of a fancied restoration of the primitive Church."[24] Correlative patterns of action associated with individualism as a dominant value tended to involve an explicit contrast and antagonism to European institutions:

The chief virtue of the primitive Church was held to be simplicity of ordinance, moral conduct, manner, dress, speech . . . above all, the devil accomplished his wiles in the guise of a princely gentleman — suave, sophisticated, cultured, aristocratic, accustomed to power and authority. The chief enemy of simplicity . . . was the habitude of authority. Colonists increasingly contrasted a natural simplicity and freedom with compulsion, restraint, artificiality, and self-seeking and associated the vices of authority with intellectualism, worldly extravagance, irreligious lasciviousness, indolence, dilettantism, drunkenness, and deceit. Massachusetts and Virginia passed strict laws against such vices as part of the campaign to restore a condition of primitive innocence.[25]

The injunctions favoring productive efforts and condemning frivolous utilization of the fruits of these efforts were, of course, conducive to economic growth. Their reference in the early years, however, was to an agrarian-based society in contrast to the demoralizing spectacle of European industrialism with its large segment of propertyless, dependent, urban poor. Industrialism was seen as inimical to America's special virtues, best exemplified by the independent producer relying on his own devices to earn his livelihood. Jefferson's early views, later to be modified, represented these ideals in his pronounced anti-industrialism accompanied by a repugnance for urban living.[26]

The individualistic emphasis and institutionalized controls on extravagance were well suited to early American social structure made up, as it was, of highly self-sufficient units of production. The family was the basic unit; in the artisan's shop as well as on the farm.[27] Training of the young was primarily carried out in the family.[28] "The son not only accepted the beliefs of the father but accepted them as an expression of the loyalty that a son owes a father."[29] In the rural community:

> The attitudes and beliefs consciously and unconsciously inculcated in children were similar to those acquired under their parents. The formative contact of children and youths was, therefore, that with their parents and with each other. Children constantly were enjoined to do and think like their elders.[30]

Self-reliance was explicitly inculcated by rural parents. Whether or not the son followed his father's calling, and it was generally expected that he would,[31] the role model of the independent enterprise — farmer or artisan — was highly visible. The success of the enterprise, in each case, depended on the individual abilities of the family head in planning, coordinating, and executing the work to be done. It was his skill and judgment in all phases of the productive process on which the farm or shop stood or fell.[32]

Before the advent of wide market extensions and a "money economy," the success value merged easily with the antiauthoritarian injunctions of individualism. Success applied to an individual's accomplishments as an independent enterpriser.

Self-management, work, and type of property coincided, and in this coincidence the psychological basis of original democracy was laid down. Work and property were closely joined into a single unit. Working skills were performed with and upon one's property; social status rested largely upon the amount and condition of the property that one owned; income was derived from profits made from working one's property. And, as the power which property gave, like the distribution of property itself, was widespread, their coincidence was the source of personal character as well as social balance.[33]

Those without property, those who "worked for a boss," conceived of their position as temporary or prerequisite to accumulating the capital with which to become "one's own boss." Cheap land and the relatively small investment in equipment made the move from farmhand to farm owner fairly easy in the early years. Similarly with urban craft pursuits, "An artisan just starting out for himself did not need to make a large investment; tools and materials were not costly."[34] Thus, the movement from apprentice, to journeyman, to master craftsman with one's own shop, was both an ideal expectation and a highly probable sequence.

The traditional attitude toward employee status, then, was that it was a temporary condition prior to self-employment. The scarcity of labor, especially the unskilled kind, was a consequence of this. Abundant opportunities for independent proprietorship, supported by the value of individualism, help to explain this scarcity in spite of relatively high employee wages.

It was earlier noted that labor scarcity proved a stimulus to innovations in productive techniques when market extensions made increased output practicable. Alternatives to current practices were available in the form of British and other productive technologies from abroad, and those with capital sought to procure them while simultaneously innovating independently. With a highly decentralized social structure, it was quite likely that independent producers would become entrepreneurs, i.e., those who brought about "new combinations" of productive factors, thereby altering the character of business organization such that contemporaries had to follow suit to survive.[35]

A highly decentralized system of production buttressed by Puritan values centering upon individualism thus produced a stress toward innovation which functioned to undermine these very patterns. The classic expression of this change is summed up by the paired concepts of "old" and "new" middle class, respectively referring to the owner-operator and white-collar salaried bureaucrat.[36] A more appropriate and general distinction is simply that of the self-employed as contrasted to the employee occupational role.

Large-scale manufacturing was initially introduced in this country with textile production. "This industry brought the factory system to the United States and furnished the laboratory wherein were worked out industrial methods characteristic of the nation."[37] The inception of such new methods of production took place in a setting distinctly hostile to them and entrepreneurs were hard pressed to secure acceptance within the communities in which the new factories were established. Such acceptance was, of course, essential if labor was to be recruited in local areas. The antipathy, already mentioned, to European institutions, had become strongly nationalistic following the Revolution and the War of 1812.[38] Industrialism, as evidenced by the British, no less than other European institutions, had to be repulsed if the unique qualities of American society were to survive. "The strongest and most lasting prejudice rested on a horror lest the factory system in America should degrade the worker as it had in England and become a menace to American social and political ideals."[39] This antagonism stemming from ideal patterns associated with individualism was to continue far into the nineteenth century.

Marx asserted that a stratum rising to prominence must legitimate the changes it is initiating by representing such changes as in the interests of all and not only the initiators.[40] In England, the rising entrepreneurs enlisted the aid of workers in their efforts to repeal the Corn Laws and claimed themselves to be "the spokesmen for the people as a whole at the same time that they were the avowed representatives of industry."[41] In the United States, the antagonism to European institutions ironically served as a basis through which entrepreneurs could claim industry as a means of maintaining national integrity. It was on this principle that Jefferson himself came to regard manufacturing, within limits, as desirable.[42]

In putting forward their claims, entrepreneurs were not unmindful of the image of depressed European labor which ran so counter to the strongly held value of individualism in the United States. They insisted that American enterprise need not follow the British pattern, need not undermine domestic ideals. They claimed to be as much against transferring European industrial conditions to the United States as their opponents and argued that a distinctly American pattern of manufacturing could emerge which would safeguard, even enhance, "moral progress" by identifying it with "material progress." Many early entrepreneurs had rural backgrounds which, and in contrast to a later generation of businessmen, were steeped in the traditions earlier spoken of. An explicit regard for the well-being of their employees, without undermining rural traditions, was a hallmark of much early textile manufacturing in New England. To be sure, the "economic self-interest" of these men was not a small part of their initial calculations, but by joining these with patriotic appeals and demonstrated responsibility in labor management, they were able to introduce factory production methods to a doubtful population.[43]

Finally, the nature of the product for which the factory system was first introduced proved to have minimal dislocating effects on craft skills. The replacement of homespun materials by inexpensive factory produced fabrics released farm women from an activity that consumed a considerable amount of time at home. Farm girls were early employed in the mills, but their stay in the factory was explicitly temporary and their ties with home were deliberately maintained. Since the early operatives were mostly American, mutual understandings were more easily arrived at than later when conditions changed and the inevitable spread and growth of factories to other industries as well as within textiles proved disintegrative to traditional patterns. We return to this shift in discussing the employer-employee relationship patterns in the following subsection, but the point to be made here is that factory production gained a foothold in an industry that required few adjustments on the part of prior producers and a slight threat, at most, to prior craft traditions.[44] But once factory techniques were begun, enterprising individuals with capital were quick to recognize their superior efficiency in other areas, and the revolutionary changes that have been discussed previously were well under way by the end of the Civil War. This process was briefly described in Chapter 3. We examine its consequences now by viewing the altered employment situation.

The Employer-Employee Relationship Structure Prior to Modernization. It has been pointed out that the role of employee was generally viewed, by early Americans, as a temporary expedient, a preliminary to operating a small business of one's own. The small scale of producing units together with low capital requirements made such a sequence a not unreasonable expectation. Further, the scale of these units also conditioned the relationship between employer and employee. When the methods of production changed, heretofore institutionally expected behavior, from the point of view of the employee, failed to be realized, and the probability of moving toward previously assumed goal states became severely restricted.

The modernization of production essentially involves the explicit introduction of rational methods in the output of goods and services.

The great difference between emphases on rationality and traditionalism has not to do with whether a given activity is in fact rational or not. It has to do with an attitude, with whether people feel it should be rational or not. If traditionalism is emphasized, even though the actual practices are in fact rational, the implications of this emphasis are important. Problems of efficiency are not immediately posed, but if the means change and what was formerly done is no longer rational, traditionalists are likely to continue the old methods although they are now irrational. When available means are likely to be changing, this distinction means more.[45]

The emergence of a rational emphasis is not independent of other social structural aspects which are also likely to be changing.

Emphases on rationality, functional specificity, universalism, and avoidance are likely to cluster, and if they fail to, one can make further predictions from that variation. When rationality is involved, both ends and means must be empirical and to a high degree explicit. Functionally diffuse elements are likely to interfere with rational emphases and force inclusion of traditional or nonrational elements if only by adding vagueness to an otherwise explicit situation. Again rational factors are likely to be interfered with by particularistic selections, especially if the particularism is not germane particularism, since such selection will not maximize or safeguard the ability of members of the relationship to carry out rational action in terms of the relationship. Intimacy, as opposed to avoidance, is more likely to involve departures in the direction of traditionality [or nonrationality], functional diffuseness, and particularism. It is difficult to confine activity to rational considerations or to specifically defined and delimited factors or to objective selections when a person is intimately involved with others.[46]

Much has already been said regarding the traditional orientation of early Americans to their work situation. As is clear at this point, the widespread goal of self-employment was at variance with the intrinsic features of modern production and an apparent diminution of such opportunities was a likely point of resistance. The goal of self-employment depended on the maintenance of traditional craft skills which in turn was associated with the persistence of small-scale productive establishments. Innovations in production undermined the viability of individualistic values, at least as expressed in the ideal of the owner-operator.

As might be expected from the foregoing remarks, the relation between employer and employee in the small producing unit was predominantly particularistic. The most obvious manifestation of this was of course labor recruitment from within the family. As was indicated earlier, sons were frequently expected to follow the father's calling, often succeeding to proprietorship of the family enterprise when the parent grew old. Beyond this, however, the fact that production took place primarily in terms of the family unit meant that where "outsiders" in the form of apprentices or journeymen were recruited, they became part of the household. Further, although abilities are never entirely to be discounted, minute skill distinctions are inapplicable in relatively nonmodernized productive settings. Thus Bridenbaugh's somewhat facetious remarks concerning the recruitment of apprentices:

The system seldom took aptitude into account, for colonial artisans were as yet innocent of that modern institution called vocational guidance. Prospective apprentices were never made to play with blocks or given I.Q. tests.[47]

Thurnstrom, speaking of pre-1850 Newburyport, asserts that: "In the household-based economy even the lowliest laborer was customarily attached to a particular master."[48] And, in somewhat larger operations, the probability was still high that "personal relations" would predominate between worker and employer.[49] The cognitive problem of the small mill owner "knowing his employees as individuals" was not great. Thus, in Holyoke, Massachusetts: "In the seventies and early eighties plants were small enough so that employers knew their workpeople as human beings."[50] In one area where truly large-scale production was under way, a different sort of particularism prevailed. To induce New England farm parents to release their daughters for millwork, textile owners sought to employ only a "higher type" of "respectable" worker. By providing closely supervised boardinghouses for the young women and carefully recruiting operatives whose "pride of character" could be relied upon, millowners hoped to alleviate the suspicion of industrial corruption earlier alluded to. Similarly, prospective employees were likely to know the "reputation" of the mill before placement, often after a personal visit by a mill agent to their home.[51] Thus, in the one area where large-scale production was quite general, particularistic "guarantees" ensured the early recruitment of female operatives.

The employer-employee relationship was functionally diffuse during this early period. That is to say that the substantive definition of the relationship was not precisely defined or delimited. The obligations of each party extended beyond the productive roles performed by one and the managerial roles performed by the other. Although apprenticeship was often attended by a contract, the obligation of the youth involved fairly complete servitude. Restrictions involved even behavior not related to work.[52] Similarly, the master had to provide a variety of nonwork-related service for his charges. For example, he "was responsible . . . for the education, housing, feeding, and clothing of his apprentices, and customarily for the boarding and lodging of journeymen, as well as for the health, comfort, and moral welfare of his entire household."[53] Even when the size of such units grew beyond the household, "the relation of the employing family to employees . . . tended to remain 'paternalistic,' covering actually, if not legally, far more than what we now understand by a contract of employment."[54] Thus, mill girls in New England were required to live in boardinghouses strictly supervised by matrons who in turn were carefully recruited and controlled by the millowners.[55] The "employment contract" included requirements for public worship, and various injunctions against "improper conduct." "Such rules were intended as an attraction to the girls and as guarantees to their parents of a protected life in the mills."[56] Although the employers supplied a "moral atmosphere" which might be interpreted as "far more than what we now understand as a contract of employment," the demands made on the women were also of substantial latitude. Ware makes mention of one company "regulation" which may be taken as coming very close to a pinnacle of functional diffuseness: "The Cahero Manufacturing Company required the worker to agree to 'conform in all respects, to the regulations which are now, or may hereafter be adopted, for the good government of the institution; to work for such wages as the company may see fit to pay, and be subject to the fines, as well as entitled to the premiums paid by the company.' "[57]

Although a fairly wide degree of variation was evidenced in the affective aspect of the employer-employee relationship, the small scale of even the larger establishments would indicate that intimate (emotional content being part of the relationship) as opposed to avoidant (emotional content is excluded or overt contact is minimized) relations were fairly common in the early years being considered.

In Holyoke in the 1830's and 1840's: "It was business on a small scale and an intimate relationship that existed between employer and employed."[58] Supervisors here were frequently the recipients of gifts and "surprise parties" from their charges which indicates to Green that: "Unquestionably the general tone of relations between employer and employee was friendly."[59] Even as late as the eighties in Holyoke:

Sometimes the head of the mill ate his dinner at the Company boarding house. The families of her husband's help the owner's wife could know, sometimes in the role of Lady Bountiful doubtless, but also as a humanly interested neighbor.[60]

It is quite probable that in the New England "Boarding House Mills" the degree of intimacy was more restricted than in an all-male shop, given the various Puritan strictures on work, discipline, and "appropriate conduct" so assiduously applied by the owners. Because these were the earliest of the large-scale enterprises, such conditions were to be sought in any event, and were acceptable so long as operatives viewed their work as temporary. But elsewhere, large enterprises were the exception rather than the rule, and Cochran speaks of the "pleasant personal relations and working conditions of the owner-run plant" as fairly general, if not universal, prior to the 1860's.[61]

The master-journeyman-apprentice system permitted the greatest degree of intimacy between employer and employee[62] during this period and possibly the modal form of industrial production as well. The "fraternity of the shop" and the close identity between employer and employed (journeymen especially) was to represent the ideal model during severe changes in working conditions later in the century.

Given the preceding remarks, one might reasonably infer that during the pre-Civil War years, the employer-employee relationship was predominantly responsible (the actor attempting to safeguard the goals of others in his relationships) rather than an individualistic effort (the actor attempting to maximize his own ends even at the expense of other parties to a relationship).

Indeed, the "paternalism" of the larger-scale productive units indicates that these patterns prevailed outside the workshop into the larger factory setting. It will be remembered that the inception of these units explicitly provided for responsible action on the part of employers in the one area where truly large units were general, namely the New England Boarding House Mills. Here the employer assumed a degree of responsibility for his "charges" that was quite unique in

American industry. As indicated, he expected — or better put — demanded responsible behavior on the part of his workers. Such institutions, explicitly designed to permit the rapid growth of large-scale production in textiles, in turn broke down earliest in these factories when conditions of employee recruitment altered.

Elsewhere, as in Federalist Newburyport, the unskilled laborer could rely on the knowledge that "the fixed personal relationship between laborer and master had provided a modicum of protection; the master's knowledge that the man who lived in the room over the stable had five children to feed in the winter as well as the summer was some incentive to find work for that man."[63] The ironworker living in rural Pennsylvania enjoyed a degree of responsibility from his employer that was not the lot of workers in Philadelphia. In fact, his position is likened by one writer to that of the medieval serf rather than a manufacturing employee. He was "never as completely at the mercy of those fickle economic forces which brought so much misery and unrest to the city worker ... the ironworker and his family were sometimes provided not only with a home but with a sizable plot of land for gardening, pasturing his animals, and firewood."[64]

Although the above remarks indicate that there were exceptions to the responsible orientation outlined, the latter appears to have been quite general during the period under consideration, being manifested by both employer and employee.

In the great majority of cases the plant manager was also a heavy investor in the enterprise. Under such conditions he could dispense a sort of compensation insurance out of his own pocket. Knowing the lives of his permanent employees, he could aid them when sickness came or care for them or their families in case of injury. Unconsciously the older workers and the boss entered into semifeudal relations. The worker gave the boss loyal support in his battles with competitors and he in turn regarded them as "his men."[65]

Similar patterns were observed between masters and journeymen where perhaps the most pronounced expression of a predominantly responsible relationship was evidenced. Master artisans often passed increases in costs on to the buyer, thereby protecting the wage level of their employees.[66] Similarly:

The journeymen were fully aware that wages could best be maintained and advances secured by co-operating with the retail merchant-employers in suppressing "unfair" competitors. Hence, we find them actively supporting their employers against those master merchants who refuse to abide by established standards.[67]

Much of the foregoing discussion has, by implication, indicated that the stratification aspect of the relationship structure of employer and employees was predominantly hierarchical; that is, their rankings were different and related to the roles they performed. The dominance of small-scale operations, especially the artisan's shop, and the intimate relations that generally prevailed even in the small mill, suggest that the extent of differential ranking was, as yet, not severe in most cases. Control, however, rested with the owner-operator and the expectations on the part of his employees confirmed the right to manage and decide the disposition of productive property. Although he worked alongside his employees and his relations with them were friendly, "they did not think of challenging his right to run his business as he saw fit."[68]

Discontinuous Social Change and Mobilization. A major difficulty or "obstacle" to modernization, it has been claimed here, rests with alterations in patterns of action that disrupt previously institutionalized expectations and render behavior in terms of them anachronistic. The direction in which modernizing social structures move with respect to the relationship aspects was indicated in Chapter 1. Above, the relatively nonmodernized form of the employer-employee relationship in the United States has been briefly characterized. We consider now the strains associated with the discontinuous features of modernization as they manifested themselves in the United States.

A point of strain or tension-producing focus is likely to occur when a lack of symmetry is manifested in the actions of a party to a relationship relative to what have come to be the legitimate expectations of other parties to that relationship. This is one manner, among others, in which the "leads and lags," so often discussed with respect to modernization, may be observed. Thus, when one actor in a relationship alters his orientation to it, he, in effect, is deviating from institutionally prescribed patterns of action and an effort on the part of other implicated actors is likely to be made to restore the previous pattern.[69] In the employer-employee relationship, these changes occurred on the part of the employer, who in carrying forth entrepreneurial activity or being forced to emulate those who did, would, or could, no longer adhere to traditional expectations on the part of his employees.

A rational orientation on the part of the employer was quite likely given the conditions that were indicated above. This, again, is not to suggest that the previous action itself was objectively nonrational but rather that the orientation to such action was. Of special importance here is that initially the emphasis on rationality is likely to be variable among the parties to a relationship and, given our concern with the employer-employee relationship, will generally be seen earliest in a capitalistic setting on the part of the employer. Weber's notions concerning the relationship of calculability as part of the process of productive rationalization has earlier been alluded to. Such calculability is in part dependent on a generalized medium of exchange and, where such exists to any extent, "an element of rationality is exceedingly likely to be injected into the society even though tradition is emphasized."[70]

Rational calculation, dependent on some basic standard of value, is indispensable if the actor is to assess the effectiveness of alternative methods or techniques. Involved in alternative methods or techniques of production is, of course, labor, which must also be calculable. The tendency then is to "reduce" such inputs to a form amenable to accounting operations along with other elements in the productive process. Thus, the condition in which effort is exchanged for specified remuneration (labor market) thereby being measurable as a "cost of production" is a concomitant of modernization. Further, if calculability is to be maximized, "extraneous" considerations must be minimized in recruiting labor, and ability to perform becomes the central criterion for inclusion or exclusion in the productive organization. In brief, then, "free labor" the relationship of which to employment emphasizes a "cash nexus" which is differentially allocated with respect to skills reflects the "clustering" suggested earlier of rationality, functional specificity, universalism, and avoidance.

In elaborating here on the theoretical basis of this clustering with respect to the employment situation, the emphasis has been placed on "rationality" as a leading factor. It has been noted that the stress on rationality is most likely to emanate from the employer side and be resisted on the part of employees whose position relative to traditional patterns is called into question and whose access to formerly established ends is inhibited. Thus it has also been indicated that, as actual patterns of action move in the direction of rationality, ideal traditional patterns, though they eventually may be abandoned, serve as the basis with which an attempt may be made to bring actualities back into line. It is this latter feature which partially constitutes, according to the argument developed here, the often-observed "resistances" to social change.

The goal orientation and the stratification aspects are of peculiar significance when discussing the modernization of the United States. In considering the first, we note that individualism was a dominant value in early America and one that involved special consequences:

When individualism is emphasized, the goal orientations of individuals are likely to be individualistic rather than responsible. That is to say, an individual is more likely to pursue his own ends without regard to whether others with whom he is interacting achieve their ends or not.[71]

It should be noted that individualism as a value and a predominantly individualistic relationship are not necessarily related, nor do they, as these remarks imply, refer to the same phenomena. Thus, at a time when individualism as a dominant value could most readily be approached via small business, the employer-employee relationship was most likely to emphasize responsibility.

A paradoxical issue emerges. It relates to the fact that the very operations associated with individualism as a value were dysfunctional for the persistence of a major structural component in the intermediate means-end chain of approaching that value, namely, the owner-operated business enterprise. The decisional latitude permitting productive innovation ultimately resulted in a situation whereby modern productive operations were beyond the capacities of the ordinary workman, thereby undermining the value accessibility of one party to the employer-employee relationship. "Out of small property," as Corey puts it, "arises big property: the right to one includes the other."[72] Thus, an individualistic relationship was in fact related to modernization which, if it was to be carried through on the basis of "private enterprise," of necessity undermined the accessibility of the employee to attain independent proprietorship for himself. His goals were no longer safeguarded.

Discontinuity, Mobilization, and Social Origins

Finally, with respect to the stratification aspect, there is some reason to infer that the initial bipolar widening previously considered involved a more severe departure from earlier patterns in the United States than in societies which had a feudal legacy. Indeed, as early as the thirties Tocqueville made note of the new "aristocracy" based on manufacturing. He was too astute, however, to liken it to a feudal elite. It did not include a fixed hereditary class and, although the poor might not rise to wealth, the wealthy might very well experience poverty in the course of their careers. But of greater importance from the point of view of the present discussion, Tocqueville noted the relationship between this "aristocracy" and the poor:

Not only are the rich not compactly united among themselves, but there is no real bond between them and the poor. Their relative position is not a permanent one; they are constantly drawn together or separated by their interests. The workman is generally dependent on the master, but not on any particular master; these two men meet in the factory, but do not know each other elsewhere; and while they come into contact on one point, they stand very far apart on all others. The manufacturer asks nothing of the workman but his labor; the workman expects nothing from him but his wages. The one contracts no obligation to protect nor the other to defend, and they are not permanently connected either by habit or by duty. The aristocracy created by business rarely settles in the midst of the manufacturing population which it directs; the object is not to govern that population but to use it.[73]

Tocqueville went on to assert a lack of concern on the part of the manufacturers for the welfare of their employees as opposed to the "aristocracy of former ages" who felt bound to relieve the distresses of the men who served them. He suggested that the "manufacturing aristocracy" was "one of the harshest that ever existed in the world," but, importantly at this early period of his observations, noted its as yet confined domain while cautioning a continuing attention to its operations by the "friends of democracy," for he envisioned the possibility of a permanent inequality resulting from its spread.[74]

Tocqueville's profound insight quite early assessed many features of modern American industry indicated in the preceding discussion and provided a "preview" of what was to prevail more generally in later decades. As he noted, however, these conditions were far from general at the time of his observations. Nevertheless, large-scale manufacturing in the few sizable cities of the time had already got underway and, as in New England, textiles led. The very conditions which New Englanders, whose sensibilities employers attempted to assuage, resented were quite evident already among Philadelphia's textile operatives.[75]

Although factory production was quite limited at this point, market extensions and the development of new techniques stimulated the spread of modern production to an increasing variety of undertakings. This early growth in markets produced changes in the organization of production and distribution which, according to Commons, follows a definite pattern typified by the shoe industry.[76]

In this scheme, Commons initially sees the craftsman who produces and sells his goods locally to the order of his customer. This "custom-order" stage is characterized by the artisan being "in his own person master, custom-merchant, and journeyman."[77] The "retail shop" stage entails production of certain standardized articles for stock and eventual sale to customers as they happen into the shop. It requires the employment of journeymen, and the master is here both a retail merchant and an employer.[78] The "wholesale order" stage involves taking orders from distant merchants for goods to be made and delivered later.[79] Although role differentiation as between employer and employee is fairly distinct in the retail shop situation in that the employer is primarily a merchant interested in prices and quality while the employee is interested solely in wages, "Profit is still dependent on increasing prices more than on reducing wages."[80] With the wholesale order stage, however, the merchant employer "meets competitors from other centres of manufacture, which prevents him from passing along his increased expenses." He must reduce wages to meet price competition, Commons argues, concluding that it is at this point that the "conflict of capital and labor begins."[81]

The distinguishing feature of the custom-order, retail-shop, and wholesale-order stages of industry is that the financial and marketing direction of business is still in the hands of the mechanic. He has come up through the trade as a journeyman and master, and even when, as a merchant, he solicits wholesale orders, he does not lose his position as a mechanic. In his shop, at one and the same time, the journeyman may be engaged on "bespoke," "shop," and "order" work. His profits come from his management of the production, or "manufacturing" side of the business more than from the mercantile side. But with the extension of the market he is entering upon competition with other centres of industry, which compel him to give attention both to better methods of production and to larger methods of financing and marketing. Hence it is that the wholesale-order stage of industry is marked by organizations designed to lower the costs of production, and to secure both capital and credit for the capture of distant markets, and protection against foreign competition.[82]

Still and all, Commons continues, this stage "held out to the journeyman the familiar and often realizable prospect of advancement to the position of master." Not until the 1830's, he suggests, did this prospect begin to be curtailed as "outsiders" entered the industry in the role of the "merchant capitalist."[83]

The bargaining specialist, or the merchant-capitalist, need no longer be one who has a knowledge of the technical processes of the trade. These he turns over to a subordinate or to the master workman, who now becomes merely the labour contractor; while for himself the merchant-capitalist retains those functions calling for his special skill in sizing up a market, driving a bargain, and commanding credit.[84]

The merchant-capitalist was able to effect production savings by more efficient division of labor, that is, by splitting the various processes of production among the skill gradations of the workman.[85] The masters, who had to accept merchant-capitalist prices,

Discontinuity, Mobilization, and Social Origins

... organized their workmen in teams, with the work subdivided in order to lessen dependence on skill and to increase speed of output. They played the less skilled against the more skilled, the speedy against the slow, and reduced wages while enhancing exertion. Their profits were "sweated" out of labour, their shop was the "sweatshop," they the "sweaters."[86]

A rise in the wage scale of unskilled labor is associated with a reduction in skilled remuneration and gave rise to union activity on the part of skilled artisans seeking to retain their relative positions. These attempts, however, were not the result of lack of opportunity to engage in independent enterprises, since the artisan's skill was still, apparently, a viable asset for such ventures. Rather, it appears to have been, according to Commons, from those who could most easily set up a business that the attempt was made to hold the line on income and, one might surmise, amass the financial wherewithal for a future business establishment.[87] Pessen's remarks affirm this conclusion:

The Philadelphia, New York, and New England groups were similar to the numerous other labor organizations which sprang up in northwestern cities during this period. They were unlike the unions of today which have a more or less similar range of union activities and job objectives. What has been called the labor movement of the period 1827 to 1837 consisted of varied organizations with all-embracing social programs. In their complexity and scope they reflected the situation and the mood of the American workman of that era: a man who while a worker today might become a master tomorrow; a man who dreamed of ascending into a higher social stratum as he simultaneously demanded the right to organize and strike.[88]

This type of movement was to reach a peak in the two decades following the Civil War but was indicative of important changes already under way at this early period in the structure of productive enterprises.

Ulman, in considering the Commons thesis, asserts that there are important exceptions to the proposed characterization of stages. The introduction of the merchant capitalist might not, Ulman argues, always reduce income. Of further importance is that the merchant capitalist may not singly be able to command the price bargain because other competitors in the area may provide the manufacturer with access to more than one buyer. Since this was the case in New York and Chicago, where clothing-worker wages were in fact reduced, the special characteristics of the merchant capitalist as sole buyer do not explain the reduction. By pointing up such exceptions, Ulman concludes:

What emerges as the truly significant consequence of the extension of markets, therefore, is not the succession of "classes" and "stages," so much as the forces of specialization and dilution. The debt which Commons acknowledged to Schmoller and Bucher was of much less consequence than his debt, unacknowledged, to Adam Smith.[89]

A further word might also be added concerning Commons' contention that extension of markets is a necessarily prior development to larger-scale productive enterprises. The stages he puts forward suggest that role differentiation on the basis of production is a function of gradual market extension. There is an implicit assumption that the demand side of the market situation is the determining factor here. Transport improvements are normally taken as the main source of market extension in that increasing scope of potential buyers affects the decisions made by various producers. Thus widely scattered producers may come to compete with one another as a result of the fact that costs arising from making goods available to consumers over a wider area become less of a prohibitive factor in price determination. This results in innovations among competitors which emphasize rationalization of production.

The discussion in Chapter 3 affirmed the importance of improved transport in the creation of "mass demand" which, in turn, generates changes in the organization of production. The reasoning, however, may be reversed. If one were to take a transport system as given, however inefficient by later standards, the introduction of modern technology might, as it were, "create a market" by providing goods cheap enough to offset transport costs and do away with less-efficient producers despite the constancy of the transport system. Thus the supply side may affect the "state of the market" as well as the demand side without contradicting the assertion of the necessity of "mass demand" for large-scale production.

The one major example (and major exception to the Commons thesis on stages) of these remarks was textile production. Modern British technology in textile production was removed "full-blown" to the United States without requiring the step-by-step innovations involved in other areas. Large-scale factory production characterized this field early in the nineteenth century while it was not realized in many other areas of production until some time after the Civil War. At a stroke, home production shifted to the factory without the intervening stages noted in other areas. Whereas in other areas of production, as indeed with textiles in England, gradual rationalization undermined traditional craft practices, none existed in America with respect to textiles. Very little was produced for domestic marketing. The inception of American factory-made textile products replaced, on the one hand, British imports and, on the other hand, homespun produce for home consumption.

The transfer of spinning and weaving in America from homes to factories was a greater change than their transfer from workshops to factories in Great Britain. No other industrial arts were so universally practiced by our people and no other were so suddenly taken from their hands. In spite of the occasional persistence of homespun in isolated districts until within recent memory, the short period between 1810 and 1830 saw the center of gravity of textile manufactures shift from the fireside to the factory.[90]

Although hostilities with England and curtailment of imports stimulated these changes in the textile industry, Clark asserts that development was so vigorous that "we cannot ascribe its subsequent growth entirely to the interruption of commerce . . ."[91] Indeed, textile manufacturers depended on improved transport to "extend" their market, but they apparently had the technology sufficient to exploit a large market with the turnpikes and canals in existence, while artisan methods still characterized other industries. It appears that "widening" of the market was here a function of production changes rather than distribution ones. Textiles provide one major example where the United States benefited as a "latecomer" to modernization.

Textiles were by far the exception rather than the rule with regard to factory production, and it was not until the sixties that modern industrialism became more generally evident.

The Civil War provided a dividing line in labor trends as in other economic fields. Though there were numerous factories before the war, few of them employed as many as 300 "hands." The great majority of workshops in the sixties were small, averaging less than ten workers per establishment, with most of the men sharing the same tasks and hours as their bosses and some still living in the master's house. Even in the factories the owners knew many of their employees by name, and the latter, mostly young men or women, looked forward confidently to establishing a shop of their own (or, in the case of the sixty per cent who were women, hoped to escape the mill through marriage.)[92]

The prospects for advancement to independent proprietorship were already fading, however, in such areas as textiles, mining, and railroads, where capital requirements had grown beyond the scope of the single owner-operator. Nevertheless the ideal of the independent enterprise was still viable in the sixties and in 1861 Abraham Lincoln could still assert: "The prudent penniless beginner in the world labors for wages a while, saves a surplus with which to buy tools or land for himself, then labors on his own account another while, and at length hires another beginner to help him."[93]

It was in the forties that the first signs of a "backward-oriented" attitude began to appear, and the labor movement in that decade has been characterized as "defensive" insofar as "the workers and intellectuals who participated . . . had not emancipated themselves from the traditions of an earlier economic society and were simply trying to ward off the encroachments of the new power of capitalist industry."[94] "The remedy was sought in a return to an idealized colonial system of economics dominated by agriculture and domestic industry."[95] The difficulties which workers experienced, then, were perceived as a divergence from traditional institutions and their movement in large measure expressed an attempt at bringing actualities back into line with ideal prescriptions.

. . . neither the workers nor the reformers who shared in their movements realized the inevitability of the new industrialism. They were unable to convince themselves that the old relationship of master and journeyman had to go. They saw that the condition and status of the worker were declining, but underestimated the new forces at work, and, imbued with the optimism that characterized the period, they made a strong but ineffectual effort to stem the tide.[96]

In making this effort, the close identification between employer and employed was reaffirmed. Thus the membership in the New York State Mechanics' Association included *both* workers and employers. "While this was not strictly a working-class movement in the modern sense — it included employer and employee — it was just that in the sense of the period that was passing away."[97] Various experiments and proposals on producers' and consumers' cooperatives, self-supporting communities, and free land characterized this period. These efforts were largely unsuccessful and this period, referred to as the era of "humanitarianism," gave way to a more strictly trade union movement with the upswing of business in the early fifties.

This "new trade unionism," according to the Commons group, dates the beginning of *modern* unionism. "Instead of experiments in co-operation or leadership by humanitarians we find rules for apprenticeship, closed shop, minimum wage, time and method of payment, initiation fees and dues, funds for strike benefits, union employment offices, and the exclusion of employers, politicians, and friends of labour not actually working at the trade."[98] Despite these features, the new trade unionism failed to survive the decade which witnessed a major depression toward its close, and Commons admits that no less than thirty years were to pass before the "policies of 1853 became fully justified . . ."[99] Ware concludes his book on the period by stating: "The labor movement in America finished the period 1840-60 as it had begun — practically in nothingness."[100]

These two strands of unionism expressed the dualities of commitment which were a function of the structural changes accompanying modernization. Each type of organization represented commitment to a different state of the system. The renovating form, as exemplified by the various reformist groups in the forties, was to arrive at its fullest growth in the decades following the Civil War, culminating in what has been referred to as "the upheaval" of the eighties. This was the final thrust "backward" toward ideal patterns with which actualities no longer coincided.

It will be recalled that the product market was rapidly expanding, due (in part) to the enormous burst of railway construction. After the Civil War it rapidly approached national dimensions. Thus, competing producers could now be almost a continent apart. Further, the increased means of transport meant that labor was as mobile as products and out-of-town migrants could seek jobs locally. Even where product markets were local (as in printing) the labor market might still be countrywide and national unions rapidly emerged.[101]

This nationalization of unions followed the two forms we have been discussing, i.e., the "new unions" and the renovating type. The latter were the successors to the reform movement of the forties and the former were the successors to the "new unions" which arose in the fifties but failed to survive. Of the renovating type, the National Labor Union represented the first effort. It came into being in 1866.

The two lines of agitation that dominated the National Labor Union were eight hours for work, and greenbackism. The first prevailed in 1866, the second took possession in 1867.[102]

Although the National Labor Union initially included elements from both the "new unions" (trade unions) and reform organizations, "The national trade unions, unhappy at the direction in which the National Labor Union was pointed, began to disaffiliate, and after 1870 the political and reform elements were in control."[103] Again, the renovating direction of this "reform" orientation is suggested by Grob, who significantly notes that the "basic character of the National Labor Union was in large measure determined by the background and ideological orientation of its leaders, most of whom had been born and had grown to maturity during the reform and antimonopoly crusades of the 1830's and 1840's." The most important of these leaders was William H. Sylvis, whose personal career, Grob asserts, is representative:

Easily shifting from the status of journeyman to part proprietor and then back to journeyman, Sylvis' experiences were typical of the labor movement as a whole. Growing to manhood in an era of ferment, he retained the political and social reform philosophy that was such an integral part of the ante-bellum labor movement. To him the primary purpose of the labor movement was the abolition of an impersonal and degrading wage system, which would be replaced by a co-operative society based on the dominance of the small individual producer.[104]

Sylvis, while a reformer, was also an active trade unionist who saw no contradiction between advocating "bread and butter" demands while directing his attention to broader issues. In the beginning, then, trade unionists, even those who did not entirely agree to National Labor Union goals, were willing to join forces "in the hopes that a successful national federation would result in a more thoroughgoing organization of the working class."[105]

The trade unionists and the reformers increasingly diverged, however, for Sylvis' ultimate aim was the complete abolition of the wage system. Although he saw trade unions as necessary, he felt them to be only temporary expedients.[106]

Monetary reform became an important part of the National Labor Union's ideology. Its underlying intent "was in harmony with efforts of the time to finance cooperation, to expel the middle-man and financier, and to raise the small producer to a position of independence."[107] The adherents to these programs, Grob states, "were radicals who expressed their hostility to an industrial society through a plan that offered to the workers a restoration of their entrepreneurial status as well as a just share of the national income."[108]

Numerous difficulties of organization and conflicting goals plagued the leaders of the National Labor Union. The most important of these was their relative neglect, during the later years, of the pragmatic "bread and butter" issues espoused by many trade unionists. Grob asserts, however, that the orientation of the National Labor Union leadership was in keeping with the membership's.

Its emphasis on co-operation was designed to restore a society where the simple master-workman relationship was dominant. The analysis of many workingmen brought them inescapably to the conclusion that it was at the root of all their troubles. When co-operation failed to achieve the anticipated relief, it was perhaps inevitable that the next weapon the National Labor Union would turn to would be political action.[109]

This neglect of immediate benefits lost the parent organization the support of its trade union constituency and, by 1872, it had become defunct.

The efforts of the forties and the sixties were but precursors of a dramatic final attempt to restore a previous condition. The value of individualism as expressed in the widespread desire for small business ownership was, even at the time of the National Labor Union, still viable for those in the skilled trades. Nevertheless, the trend was clear to some and the rapid growth in large-scale production following the Civil War appeared to confirm their assessment of the degradation of manual labor. The Knights of Labor represented the final major attempt to realign actualities with ideal traditional patterns.

"The Noble Order of the Knights of Labor, although it first became important in the labor movement after 1873, was formed by Uriah Smith Stephens in 1869."[110] Early in its existence the organization was kept quite secret, which may, in part, have been a justifiable tactic for an infant labor organization in that period. The traditional opposition of the Catholic Church to secret organizations and the public identification of them with the Molly Maguires (a secret labor organization reputed to be engaging in terrorist activities in mining areas until the late 1870's) militated for a change in such policy along with the expunging of objectionable religious oaths.[111]

The instructions given to each new member indicate an opposition to modernization, particularly as it involved productive rationalization. The predominantly individualistic orientation, so pronounced among American capitalist employers, is specifically recognized when it is proposed to "rescue the toiler from the grasp of the selfish . . . " Although it is affirmed that "no conflict with legitimate enterprise, no antagonism to necessary capital" is intended, some "in their haste and greed, blinded by self-interests, overlook the interests of others, and sometimes violate the rights of those they deem helpless." In contrast, the order's members would work to "harmonize the interests of labor and capital . . . to combine and co-operate in the great army of peace and industry."[112]

Grob emphasizes that the Knights were the heirs to the reform goals of the pre-Civil War labor movements and the post-Civil War National Labor Union. He sums their program up as follows:

Their primary aim, briefly stated, was to abolish the wage system and re-establish the simple master-workman relationship of an earlier era where employer and employee performed similar functions . . . Efforts to assist workingmen to secure higher wages, shorter hours, and improved working conditions were mere amelioratives . . . Emphatically opposing the developing industrial order, they sought to re-establish the simpler and supposedly more humane society of an earlier era. In turn, thousands of workingmen, who had been hard hit by the depression of the 1870's, enthusiastically supported leaders who offered them not merely a higher standard of living, but also a position of independence and respected status in the community.[113]

It was not until 1878 that a Declaration of Principles was laid down and a national governing structure was constituted. The manner in which the Knights

Discontinuity, Mobilization, and Social Origins

"grew up" to a national organization is important for understanding its operations.

The Knights of Labor differed from the national bodies representing all trades that preceded it, in that it began from the ground and worked up. It was a natural growth and not artificially created by reformers. The older bodies were simply conventions which sometimes tried to reenforce themselves by organizing labor unions from the national convention down.[114]

This natural growth involved the creation of local assemblies, the first of which was formed from among Stephens' disbanded Garment Cutters' Union in Philadelphia. By 1875, "fifty-two Locals had been organized in Philadelphia, and about two hundred and fifty in other parts of the country, principally in the mining regions of Pennsylvania, West Virginia, Indiana, and Illinois."[115]

When the work of coordinating the various locals became difficult without a higher governing unit, a district assembly was formed, comprised of delegates from the locals. The first such unit occurred, again, in Philadelphia but others followed quickly. Each was based on geographic locale, their delegates coming from the surrounding locals.

A Declaration of Principles was promulgated for the order. It asserted that many of the order's aims could only be attained by legislation but that the order itself was not a political party and supported no particular party. In its articles, wealth was decried as a standard of greatness and a demand was made for a just share of wealth for the workers who created it. The declaration pledged that, through the order, efforts would be aimed at a cooperative system to replace the wage system, equal pay for both sexes, the establishment of the eight-hour day, and the recreation of "bonds of sympathy" between employer and employee through arbitration procedures that would render strikes unnecessary. Beyond this, numerous proposals for legislative action were contained in the declaration.[116] As Grob notes, the order's ideological thrust was a clear continuation of the reform movement among labor groups in America.

The close ideological bond linking the Jacksonian labor movement with the National Labor Union and the Knights of Labor can be found first in the similarity of aims and objectives of each. All three were professed enemies, though in varying intensity, of the financial structure of the United States, and each espoused the destruction of monopoly, to be achieved in part through currency and banking reform. There was also a direct line from George Henry Evans to those of the leaders of the National Labor Union and Knights. The ten-hour movement of the 1830's and 1840's had its counterpart in the eight-hour movement of the 1860's and 1880's. In other areas as well — insistence upon the legal equality of capital and labor, the termination of foreign contract labor and convict labor, the introduction of a co-operative industrial system, the substitution of arbitration for strikes, the enactment of a weekly wage pay law and the need for labor political action — the debt of the Knights to its reform predecessors is evident.[117]

Anyone who was or who had been a wage worker could join the order except for lawyers, doctors, bankers, and those deriving their livelihood from intoxicating beverages. Thus, farmers, merchants, and masters were allowed into it. Although there was a stipulation that the membership of local assemblies be comprised of three-fourths wage earners, the provisions for nonwage-earner members, including employers, indicates the "harmony of interests" assumptions prevailing in the order as well as the "one big union" approach emphasizing the solidarity of all labor.[118]

These features led to some crucial formal organization features of the order that had distinct implications for its operation:

> Within the three organizational levels of the Knights there was much diversity. There were, for example, two forms of local assemblies, the mixed and the trade. The mixed local included men of all trades and callings, while the trade local was composed either of groups of the same craft or groups having different occupations but working at the same plant. In addition, there were mixed and trade district assemblies and also national trade assemblies.[119]

The admission of national trade unions into the Knights as district assemblies altered the geographic character of the latter. When solidarity was later insisted upon (in part by reasserting the primacy of "mixed" assemblies), a breach was to develop between the "trade element" and the order.[120] The probability of such a breach is particularly understandable when it is remembered that the leaders of the order did not conceive of their organization as a primarily collective bargaining unit centering around "bread and butter" issues, but as an instrument of reform. The guiding motto, "an injury to one is the concern of all," applied to skilled and unskilled alike. "Unlike the Federation of 1881-86, and unlike the American Federation of Labor, the Knights of Labor was an integrated body and every member was directly a member of the Order and not indirectly through an affiliated organization."[121]

This abrogation of "trade autonomy" and emphasis on the mixed district assembly, which was geographic in composition, was clearly at variance with trade union bargaining aims. The failure of the order's constitution to spell out a legitimate role for trade unions and to call for apprenticeship laws, taken together with the above, was indicative to Commons and his associates that it "started out as the antithesis of the trade unions in form of organization, and, similarly, it emphasized eduction, mutual aid, and co-operation rather than a policy of restriction . . ."[122]

The program of the order was inimical to an emphasis on craft distinctions. Its leaders felt that such distinctions were threatened by modernization. Solidarity in a movement designed to alter a deleterious course of events was in the interests of all wage earners, skilled and unskilled, since craft exclusiveness would be obliterated by modernization in the long run.

The phenomenal rise in membership in the order, and the bitter struggles that ensued, coincided with a rise in factory production. "Indeed, the factory system of production, for the first time, became general during the eighties."[123] Membership in the order rose from some 20,000 in 1879 to 60,000 in 1884.[124] Then a spectacular increase took place:

Discontinuity, Mobilization, and Social Origins

In a remarkably short time — in a few months — over 600,000 people living practically in every State in the Union united in one organization. The Knights grew from 989 local assemblies with 104,066 members in good standing in July 1885, to 5,892 assemblies with 702,924 members in July, 1886.[125]

This growth in membership was not unassociated with rather severe "labor agitation."

The idea of the solidarity of labour ceased to be merely verbal, and took on flesh and life; general strikes, nation-wide boycotts, and nation-wide political movements became the order of the day. Although the upheaval came with the depression it was the product of permanent and far reaching economic changes which had taken place during the seventies and the early eighties.[126]

Commons asserts that much of the impetus in membership and militant action came from the unskilled "rising as an elemental protest against oppression and degradation . . . The movement bore in every way the aspect of a social war. A frenzied hatred of labor for capital was shown in every important strike."[127] Ware's remarks are of further significance:

The old, master-journeyman relationship was gone forever. Great corporations owning mines and railroads, employing private police and semiprivate "detectives," calling vainly for state but more successfully for Federal protection, influencing if not controlling courts and legislatures, were set over against labor masses, ignorant and unorganized, daily losing their one possession, their craft skill, as suspicious of one another as of their common enemy, and aroused to futile action only as a result of long depression.[128]

Thus, Ware suggests that membership in the order was swelled by those whose skills had been diluted or rendered obsolescent by modern technology, or "from the specialized workers created by the Industrial Revolution . . . " He asserts that the major strikes in 1885-1886 involved railway shopmen who "had been machinists but were then specialized workers of the modern sort."[129]

It will be recalled that the model Commons used in his analysis of market "stages" and associated productive organization, was that of shoe workers, who were among the first to exemplify the trend he perceived. It was indeed this body which made up the greater proportion of the New England membership until 1884 and, as late as 1888, it was written that "nearly fifty per cent of the members of the Knights of Labor in Massachusetts, Maine and New Hampshire are of the same craft."[130]

Both the leaders and a substantial portion of the rank-and-file membership of the Knights had been socialized in a setting where their once-important skills were the basis of independent productive enterprise. The changes brought about by modernization and the rationalization of production were most evident in the wage system. The cash nexus between employer and employee was a concrete expression of rationality, functional specificity, avoidance, and universalistic membership criteria. This latter aspect, of course, relegated those with obsolescent skills, regardless of how sophisticated, to an inferior position and rendered aspirations for independent productive establishment highly doubtful. Further, the individualism initially adhered to by all now had resulted in an individualistic relationship between employer and employee. The selfishness often pointed to by the Knights' leaders explicitly emphasized this change.

Alternative goals may lessen disruptive behavior insofar as individuals unable to achieve one may turn to another. Those whose skills remained valid, although also less able to approach individualistic goals, could nevertheless orient their activities to the now distinctive alternative of success within the confines of large-scale enterprises. Those whose craft traditions were no longer significant faced failure on both counts. They provided the core of the renovating movement. To them modernization obliterated the advantages of the "good old days" and their expectations of private, small-scale, productive units guided by the value of individualism was the basis of their renovating orientation.

The leadership of the Knights exemplifies this adherence to older patterns, as Grob points out:

The Knights, on the whole, were led by men who had been born and grown to maturity during the eventful decades preceding the Civil War. The humanitarian crusades of the 1840's and 1850's had laid the foundation for an irrevocable hostility toward industrial society and the wage system. Belonging to an America where the development of an industrial economy had not yet overwhelmed a predominantly rural nation, these leaders did not think in terms of a permanent wage-earning class and its needs. Regarding the workers as the only legitimate members of the community, they sought to establish a co-operative society based upon a large number of small producers, for only under such conditions could the American democratic ideal be realized.[131]

While many of the more prominent leaders of the Knights espoused a rapidly receding state of affairs, many of the trade union leaders, Grob notes, "were foreign born, and were therefore little affected by ante-bellum reformism."[132] There is some evidence that suggests that these orientations were reflected on the part of the rank-and-file membership. In some areas, the Knights' membership appeared to be made up largely of the American born. In 1886, 45 percent of the members in Illinois were American with the next highest proportion (16 percent) being German born.[133] On the other hand, the trade unions in the same state counted only 20 percent American-born members.[134] "Having grown to maturity during years of social ferment, most native American workers proved to be highly receptive to the reform philosophy of the Knights."[135]

The demise of the Knights followed numerous unsuccessful strikes (which were inimical to the principles of the order and received only lukewarm support from the central leadership), the ultimate failure of the eight-hour movement, capped by the Haymarket bomb catastrophe, and the growing rift with trade unionists. "Indeed, after 1886 many national trade districts left the Order because of their inability to function within the framework of that body."[136] But of even more importance, the unskilled membership dwindled precipitously, its strength especially declining in the large cities. According to Commons, the order "fell from a membership of 700,000 in 1886 to 500,982 in 1887, 259,578 in 1888, 220,607 in 1889, and 100,000 in 1890."[137] At the same time, the trade unions grew in strength. Ulman assesses the situation as follows:

> In theory, both the Knights and the national trade unions were unsuited to the total dynamic environment, because each was adapted to only one aspect of that environment and was not well equipped to cope with the other. In fact, however, it seemed that a labor organization's failure to orient itself to the extension of market areas, as exemplified by the district-dominated Knights, was fatal; while failure to be oriented to the possibility that changes in products and methods would uproot existing craft jurisdictions was not necessarily fatal, since craft obsolescence was not an inevitable concomitant of economic change, at least in the short run. The Knights, relying for their strength upon the solidarity of all trades, were obliged to gamble that the leveling influence of technological change would be great enough to make membership in the Order a matter of self-interest to the unions' members. The trade union, on the other hand, relying for its strength upon the economic isolation of its membership, was obliged to gamble on the permanence of that isolation. The Knights lost this bet.[138]

But the Knights lost not only the skilled element in their membership but the unskilled as well, who, it will be recalled, had swelled the order's rolls to begin with. In fact, Commons notes that, after 1887, "the bulk of the unskilled-labourers having left the Order, the struggle between the Knights and the Trade Unions ceased to be one between the unskilled and skilled portions of the wage-earning class for control of the labour movement, and became instead a mere fight between two rival organizations."[139]

It is, therefore, on the circumstances surrounding the less-skilled members of the industrial labor force that attention must be focused. The following chapter will pursue this issue with respect to the events we have just reviewed.

Conclusion

It has been suggested that the point of discontinuity in the course of American modernization centered on the value of individualism, ultimately undermined in practice by the very patterns associated with it. "Middle class producers were increasingly harassed and wiped out by the economic effects of the relations and ideals they glorified."[140] The inception of the Knights of Labor involved the recession of this value for a substantial portion of the American labor force.

The appeal to the past was thus the outstanding characteristic of the reform unionists. In their eyes the primary function of the labor movement was the restoration of the independence of the working class, and they constantly sought to develop appropriate means for their purpose.[141]

The inception and growth of this unit made it an outstanding bet for an ultimately radical industrial union. Yet it failed to survive, losing precisely those members whose eventual adherence to a radical ideology was most probable.

IMMIGRANT WORKERS

The demise of the Knights and the more thorough unionization of the skilled workers occurred at a time when immigration was rising to unprecedented heights. This association, it is held here, was not fortuitous, and Chapter 5 will continue the present discussion by examining the impact of immigration on the fate of the Knights.

NOTES

1. Talcott Parsons, "The Present Position and Prospects of Systematic Theory in Sociology," in *Essays in Sociological Theory* (rev. ed.; New York: The Free Press, 1954), pp. 228-231.

2. Wilbert E. Moore, *Social Change* (Englewood Cliffs, N.J.: Prentice-Hall, 1963), pp. 93-94.

3. Marion J. Levy, Jr., *The Structure of Society* (Princeton: Princeton University Press, 1952), pp. 173-183.

4. Marion J. Levy, Jr., *Modernization and the Structure of Societies: A Setting for International Affairs* (Princeton: Princeton University Press, 1966), Vol. I, p. 79.

5. It will be recalled that Moore and Feldman, whose remarks on this point are cited in Chapter 1, noted that old patterns are not "lost without trace" but provide a continuing challenge to the new, affecting the trajectory of change.

6. The concept "renovating change" is contained in Levy, *Modernization* . . . , Vol. I, p. 19.

7. Arnold S. Feldman and Wilbert E. Moore, "Commitment of the Industrial Work Force," in Moore and Feldman (eds.), *Labor Commitment and Social Change in Developing Areas* (New York: Social Science Research Council, 1960), pp. 11-12.

8. Levy, *Modernization* . . . , Vol. I, p. 79.

9. *Ibid.*, Vol. II, p. 387.

10. For two articles discussing the implications of such structural conditions see Talcott Parsons, "Age and Sex in the Social Structure of the United States," in *Essays* . . . , pp. 89-103, and "Certain Primary Sources and Patterns of Aggression in the Social Structure of the Western World," in *ibid.*, pp. 298-322.

11. Orville G. Brim, Jr., "Socialization Through the Life Cycle," in Brim and Stanton Wheeler, *Socialization After Childhood: Two Essays* (New York: John Wiley & Sons, Inc., 1966), pp. 18-19.

12. The distinctions being made here are, of course, of a relative nature. It is not being suggested that socialization is ever "completed" in either case. Rather, it is held that decreasing "inputs" are more to be expected among mature individuals in the nonmodern setting than in the modern. If this be the case, we are provided with some clues concerning the violent protests which frequently accompany modernization.

13. Marion J. Levy, Jr., "Some Aspects of 'Individualism' and the Problem of Modernization in China and Japan," *Economic Development and Cultural Change*, Vol. 10 (April 1962), especially pp. 226-227.

14. *Ibid.*, p. 227.

15. *Ibid.*, p. 229. Marion J. Levy, Jr., "Some Social Obstacles to Capital Formation in 'Underdeveloped Areas,' " in National Bureau of Economic Research, *Capital Formation and Economic Growth: A Conference of the Universities-National Bureau Committee for Economic Research* (Princeton: Princeton University Press, 1955), pp. 441-520. For further implications of this theme see Talcott Parsons, "Some Reflections on the Institutional Framework of Economic Development," in that author's *Structure and Process in Modern Society* (New York: The Free Press, 1960), pp. 98-131.

16. Joseph Stepanek, *Managers for Small Industry: An International Study* (New York: The Free Press, 1960), pp. 34-35.

17. Levy, *The Structure* . . . , p. 485.

18. Charles A. Reich addresses several of the elements considered in the present discussion with his notions of Consciousness I and Consciousness II. See *The Greening of America* (New York: Bantam Books, 1971).

19. C. Wright Mills, *White Collar: The American Middle Classes* (New York: Oxford University Press, 1960), p. 4.

20. James M. Williams, *Our Rural Heritage: The Social Psychology of Rural Development* (New York: Alfred A. Knopf, 1925), p. 229.

21. Mills, *op. cit.*, p. 7.

22. See *ibid.*, p. 6. Kurt Mayer, "Recent Changes in the Class Structure of the United States," *Transactions of the Third World Congress of Sociology*, Amsterdam (September 1956), Vol. 3, pp. 67-68, 79, n. 6.

23. Mills, *op. cit.*, p. 7.

24. Charles L. Sanford, *The Quest for Paradise: Europe and the American Moral Imagination* (Urbana: University of Illinois Press, 1961), p. 104.

25. *Ibid.*, p. 105.

26. *Ibid.*, pp. 126-132.

27. Carl Bridenbaugh, *The Colonial Craftsman* (New York: New York University Press, 1950), p. 126. Williams, *op. cit.*, pp. 52-53.

28. *Ibid.*, p. 66.

29. *Ibid.*, p. 195.

30. *Ibid.*, p. 197.

31. *Ibid.*, p. 86. Bridenbaugh, *op. cit.*, pp. 129-130.

32. Williams, *op. cit.*, p. 83. Bridenbaugh, *op. cit.*, pp. 126-127.

33. Mills, *op. cit.*, p. 9.

34. Bridenbaugh, *op. cit.*, p. 128.

35. Joseph A. Schumpeter, *Theory of Economic Development* (New York: Oxford University Press, 1961).

36. Lewis Corey, *The Crisis of the Middle Class* (New York: Covici-Friede, 1935), p. 15. Mills, *op. cit.*, pp. 3, 63.

37. Caroline F. Ware, *The Early New England Cotton Manufacture: A Study in Industrial Beginnings* (Boston: Houghton Mifflin Co., 1931), p. 3.

38. Sanford, *op. cit.*, p. 135.

39. Ware, *op. cit.*, pp. 7-8.

40. Karl Marx and Friedrich Engels, *German Ideology* (New York: International Publishers, 1947), p. 41.

41. Reinhard Bendix, *Work and Authority in Industry: Ideologies of Management in the Course of Industrialization* (New York: John Wiley & Sons, Inc., 1956), p. 100.

42. For a discussion of the debate over large industry, see Samuel Rezneck, "The Rise and Early Development of Industrial Consciousness in the United States, 1760-1830," *Journal of Economic and Business History*, Vol. 4 (August 1932), pp. 784-811.

43. Sanford, *op. cit.*, Chapter 9, "The Intellectual Origins and New-Worldliness of American Industry," pp. 155-175. Ware, *op. cit.*, p. 10.

44. *Ibid.*, pp. 11-14. Victor S. Clark, *History of Manufactures in the United States* (New York: McGraw-Hill Book Co., 1929), Vol. I, pp. 391, 448.

45. Levy, *Modernization* . . . , Vol. I, p. 61.

46. *Ibid.*, pp. 169-170. See also, Levy, *The Structure* . . . , pp. 296-297.

47. Bridenbaugh, *op. cit.*, p. 132.

48. Stephen Thurnstrom, *Poverty and Progress: Social Mobility in a Nineteenth Century City* (Cambridge: Harvard University Press, 1964), p. 43.

49. Thomas C. Cochran, "Business Organization and the Development of Industrial

Discipline," in Harold Williams (ed.), *The Growth of the American Economy* (2d ed.; Englewood Cliffs, N.J.: Prentice-Hall, 1951), p. 291.

    50. Constance McL. Green, *Holyoke, Massachusetts: A Case History of the Industrial Revolution in America* (New Haven: Yale University Press, 1939), p. 225.

    51. Ware, *op. cit.*, pp. 214-215.

    52. Bridenbaugh, *op. cit.*, pp. 130-132.

    53. *Ibid.*, p. 127.

    54. Parsons, "Some . . . ," in *op. cit.*, p. 108.

    55. Ware, *op. cit.*, pp. 256-257. See also, Vera Shlakman, "Economic History of a Factory Town," *Smith College Studies in History*, Vol. 20 (October 1934-July, 1935), p. 51.

    56. Ware, *loc. cit.*, p. 263. Much of the required behavior and strict supervision was in keeping with what community members would have demanded in any event. The boardinghouse system, however, maintained adherence to such strictures. According to Shlakman "any development toward a relaxation of the conventions tended to be held in check by the boardinghouse system and all that it involved." Shlakman, *op. cit.*, pp. 51-52.

    57. Ware, *op. cit.*, p. 264.

    58. Green, *op. cit.*, p. 15.

    59. *Ibid.*, p. 107.

    60. *Ibid.*, p. 225.

    61. Cochran, *op. cit.*, p. 291.

    62. Bridenbaugh, *op. cit.*, p. 132.

    63. Thurnstrom, *op. cit.*, p. 44.

    64. William Sullivan, *The Industrial Worker in Pennsylvania: 1800-1840* (Harrisburg: Pennsylvania Historical and Museum Commission, 1955), p. 59.

    65. Cochran, *loc. cit.*

    66. John R. Commons and Assocs., *The History of Labor in the United States* (New York: The Macmillan Co., 1918-1935), Vol. I, p. 57.

    67. *Ibid.*, pp. 57-58.

    68. Williams, *op. cit.*, p. 229.

    69. Talcott Parsons, *The Social System* (New York: The Free Press, 1951), pp. 303-321.

    70. Levy, *Modernization* . . . , Vol. I, p. 113.

    71. Levy, "Some Aspects . . . ," p. 228.

    72. Corey, *op. cit.*, p. 61.

    73. Alexis de Tocqueville, *Democracy in America*, ed. Philip Bradley (New York: Alfred A. Knopf, 1951), Vol. II, pp. 160-161.

    74. *Ibid.*, p. 161.

    75. Sullivan, *op. cit.*, pp. 31-57.

    76. Commons, *et al., op. cit.*, p. 103. For Commons' original "interpretive" discussion of shoe workers, see his *Labor and Administration* (New York: The Macmillan Co., 1913), Chapter 14, "American Shoemakers, 1848-1895," pp. 219-266.

    77. Commons, *et al., op. cit.*, p. 36.

    78. *Ibid.*, pp. 56-57.

    79. *Ibid.*, pp. 61-63.

    80. *Ibid.*, p. 63.

    81. *Ibid.*

    82. *Ibid.*, p. 71.

    83. *Ibid.*, p. 72.

    84. *Ibid.*, p. 101.

    85. *Ibid.*, p. 102.

    86. *Ibid.*, p. 103.

    87. *Ibid.*, p. 104.

    88. Edward Pessen, "The Workingmen's Movement of the Jackson Era," *Mississippi Valley Historical Review*, Vol. 43 (December 1956), pp. 434-435.

89. Lloyd Ulman, *The Rise of the National Trade Union: The Development and Significance of Its Structure, Governing Institutions and Economic Policies* (Cambridge: Harvard University Press, 1955), pp. 575-576.
90. Clark, *op. cit.*, p. 529.
91. *Ibid.*, p. 536.
92. Blake McKelvey, *The Urbanization of America*, 1860-1915 (New Brunswick, N.J.: Rutgers University Press, 1962), p. 130.
93. Quoted in Louis Hacker, *The Triumph of American Capitalism: The Development of Forces in American History to the End of the Nineteenth Century* (New York: Columbia University Press, 1940), p. 279.
94. Norman Ware, *The Industrial Worker: 1840-1860* (Chicago: Quadrangle Books, Inc., 1964), pp. x-xi.
95. Commons, *et al., op. cit.*, p. 493.
96. N. Ware, *The Industrial . . .* , pp. 198-199.
97. *Ibid.*, p. 201.
98. Commons, *et al., op. cit.*, p. 576.
99. *Ibid.*
100. N. Ware, *The Industrial . . .* , p. 240.
101. See Ulman, *op. cit.*, pp. 49-152.
102. Commons, *et al., op. cit.*, Vol. II, p. 87.
103. Gerald N. Grob, *Workers and Utopia: A Study of Ideological Conflict in the American Labor Movement, 1865-1900* (Evanston, Ill.: Northwestern University Press, 1961), p. 12.
104. *Ibid.*, p. 14, quoted with permission.
105. *Ibid.*, p. 15.
106. *Ibid.*, p. 20.
107. Commons, *et al., op. cit.*, p. 121.
108. Grob, *op. cit.*, p. 16.
109. *Ibid.*, pp. 32-33, quoted with permission.
110. Commons, *et al., op. cit.*, Vol. II, p. 197.
111. Norman Ware, *The Labor Movement in the United States: 1860-1895* (New York: Appleton-Century-Crofts, 1929), pp. 73-80, 91-102. Difficulties persisted, however, and differences between the leaders of the church and the order were a continual source of strain.
112. These instructions are reproduced in Carrol Wright's "An Historical Sketch of the Knights of Labor," *Quarterly Journal of Economics*, Vol. 1 (January 1887), pp. 142-143.
113. Grob, *op. cit.*, p. 38, quoted with permission.
114. N. Ware, *The Labor . . .* , pp. 63-64.
115. Wright, *op. cit.*, pp. 145-146.
116. Reproduced in *ibid.*, pp. 157-159.
117. Grob, *op. cit.*, p. 39, quoted with permission.
118. Commons, *et al., op. cit.*, Vol. II, pp. 335-336.
119. Grob, *op. cit.*, pp. 35-36, quoted with permission.
120. Commons, *et al., op. cit.*, Vol. II, pp. 342-343.
121. N. Ware, *The Labor . . .* , p. 65.
122. Commons, *et al., op. cit.*, Vol. II, p. 336.
123. *Ibid.*, p. 358.
124. *Ibid.*, p. 381.
125. *Ibid.*, pp. 343-344.
126. *Ibid.*, p. 357.
127. *Ibid.*, pp. 373-374.
128. N. Ware, *The Labor . . .* , p. 50.
129. *Ibid.*, p. 71.

130. Frank K. Foster, "Shoemakers in the Movement," in George Edwen McNeill (ed.), *The Labor Movement: The Problem of To-Day* (New York: The M. W. Hazen Co., 1888), p. 196.
131. Grob, *op. cit.*, p. 39, quoted with permission.
132. *Ibid.*, p. 43.
133. Commons, *et al., op. cit.*, Vol. II, pp. 381-382.
134. *Ibid.*, p. 315. However, New Jersey figures do not show marked differences. See Grob, *op. cit.*, p. 43, n. 21.
135. Grob, *op. cit.*, p. 43.
136. *Ibid.*, pp. 118, 377.
137. Commons, *et al., op. cit.*, Vol. II, p. 482.
138. Ulman, *op. cit.*, p. 377.
139. Commons, *et al., op. cit.*, Vol. II, p. 482.
140. Corey, *op. cit.*, p. 8.
141. Grob, *op. cit.*, p. 8, quoted with permission.

5

Immigration and the Decline of Renovation

The present chapter pursues the first part of the argument developed in Chapter 1. It will be suggested that immigration muted the strains of discontinuity, spectacularly demonstrated by the rise of the Knights of Labor. We examine the entry of immigrant labor into American industry and the orientation this body of workers had toward both industrial employment and the society in which it was experienced. It will be argued that, not possessed of traditions to which native-born workers adhered, immigrant laborers proved to be little or no obstacle to the changes being wrought by modernization. In fact, their entry into mines and mills functioned to facilitate such changes.

Data presented in Chapter 3 showed that a substantial part of the nonagricultural work force was recruited from among those who were not native born. Further, these individuals were disproportionately concentrated in the least remunerative occupational roles. An upswing in immigration occurred at precisely the period when the United States was experiencing the "great upheaval." Over five million immigrants entered this country during the decade of the eighties, or more than twice the number that came in the preceding ten years.

It has been pointed out that the conditions confronting the immigrant were vastly different in the later period than in the earlier years of the nineteenth century. Rural migrants coming early in the century were generally able to resume farming in America. Thus arrivals from Scandinavia and Germany generally eschewed the eastern seaboard and went westward to settle beyond the Alleghenies.[1]

The one major exception to this pattern were the Irish, who left their homelands under the most pressing circumstances of famine and poverty. Arriving on the east coast of the United States without money and in desperate straits, there was no question of "pushing west." The Irish peasants stayed in the eastern cities and became the first of the large groups of immigrants to settle in America's urban areas. For them the settlement was relatively permanent.[2]

As was asserted earlier, the alterations in the relationship between employer and employee were likely to be initiated by the employer in an effort to rationalize production. The early larger-scale enterprises, where such changes were likely to occur, were among the New England textile manufacturers. As early as the forties, in fact, difficulties were beginning to manifest themselves in the "model" New England mill towns.

This increasing tension was the result of both social and mechanical changes, the development of a policy of speeding up and of improvements in the machinery that permitted greater efficiency. As the control of the corporations passed out of the hands of the original owners, and a chiefly exploitive purpose came to dominate their policy, wages were cut, hours were not appreciably reduced, and the numbers of looms per worker or the speed of the looms, the noise and the dust, constantly increased. The New England girls found the old factories and their laxity not unpleasant and quite remunerative. They continued so to regard them while they played at mill work for a year or so. But in proportion as they came to regard the work of the mills as their permanent occupation and found themselves involved, year after year, in a severer discipline, the whole matter took on a new complexion.[3]

These girls were committed to a previous set of circumstances that was beginning to change. It was this previous condition that convinced them to first come to the mills. The immigrant provided the employer with cheap labor and the means to finally divest himself of what were becoming irksome demands and impediments to change. "Only when the advent of the immigrant made it no longer necessary for the manufacturer to gain the respect of the community in order to secure his labor force, was he freed from the need of guaranteeing the social welfare of his workers."[4] Where previously the employer was institutionally expected to enter into what amounted to a predominantly diffuse and responsible relationship with his employees, he was now "only too eager to be relieved of that necessity by the advent of a class of labor which had no standing in the community and no prejudice against mill work."[5]

The rapid influx of Irish immigrants in desperate need of work, and outside of the orbit of local traditions, provided the manufacturer the means with which to reorganize the management of labor. "Within the space of a decade they became the dominant element in the labor force of the cotton mills and both the companies and the communities found themselves with a labor situation radically different from that of the industry's beginning."[6] Although, after their entry into the labor force, prejudice may have hastened native departures, the immigrants were not the source of the exodus but rather took the places of those who left. Nor does wage competition appear to have contributed substantially to the native outflow.[7]

Immigrants thus provided a ready and willing labor pool with which the manufacturer could effect desired changes. The ethnic differences between employer and employed facilitated such changes. Lawrence, Massachusetts, "society" of the 1850's was summed up by Cole in the words, "Yankees at the top and Irish at the bottom . . ."[8] and Clark notes that "immigration with its resulting differences in language and custom has weakened ties of sympathy and understanding between employers and employed."[9]

The solidarities among these early factory operatives were more likely to be among fellow immigrants than with anyone else. Their orientation toward their native-born employer, on the other hand, was quite likely to be precisely limited and to revolve around one aspect, namely the cash nexus of employment. Thus was the rationalization of textile production facilitated. Later the Irish would man the supervisory posts while newer and similarly alien groups moved into operative positions.

But the pre-Civil War period was one of restricted factory production. It was not until the 1880's that such units started to become fairly common to industrial production. The significance of the vastly increased post-Civil War immigration lies in its coincidence with the inception of modern industrialism and the "great upheaval" which indexed the strains that such changes engendered.

As mentioned previously, the later immigration was conditioned by opportunities for employment and fluctuated considerably when such opportunities altered. Later immigrants came during a period when the more abundant possibilities for land settlement had passed and, furthermore, possessed little or no resources with which to start an enterprise, rural or urban.[10] Finally, due to the relatively less expensive and more convenient modes of transportation in existence after mid-century, it was not unreasonable for the migrant to view his crossing as a temporary measure designed to improve his position in the home society. Many immigrants came with the initial intention of later returning.

This last point (i.e., the immigrant as a "sojourner") is quite important because it had a considerable bearing on the immigrant's orientation to American society. Thus, in discussing Italian migration, the MacDonalds state:

They left Italy, for the most part, in order to return to their birthplace with money to buy land and a better house and to raise their social status. They did not intend, at first, to enter American society and raise themselves in its terms. They had little contact, other than impersonal service relationships with the host society, and it was many years before they were assimilated to it.[11]

Of Poles, Thomas and Znaniecki claim:

... there are few peasants who do not intend to return. Temporary absence changes into permanent absence slowly, but there is always a latent feeling of obligation to return.[12]

... the emigrant who goes to America means to return a different man, to obtain — by earning much and spending little — the economic foundation on which to build a new and superior career. If he is a landless peasant, i.e., manor-servant or komornick, or will be landless because his parents have not enough land to give some to each child, he wants to save for a farm. If his farm is too small to live on without hiring himself as a laborer, he intends to buy a larger one so as to be completely his own master. If he is a hard-working journeyman, he dreams about establishing a prosperous business of his own.[13]

Saloutos observes the following of Greek migrants:

The immigrant lived a hand-to-mouth existence. He needed cash and he needed it quickly in order to provide for himself, for his anxious parents, or for the family he had left behind. Time and ready money were of the essence. Urban employment and street vending, not farming, offered the best opportunities to obtain ready cash. Certainly at first, when the immigrant came "to grab a few riches and hurry home" the thought of engaging in a long range operation such as farming hardly entered his mind. Cash, mobility, and the dream of going home at the earliest opportunity dominated his thoughts.[14]

Brody, commenting on immigrant steelworkers, notes:

The Slavic influx shaped the labor stability at the unskilled level. A lowly job in the mills, however ill-paid and unpleasant, was endurable if it enabled the immigrant to leave in a few years with enough funds to resume his accustomed place in his native village. That was his original purpose.[15]

The immigrants ... counted the value of their hoards in terms of the increased buying power in their native villages. Mentally converting dollars into roubles, they estimated carefully that a few years of steady work would bring enough to buy a piece of land. "If I don't earn $1.50 a day," figured a prospective immigrant, "it would not be worth thinking about America." He could surely get that much in a steel mill.[16]

In spite of the growing ease in gaining access to cheap and efficient transportation, the immigrant who came and planned to return had to assume a relatively long period of *steady* work if he was to accomplish his ends. Thomas and Znaniecki state that "even the immigrant who has firmly decided to return counts on at least two or three years here."[17]

Without funds to sustain him very long after arriving, the immigrant was anxious to find work at the earliest possible moment. Herein lay his ready induction into the American labor market even at less than the prevailing standards. In spite of efforts at "racial" explanations, the Immigration Commission appeared to have a clear understanding of these circumstances when they wrote:

Still another salient fact in connection with the recent immigrant labor supply has been the necessitous condition of the newcomers upon their arrival in American industrial communities in search of work. Recent immigrants have usually had but a few dollars in their possession when they arrived at the ports of disembarkation. Consequently they have found it absolutely imperative to engage in work at once. They have not been in position to take exception to the wages or working conditions offered, but must needs go to work on the most advantageous terms they could secure.[18]

As already noted, these wages appeared to satisfy the relevant standards of the immigrant. At one and the same time, the spread of large-scale productive enterprises undermined American traditions while providing the means with which the unskilled immigrant could approach his own. He was not likely to oppose the "wages system" or the skill dilution and obsolescence which accompanied it. The former was what attracted him in the first place and the latter was what permitted him access to it.

The conditions of modern capitalist enterprise, free labor mediated by a cash nexus, fitted the immigrant's scheme precisely. Without a generalized medium of exchange with which to calculate his relative advantage, without the freedom to move in and out of employment with minimal obligations, without a social setting that positively sanctioned parties to a relationship pursuing their own goals regardless of the goals of others, migration would have been a completely unsatisfactory alternative for the European peasant.

Given the foregoing, the peasant immigrant of the latter nineteenth and early twentieth centuries may reasonably be considered an expedient member of American society, operating in terms of its patterns, but primarily oriented to his parent society. His contact with native Americans was most likely to be within an employment relationship and that relationship was predominantly rational, functionally specific, universalistic, avoidant, and individualistic. Wage labor was entirely acceptable to the new immigrant.

Again, migration was conditioned by economic circumstances. As pointed out in Chapter 3, employment opportunities, as indicated by business cycles, were a determining factor in levels of immigration. A second feature, the return movement, increased proportionately and amounted to nearly a third of the arrivals by the turn of the century. Of importance here is that these movements also fluctuated with the business cycle. Depressions, then, were not only associated with decreased immigration but also with increased emigration. To quote Jerome: "When industry booms, immigration increases and emigration decreases, when industry is dull, immigration declines and emigration increases."[19]

Although Jerome concludes that emigration did not sufficiently offset immigration during depression years to prevent further aggravation of unemployment,[20] Brinley Thomas presents a much different picture of its consequences.

Countries of emigration suffered quite as severely, if not more severely, from cyclical unemployment as countries of immigration. The United States would have experienced the business cycle even if it had no immigration, and if, in addition, the expansive influence of its population growth had been low its depressions would have had the chronic character associated with secular stagnation and its unemployment would have been correspondingly heavy. Indeed it was in the early thirties, a few years after the immigration barriers had been erected, that America had its most catastrophic experience of unemployment. The outstanding fact is that immigration in its upward phases was a powerful factor pushing up the rate of growth of investment, income and employment, while in its downward phases, unlike internal population growth, it automatically contracted and thus relieved pressure in the labour market.[21]

Comparing "new" and "old" migrants for the years 1908-1910, the Immigration Commission found a greater rate of departures for the "new" (37 per hundred admitted) than for the "old" (13 per hundred admitted).[22] It may be noted once again that the "old" groups were entering a society that was quite isomorphic with their parent one. The "new" groups, on the other hand, were entering one that was structurally quite dissimilar from that which they had left. They were therefore less likely to orient themselves to the American social structure in general. Further, there were some exceptions to the overall breakdown of "new" and "old" with regard to emigration rates. Jews and Armenians, migrating for political reasons, evidenced a distinctly lower return movement than most of the "old" groups, while the French return movement was higher than that of many of the "new" groups.

In general, however, those coming from the southern and eastern countries of Europe returned in larger proportions than those from Northern and Western Europe. At the time the Immigration Commission made its study the peak of "new" immigration had recently been attained. Since the return movement was associated with recency of arrival (95 percent of the returnees of all groups left within ten years of arrival), there was a greater pool of "new" arrivals in the country than of "old," the former thereby providing the bulk of the departures.[23] The commission, in attempting to show the higher transience of "new" as compared to "old" immigrants failed, as with other similar comparisons, to take a historical perspective. Comparing the two categories at one point in time, it concluded something about the qualities of recently arrived "new" immigrants as compared with the "old" who, as a group, had been in the country longer and therefore formed less of a "stranger" element.

But of further importance were the conditions governing immigration after the Civil War. First, the United States was rapidly modernizing and offered a distinct opportunity for temporary, if long-term, employment in its industrial establishments. There was a demand for nonagricultural labor:

In other words, the United States after 1882 was more fully settled and immigration had to be adjusted to a partially industrialized country. Conditions had changed more than the nature of the immigrant.[24]

Further:

It is also important to recognize that it was the steamship, and not the shift in the sources of immigration, that was responsible for the beginning of temporary European immigration to the United States. No sooner had the Atlantic crossing become regular, fast, and tolerably comfortable than a substantial transient movement set in.[25]

For the "new" immigrants, starting to come in the eighties, the social setting was vastly different than it had been for their predecessors. That the later group took the altered circumstances into account and provided a fluctuating labor force, sensitive to employment changes, was entirely in keeping with the changing context in which they had to operate. They, as well as many "old" immigrants, could reasonably contemplate a temporary move that would provide the wherewithal to approach their goals elsewhere without permanently committing themselves to American society or the industrial work context. Finally, it must be noted that, although over 30 percent of those arriving after the eighties later left, the majority remained. At the moment, however, we are considering the immigrants' *initial* and quite rational orientation to the American scene in the decades just before and after the turn of the century. Many, and perhaps most, immigrants entering American society at this time came in quite consciously as expedient societal members.

Immigration and the Decline of Renovation

Steamship companies were anxious to benefit from potential migrants in Northern as well as Southern and Eastern Europe. Many such lines set up labor bureaus and as early as the seventies advertised for prospective Scandinavian passengers. Also there were private emigrant agencies whose representatives offered industrial jobs to migrants with a view toward commissions on steamship tickets and the like. Sometimes these agents advanced passage money to be reimbursed from immigrant wages after arrival. Often, owing to difficulties in securing jobs for the newcomers, such ventures were a failure. Similar operations were carried on in England and Germany.[26]

It will be recalled that one of the legislative demands made in the Constitution of the Knights of Labor was for an anticontract labor law. Erickson indicates the reasons for this and the erroneous assumptions:

The discussions of immigration which preceded the Foran Act to prohibit the importation of contract labor in 1885 were based on the assumption that radically different forms of recruitment of agricultural workers were being used in Italy and Hungary, that mine operators and railroad companies were actually engaged in importing unskilled workers on contracts. The evidence . . . suggests, on the contrary, that what was really happening was that steamship companies, emigrant agencies, and independent commission men were merely expanding their base of operations into new areas, using much the same inducements and methods which had been developed in northern Europe.[27]

Erickson makes clear that American industrial operators did not recruit unskilled European labor. Other agencies, as noted, often did, and occasionally they did arrive under contract wherein they agreed to repay loans for passage out of their wages. The risks here were often greater than profits and the practice did not persist for long.[28]

What was more characteristic of the recent immigrant was indicated by early Italian arrivals, as yet without many predecessors in this country:

Employers of his own nationality are scarce, and unfamiliarity with the language prevents him from applying to others for work, so he turns to one of that numerous fraternity who make it their vocation to supply contractors with cheap labor, the bosses. The common laborer . . . recognized only the middlemen as bosses, not the contractors themselves, unless they happen to be Italians, in which case they are distinguished as boss contractors.[29]

What was true for the Italian appeared to be true for most other pioneer immigrants:

Some form of bossism seemed to be typical of the newly-arrived non-English-speaking immigrant groups in industrial America in the years after 1880. Bossism operated not only among Italians. It was found also among Greeks, Austrians, Turks, Bulgarians, Macedonians, and Mexicans. It was the method by which these groups overcame the problems of language, of quickly finding jobs, and of differences in labor practices. It was, in fact, part of the price that the newcomer had to pay for his strangeness.[30]

This arrangement has often been referred to as the *padrone* system, as it flourished widely among Italian immigrants. Erickson distinguishes between the boss who hired his men directly, provided them with room and board until work was available, often advanced them money to come over, and collected the wages from the employer and paid the men a previously agreed-upon rate. Another type of boss worked for a labor agency and acted as an interpreter but, in this case, the men were hired and paid by the employer.[31] Bossism, further, did not begin with the "new" immigrants but had appeared shortly after the Civil War among Scandinavians in Chicago and among Swedish and German laborers in New York.[32]

Frequently the agent operated in conjunction with a "banker" who financed transportation to the job site and other initial costs. Abuses were many. The agent often profited from the transport, food, and living quarters with which he provided his men at inflated prices. He frequently failed to come up with the work promised or discharged men after only a few days in order to hire others, thereby collecting extra initial fees.[33]

The *padrone*, or labor agent, however, provided an important service for the newly arrived immigrant who had not been in the country long and had virtually no other contacts. He was therefore well regarded by many of his charges who would otherwise have been severely handicapped in finding work. A primary function performed with this arrangement, as the MacDonalds point out, was that the labor agent, in making all arrangements with the employer and frequently supervising the men, "isolated new arrivals from American society," and "kept his *paesani* together."[34]

Earlier, the labor protests of the thirties were shown to have a dual character; i.e., men aspired to independent producer status at the same time as they attempted to improve their condition as employees by organizing and striking. Similarly, many members of the Knights, despite opposition by the leadership, engaged in a wave of strikes, often spontaneous attempts to ameliorate local grievances, during the eighties. Although such strikes appeared to indicate, as Grob notes, that those involved were "implicitly acknowledging the permanency of their wage status," he also asserts that "workers persisted in retaining a middle class viewpoint."[35]

The basis of an (old) "middle class viewpoint" necessarily rested on the skills required for small enterprise and on the persistence of the viability of such kinds of productive units. But individualism of this sort was precisely what gave rise to competitive innovations in order to "capture the market." Entrepreneurship, as defined earlier, is a highly likely outcome of such individualism. In moving into a skill-diluted labor market, the inexperienced immigrant competed, for a brief time, with those whose skills were being undermined by new technology.

It was unlikely, as Erickson asserts, for an employer to be able to introduce new equipment rapidly enough to break a strike by doing away with the need for the strategic skills of the strikers.[36] In an expanded product market, however, new firms could emerge with more efficient technology calling for expanded increments of lower skill-rated employees. This, on the one hand, would force a

Immigration and the Decline of Renovation

lowering of direct costs of production on the older firms if they were to compete effectively and, on the other hand, make for their ultimate adoption of the new production techniques. Although immigration cannot be credited with the modernization of industrial production, given the alternatives of more efficient methods, as Habakuk has indicated, a supply of such labor as immigrants afforded provided the means with which to give effect to such methods.

In this manner the craftsman's position was undermined as violence was done to his skill-based income standards and as the altered nature of production wiped out his chances to approach goals inhering in the old order. Immigration provided the employer with the required unskilled labor to man his new equipment. This process of immigrant succession to new productive roles in America was not begun with "new" immigrants, but, as indicated, it had been in operation for some time. Thus, as Handlin notes of one Boston industry, after the arrival of the Irish in large numbers:

No matter what degree of standardization the technical process of manufacturing reached, the absence of a cheap labor supply precluded conversion to factory methods. Machines alone could not create a factory system in Boston when only 473 tailors employed in 1845 were available to man them . . . Erstwhile peasants were unskilled, of course, and knew nothing of tailoring. But the simpler parts of the trade were not difficult to learn and it was profitable to press the raw immigrant into service at wages which no true tailor would consider.[37]

Thus, employers simply refused to arbitrate strike differences with journeymen tailors in 1849, "for an abundance of other labor sources were available to them."[38]

Once modernization was under way, the demand for unskilled and semiskilled workers increased and gave rise to further innovations as well as the spread of existing ones. Thus, Brinley Thomas notes a close relation between invention (as measured by patents granted) and immigration. "It seems that the outstanding bursts of invention took place at the same time as the big upswings in immigration."[39] Immigration provided a pool of labor from which manufacturers could draw in bringing into play more efficient production alternatives. In the eighties there occurred an upswing in immigration followed by a downswing in the nineties and another final upswing after the turn of the century:

Now it happens that the eighties were a period of upswing in investment, for example in railroad construction, building and bituminous coal, as well as immigration, whereas the nineties saw a downswing in these indices.

The upswing in the investment cycle in the early years of the century coincided with the fulfillment of technical innovations, for example in electricity and chemistry; thanks to immigration of cheap labour the United States was able to take full advantage of those innovations by "widening" her capital structure with enormous benefit to her physical productivity and economic power.[40]

The important issue here is that these technological innovations undermined previous practices and individuals who had been socialized to them were the most likely to protest. Again, their demands were entirely legitimate, given the institutionalized expectations that had heretofore been inculcated in societal members. The implications of such changes, when they are rapid, are quite profound, as Moore's remarks affirm:

> The demand for those skills particularly relevant to industrial production has implications both for the worker's sense of security and for his hope of advancement. The problem of security arises especially with the loss of skills involved in the shifting of handicraft workers into the factory. In general, little effort has been made in recruitment and initial placement to utilize those skills already developed in the preindustrial economy. Although there is virtually no evidence to support the idea, it may be guessed that this circumstance has led to considerable frustration and loss of confidence on the part of the worker whose skills are not recognized.[41]

In the eighties, then, immigration coincided with the spread of modern productive techniques and the phenomenal rise and subsequent decline of a labor organization which, at the time, was the largest ever achieved in the United States.

The Knights of Labor, as an organization in which the solidarity of *all* labor was emphasized, approached, for a time, the Marxian conception of social class, i.e., a concrete structure oriented to the common ends of its membership which constituted a group occupying a particular position in the structure of production. Indeed, the ideology of the Knights, although not Marxist, adhered to a Marxist notion that modern industrialism would obliterate craft skills and concentrate the means of production in fewer hands (the "monopolists"). The members of the Knights "could be simultaneously hostile and favorable toward capitalism, depending on whether it was defined in post- or pre-industrial terms."[42] And it was, of course, toward "post-industrial" capitalism that they were hostile.

The Order's Constitution, as previously noted, made explicit reference to legislative goals and, if the national leaders did not favor aligning the organization with a third party or one of the two major parties, local units did become so aligned. There were independent tickets in some twenty-six states that were backed by various assemblies in 1886, and an attempt was in the offing to solidify scattered successes into a permanent party structure.[43] Thus, a relative deterioration of the worker's position led to a strong protest movement that gained enormous momentum and evidenced all the earmarks of a nascent "politicization" of the American labor movement.

Again, this critical period in American history coincided with the introduction to the labor force of thousands of immigrants. Erickson asserts that, beyond leadership ineptness, ill-defined aims, and hysteria produced by the Haymarket affair, a "constant undermining of Knights' locals through strikebreaking with immigrant labor furnished by the labor exchanges has probably not been sufficiently recognized as an important factor in the defeat of the 'one big union' which for a short time seemed likely to organize the bulk of the American labor force."[44] In the bituminous coal mines of Pennsylvania and Ohio, "the importation of migrant strikebreakers became a feature of nearly every important strike, official or unofficial, by members of the Knights of Labor."[45] In other areas where new machine methods were even more extensively utilized, an even greater demand for unskilled labor developed. In iron and steelmaking and in textiles, skilled operations were obliterated by the introduction of new machinery and the employer's constant use of immigrants to subvert strikes. In Erickson's words, they "taught trade-unionists to fight not the machine but the immigrant in their attempts to cling to privileged positions in the labor force."[46] Perlman notes, further, that worker animosity was directed more toward the newcomer than toward the employer.[47] Thus a kind of "diverted aggression" occurred among resident workers who associated immigrants with changes that would have rendered their skills obsolescent even without foreign-born entry. "But for the constant strikebreaking, the process might have gone on without arousing prejudices against new immigrants."[48] Instead, "the methods adopted by many employers . . . for making transitions to new machinery contributed to fear and insecurity with respect to the immigrant, inflaming prejudices to the point that craft workers were prepared to believe almost anything about new immigrants, even that they were contract laborers."[49]

This assessment of the native-born workingmen contributed to a rise of nativism among them which further weakened the potential for working-class solidarity and diverted attention from more fundamental explanations of the skilled worker's plight. Nevertheless, these fears did not, at this point in time, blossom forth into a full-blown antiforeign movement. Higham notes that labor leaders did not seek to restrict foreign-born entry as a whole. They were primarily concerned with foreign contract labor, and the enactment of the law restricting it in 1885 served to abate their activities regarding immigrant workmen.[50]

The insulation of the immigrant from the society he was entering, an isolation partly a function of the *padrone* system of labor recruitment, frequently kept the fresh arrival from even knowing that a strike was in progress,[51] and employers often utilized elaborate means in order to prevent contact between the newly arrived and those who were striking.[52] But of more fundamental importance is the fact that immigrant strikebreaking was symptomatic of the issue here considered. Part of the sociological relevance of the strikebreaker is that he is, almost universally, an "outsider" unfamiliar with and/or uncommitted to the aims of the strikers. As suggested in the foregoing comments, the grievances associated with many of the strikers, where immigrants were implicated, were rooted in changes brought about by the onset of modern industry. These *changes* were not, and could not have been, meaningful to the immigrant. He was not prepared to protest altered circumstances that simply were not part of his frame of reference. Though the immigrant often acquiesced to direct appeals from strikers,[53] the significant issue here is that, barring such appeals, the conditions of employment were quite acceptable to him.

Though the direct impact (via strikebreaking) of immigration on the Knights was severe, their presence muted labor mobilization in more profound ways. Recruitment of immigrants into the industrial labor force was not solely, or even largely, accomplished with their entrance into strikebound activities. Immigration provided substantial increments of labor to meet increased demand in new or expanded manufacturing and mining enterprises and permitted the employers to get these establishments under way relatively smoothly and without having to contend with disruptive worker expectations. Again, the uncommitted immigrant saw in his employment the wherewithal to approach his ends in another system. His attachments to American industry and, indeed, his actions within American society generally, were predicated upon the opportunity to earn wages from which a surplus could be extracted for use elsewhere. Thus, even after having worked for a time, immigrants were unlikely to form unions or to strike. Insofar as they viewed their position as temporary, and the originally stipulated conditions of employment continued to prevail, immigrants sought not to interrupt their work except under extreme circumstances.

Uncommitted to a permanent life in the mills . . . the immigrant did not find the arguments for joining a union persuasive. He knew that unions spelled dismissal or at least a prolonged strike . . . What was a dubious small increase compared to several months of idleness, when each day out of the mill added two days to his exile? There was no interest in trade unionism among recent immigrants in steel towns.[54]

The alternative of keeping current consumption at a minimum in order to accumulate as much saving as possible was far preferable to the recent arrival who initially intended to return home. In labor camps, Italians, Slavs, and Hungarians could save a substantial portion of their quite meager earnings.[55] Different arrangements in other work contexts were used to keep living costs low. The "boarding-boss" system, in which a number of immigrant workmen would board and lodge together in a building operated by a fellow immigrant whose wife had accompanied him to America, was fairly prevalent among recent arrivals. By pooling their resources in such an arrangement, the Immigration Commission indicates that:

. . . the entire outlay for necessary living expenses of each adult member ranges from $9 to $15 each month. The additional expenditures of the recent immigrant wage-earners have been small. Every effort has been made to save as much as possible. The life interest and activity of the average wage-earner from southern and eastern Europe has seemed to revolve principally about three points: (1) To earn the largest possible amount of immediate earnings under existing conditions of work; (2) to live upon the basis of minimum cheapness; and (3) to save as much as possible. The ordinary comforts of life as insisted upon by the average American have been subordinated to the desire to reduce the cost of living to its lowest level.[56]

Further indications that immigrants were able to wring surpluses from their meager earnings come in the form of money transfers overseas. It was estimated that some $275 million was sent abroad by means of postal money orders, so-called "immigrant banks," and other avenues during 1907.[57] The total value of postal money orders sent to European countries during the period 1900 to 1909 was $419 million and, according to postal authorities, much of this money came from the earnings of immigrant workers.[58] Although the average amount of each money order was small, it has also been noted that these represented "but a small proportion of the total amount transferred and carried over in person."[59]

The recent immigrant was, ironically, upwardly mobile, but not with respect to American society. He was able to "defer gratifications" in America in order to attain them in his home country. To do so it was not only necessary that he find work almost at once after landing, but that he *remain* at work keeping interruptions to a minimum. Without a set of institutional expectations that were applicable in the new setting, the immigrant was likely to be an uncommonly hard worker. Commons recognized this important feature of immigrant behavior — though it did not receive prominent attention in his conception of the American labor movement:

Not only does immigration bring to America the strongest, healthiest, and most energetic and adventuresome of the work-people of Europe and Asia, but those who come work much harder than they did at home. Migration tears a man away from the traditions, the routine, the social props on which he has learned to rely, and throws him among strangers upon his own resources. He must swim or drown.[60]

Commons goes on to indicate that such workers, in actually making progress in approaching their goals, were moved to greater activity in order to achieve them. He assured his readers that, in watching the recent immigrant at work,

... you shall see such feverish production of wealth as an American-born citizen would scarcely endure. Partly fear, partly hope, make the fresh immigrant the hardest, if not the most intelligent, worker in our industries.[61]

The immigrant from a rural background was, in fact, less likely to exhibit the characteristics of noncommitment, such as absenteeism, that his rural American counterpart did. Both, no doubt, found the discipline of modern industry irksome, but temporary visits home were obviously not equally possible for both groups. Lantz indicates that native workers in a new mining operation frequently absented themselves from work owing to their general indifference to steady employment and production schedules and to the fact that, in mining, they could earn in two days the equivalent of two weeks' income on the farm.[62] This author notes that the immigrant, on the other hand, who also entered such employment because of a "narrowly economic incentive," was, paradoxically, especially hardworking and frugal due to "the feeling that [he] might shortly leave."[63] Native workers were thus antagonistic to the pace set by immigrants and complained of the latter's zealous work habits and willingness to take what they felt to be unnecessary risks.

Hard work and frugality on the part of the immigrant contrasted sharply with native attitudes against the disciplines imposed by modern industrialism.[64] Ironically, the immigrant, who initially defined his position as neither committed to industrial labor nor to American society, was a more stable employee whose discipline could be relied upon. Since it was imperative to remain at work, he "tried to adjust by following rigidly the orders of management."[65] Warner and Low similarly note of Yankee City factory employees that job insecurity of the recently arrived immigrants "leads them to be more compliant, less self-assertive, than persons who are firmly rooted in Yankee City Society."[66]

This greater "zone of acceptance" with respect to managerial authority, then, was a function of the migrant's lack of specifically American normative standards with regard to work which rendered him often a more desirable job candidate than the native American.[67] Brody notes, with respect to steelmaking, that:

The stability in the unskilled ranks thus rested on mobility. The newcomers either moved up into the skilled force, or they moved out at the first depression or with a satisfactory accumulation. Despite the harsh terms of work therefore, steel companies enjoyed peaceful relations with their common laborers.[68]

It was not that steel manufacturers undervalued the immigrants. Although claiming natives to be superior workmen, employers understood very well their good fortune. They dealt with the immigrant steelworkers as they did because nothing else was necessary. Developing without any effort on their part, the unskilled labor patterns of mobility fitted perfectly into the scheme of economical steel manufacture. The steelmakers were content.[69]

The Knights of Labor represented a short-lived mobilization of American workers protesting the revolutionary changes taking place in United States society. The immigrant, entering the domestic labor market, muted the strains of discontinuity. Lacking inhibiting American traditions, immigrants readily manned the new mechanized productive facilities. The immigrant did not protest innovations but, rather, abetted their smooth institutionalization. Commons recognized this when he testified that " . . . in America, in the past 20 years, with its mixed races there has been neither organization nor tradition, or, rather obstacles imposed by tradition and organization have been easily broken down." The immigrant, Commons goes on to note, has not opposed mechanized production, but has, in fact, ". . . removed all obstacles to its free and rapid introduction, and so has stimulated invention and business organization . . ."[70] Commons goes on to suggest that objections of experienced workers to the introduction of machinery were doomed as competing establishments would ultimately force such changes on others in the industry if they were to survive. In the end, these workers would have to accept change or lose their jobs.

As noted above, immigration was inversely related to internal migration. Immigrants, by moving into industrial employment in the United States, provided a substantial increment of unusually stable workers when compared to their rural American counterparts, though the former were equally uncommitted to industrial labor initially. In fact, the low-status immigrant worker, due to his circumstances, strikingly exhibited the virtues of hard work, frugality, and calculation within the American industrial setting. His coming checked a growing

Immigration and the Decline of Renovation

mobilization of the American work force embodied in the Knights of Labor which declined precipitously in the late eighties. As Commons notes:

> After 1887 the Knights of Labor lost their hold upon the large cities with their wage-conscious and largely foreign population, and became an organization predominantly of country people, of mechanics, small merchants and farmers, an element more or less purely American and decidedly middle-class in its philosophy. This change serves more than anything else to account for the subsequent close affiliation between the Order and the "Farmers" Alliance, as well as for the wholehearted support which it gave the people's party.[71]

This is a telling remark. Indeed, the association of "wage consciousness" and the "foreign population" suggests that a "mature trade unionism" was not solely a result of peculiarly American traditions.

This chapter has constituted an attempt at analyzing the immigrant impact on labor mobilization in the United States. The immediately foregoing comments anticipate what will be taken up in the next chapter, namely, the consequences of immigration for American business unionism. We turn directly to this problem following some further remarks that are now in order.

The analysis in this and the preceding chapter has taken the notion of structural discontinuity associated with modernization as the precipitating factor in labor mobilization. In asking why this should be the case, we make the important distinction between social structure, or patterns of action, and those who operate in terms of these patterns. We note that individuals *socialized to a preexisting set of structural arrangements* are likely to perceive altered circumstances as deviating from their *legitimate* (institutional) expectations and to protest such divergences. This is held to be the explanatory key to empirical generalizations which point to more extreme labor radicalism occurring during the *initial* stages of modern industrialism.

Mobilization of the work force into a radical labor movement depends, therefore, on that generation of workers who *experience the discontinuity* between the patterns of action characterizing new modes of production and those patterns that characterized the relatively nonmodernized "state of the system."

The clue to mobilization, then, lies precisely in *alterations* in previously institutionalized patterns of action to which the vast body of societal members have been socialized and to which they demand adherence. The Knights of Labor (and to a lesser extent, its reform predecessors) grew out of this divergence between past ideals and present actualities. Immigrants, however, having moved into work roles in American society, and without having been basically socialized as to its preexisting structure, were not likely to protest changes. They had no prior legitimate expectations to call upon. To be sure, they were socialized to traditional European patterns of action, but their move was designed to preserve these patterns *in Europe*, that is, in entirely different systems of action. Thus there could be no legitimate protest on their part concerning the breakdown of specifically American traditions.

Though immigrants often reacted angrily to severe abuses, it was not modernization per se that produced these grievances. However uncommitted immigrants were to industrial labor, it provided them with just those conditions that they required to approach their own ends elsewhere. As uncommitted workers, they could enter the American labor force on an explicitly nonpermanent, if somewhat long-term basis, feeling assured that they could ultimately return to the fold of traditional patterns in their home society — though, in the end, the majority remained. As Higham puts it:

The immigrant derived not only from a more or less alien culture but also from mean, impoverished circumstances. Entering the American economy on its lowest rungs, he commonly began by accepting wages and enduring conditions which Americanized employees scorned. In time the immigrants learned to demand more, and in the long run their manpower actually created more opportunities than it absorbed in the dynamic American economy of the nineteenth century.[72]

The immigrant who initially intended to return was willing to endure hardships because his initial assessment was relative to old world patterns and, in terms of those patterns, these hardships produced a net gain.

Not so with genuine members of American society who perceived a net loss for themselves in the changing social order; and a loss that was permanent. Their antagonism to the immigrant was not only due to wage competition but also to his willing acceptance of the changes that undermined previous practices. The reform labor movement first appeared during the pre-Civil War period and, as pointed out, the Knights of Labor was its dramatic ideological descendant. The order capped previous efforts to deal with the effects of modern industrialism on American traditions.

The increasing scale of productive operations, however, called forth new occupational roles which, ultimately, American and long-resident foreign-born workers could enter, while the less-skilled occupational ranks increasingly became the province of the recently arrived immigrant. There has already been occasion to note that the immigrant was derived from a society not isomorphic with the one he was entering. Spengler spells out the occupational consequences of this fact:

... when a country of provenience is economically and technologically less advanced than a country of destination, the occupational structure of migrants tends to be inferior to that obtaining in the immigrant-receiving country ... when the cultural background of an emigrant-sending country differs significantly from that of a country of destination, this difference tends to be reflected in the immigrants, giving rise to linguistic, personality, intellectual, and other handicaps, some transient and some not entirely reversible, which at least initially exclude immigrants from the upper reaches of the occupational pyramid.[73]

Paradoxically, the immigrants were to become a "noncompeting group" as far as the more desirable occupational roles were concerned. The dislocations initially experienced by Americans were eventually resolved as they (and more probably their children) moved into the more advantageous occupational roles. "Initially," Spengler writes, "the upward mobility of the native population will increase in much greater degree than the aggregate mobility of the immigrant population."[74] The Immigration Commission duly reported on these changes. Its discussion of "racial displacements" appears to be rather one of replacement resulting from the greater ability of the native American to compete for the more desirable jobs.

In the first place, a larger proportion of native Americans and older immigrant employees from Great Britain and northern Europe have left certain industries, such as bituminous and anthracite coal mining and iron and steel manufacturing. In the second place, a part of the earlier employees, as already pointed out, who remained in the industries in which they were employed before the advent of the southern and eastern European have been able, because of the demand growing out of the general industrial expansion, to attain to the more skilled and responsible technical and executive positions which required employees of training and experience. In the larger number of cases, where the older employees remained in a certain industry after the pressure of the competition of the recent immigrant had begun to be felt, they relinquished their former occupations and segregated themselves in certain occupations. This tendency is best illustrated by the distribution of employees according to race in the bituminous coal mines. In this industry all the so-called "company" occupations, which are paid on the basis of a daily, weekly, or monthly rate, are occupied by native Americans or older immigrants and their children, while the southern and eastern Europeans are confined to pick mining and to the unskilled and common labor. The same situation exists in iron and steel and glass manufacturing, the textile manufacturing industries, and in all divisions of manufacturing enterprise. It is largely the reproach which has become attached to the fact of working in the same occupations as the southern and eastern Europeans that in some cases, as in the bituminous coal mining industry, has led to the segregation of the older class of employees in occupations which, from the standpoint of compensation, are less desirable than those occupied by recent immigrants. In most industries the native American and older immigrant workmen who have remained in the same occupations as those in which the recent immigrants are predominant are made up of the thriftless, unprogressive elements of the original operating forces. The third striking feature resulting from the competition of southern and eastern European is seen in the fact that in the case of most industries, such as iron and steel, textile and glass manufacturing and the different forms of mining, the children of native Americans and older immigrants from Great Britain and northern Europe are not entering the industries in which their fathers have been employed.[75]

Thus, the native and "older" immigrant who remained within the industries attracting new arrivals moved into the expanding supervisory posts. Natives who entered other fields were able to move into more remunerative areas of activity.[76] The employment data presented in Chapter 3 document the greater occupational advantages accruing to native Americans when compared to the foreign-born workers. "Older" immigrants, generally speaking, were also at a competitive advantage relative to the new arrivals.[77] Able to rise in the occupational hierarchy within the confines of large-scale productive organizations, the American and long-resident foreign groups would approach success goals in terms of modern patterns that, at the same time, provided a broad base of lower skill-rated occupations through which fresh recruits could approach their own goals elsewhere. As Thomas sums up the process:

The long-run consequences in America were to be different from the short-run. The native born and the second generation Americans, as they acceded to the managerial, professional, skilled and clerical posts, need a growing mass of common labour to form the base of the social-economic pyramid. Far from being a threat to the upper grades, the "new" immigrants actually bestowed prosperity on them.[78]

The short-run consequences of modernization are quite profound for those who experience them. The argument here has been that these consequences were altered as a result of immigrant industrial recruitment during basic changes in the American social structure. The alteration of these consequences involved a muting of the inception of a radical American labor movement. The demand for various grades of labor, on the one hand, eventually led to increased opportunities for upward mobility for those already here, and provided the impetus for those without industrial experience to enter at the lower rungs where they were, nevertheless, relatively gratified given their own frame of reference. This process might best be described as one of ethnic *replacement* rather than displacement in the American industrial structure.[79]

The polarization, then, occurring during the onset of rapid modernization, gave rise to violent protest on the part of those whose legitimate expectations, based on the previous state of affairs, were no longer being realized. This initial response was thwarted as the less-advantaged positions were occupied by those who assessed their gains not in terms of a previous state of affairs within American society but on an existing state of affairs in another society. Those, then, who occupied positions of greatest disadvantage during this initial polarization, willingly operated in terms of the ongoing system. They were "in the society but not of it," but this had far different consequences than had they always been in the society. In the following chapter we examine the continuing functions of this condition.

NOTES

1. Oscar Handlin, *Boston's Immigrants: A Study of Acculturation* (rev. ed.; Cambridge: Harvard University Press, 1959), pp. 35-36.

2. *Ibid.*, pp. 37-53.

3. Norman Ware, *The Industrial Worker: 1840-1860* (Chicago: Quadrangle Books, Inc., 1964), pp. 106-107.

4. Caroline F. Ware, *The Early New England Cotton Manufacture: A Study in Industrial Beginnings* (Boston: Houghton Mifflin Co., 1931), p. 8.

5. *Ibid.*, p. 234.
6. *Ibid.*, p. 232.
7. *Ibid.*, pp. 231-232. Also N. Ware, *The Industrial . . .* , pp. 149-150.
8. Donald B. Cole, *Immigrant City: Lawrence, Massachusetts, 1845-1921* (Chapel Hill: University of North Carolina Press, 1963), p. 45.
9. Victor S. Clark, *History of Manufactures in the United States* (New York: McGraw-Hill Book Co., 1929), Vol. I, p. 455.
10. Of those immigrants entering between 1905 and 1909, the majority had under $50.00 in their immediate possession. See U.S. Immigration Commission, *Report of the Immigration Commission*, Vol. IV, *Emigration Conditions in Europe* (Washington, D.C.: Government Printing Office, 1911), p. 36.
11. John S. MacDonald and Leatrice D. MacDonald, "Chain Migration, Ethnic Neighborhood Formation, and Social Networks," *Milbank Memorial Fund Quarterly*, Vol. 52 (January 1964), p. 85.
12. William I. Thomas and Florien Znaniecki, *The Polish Peasant in Europe and America* (2 vols.; New York: Dover Press, 1959), Vol. II, pp. 1493-1494.
13. *Ibid.*, p. 1496.
14. Theodore Saloutos, *They Remember America: The Story of the Repatriated Greek Americans* (Berkeley: University of California Press, 1956), p. 12.
15. David Brody, *Steelworkers in America* (Cambridge: Harvard University Press, 1960), p. 96.
16. *Ibid.*, p. 99.
17. Thomas and Znaniecki, *op. cit.*, p. 1496.
18. U.S. Immigration Commission, *Report of the Immigration Commission*, Vol. I, *Abstract* (Washington, D.C.: Government Printing Office, 1911), pp. 498-499.
19. Harry V. Jerome, *Migration and Business Cycles* (New York: National Bureau of Economic Research, 1926), p. 107.
20. *Ibid.*, pp. 113-120.
21. Brinley Thomas, "The Economic Aspect," *The Positive Contribution by Immigrants* (Paris: UNESCO, 1955), p. 171.
22. U.S. Immigration Commission, *Emigration . . .* , Tables 25 and 26, pp. 41-42.
23. Simon Kuznets and Ernest Rubin, *Immigration and the Foreign Born* (New York: National Bureau of Economic Research, 1954), pp. 28-30.
24. D. R. Taft and R. Robbins, *International Migrations* (New York: Ronald Press Co., 1955), p. 375.
25. Allen M. Jones, *American Immigration* (Chicago: University of Chicago Press, 1960), p. 187.
26. Charlotte Erickson, *American Industry and the European Immigrant: 1860-1885* (Cambridge: Harvard University Press, 1957), pp. 77-82.
27. *Ibid.*, p. 82.
28. *Ibid.*, pp. 86-87.
29. John Koren, "The Padrone System and Padrone Banks," *Bulletin of the Department of Labor*, Vol. 2 (March 1897), p. 117.
30. Herbert S. Nelli, "The Italian Padrone System in the United States," *Labor History*, Vol. 5 (Spring 1964), p. 153. See also Koren, *op. cit.*, p. 125.
31. Erickson, *op. cit.*, pp. 102-103. See also, Koren, *op. cit.*, pp. 113-116 and U.S. Industrial Commission, *Report of the Industrial Commission* (Washington, D.C.: Government Printing Office, 1901), Vol. 15, pp. 431-432.
32. Erickson, *op. cit.*, pp. 90-94.
33. See Koren, *op. cit.*, p. 118; U. S. Industrial Commission, *op. cit.*, pp. 432-435; Erickson, *op. cit.*, pp. 102-104. Erickson also makes clear (p. 105) that labor contracts, when they existed, "were usually drawn up in American cities rather than in Europe." Edwin Fenton, "Immigrants and Unions, A Case Study: Italians and American Labor: 1870-1920,"

(unpublished Ph.D. dissertation, Department of History, Harvard University, 1957), pp. 84-85.

34. MacDonald and MacDonald, *op. cit.*, p. 86.

35. Gerald N. Grob, *Workers and Utopia: A Study of Ideological Conflict in the American Labor Movement, 1865-1900* (Evanston: Northwestern University Press, 1961), p. 80.

36. Erickson, *op. cit.*, p. 171.

37. Handlin, *op. cit.*, p. 76.

38. *Ibid.*

39. Brinley Thomas, *Migration and Economic Growth: A Study of Great Britain and the Atlantic Economy* (Cambridge: Harvard University Press, 1954), p. 172.

40. *Ibid.*, p. 164.

41. Wilbert E. Moore, *Industrialization and Labor: Social Aspects of Economic Development* (Ithaca: Cornell University Press, 1951), p. 122.

42. Grob, *op. cit.*, p. 8.

43. John R. Commons and Assocs., *The History of Labour in the United States* (New York: The Macmillan Co., 1918-1935), Vol. II, pp. 450-470.

44. Erickson, *op. cit.*, p. 107.

45. *Ibid.*, p. 112.

46. *Ibid.*, p. 125.

47. Selig Perlman, *A Theory of the Labor Movement* (New York: Augustus M. Kelley, 1949), p. 168.

48. Erickson, *op. cit.*, p. 135.

49. *Ibid.*, p. 125.

50. John Higham, *Strangers in the Land: Patterns of American Nativism 1860-1925* (New York: Atheneum Publishers, 1963), pp. 48-50.

51. Herman Feldman, *Racial Factors in American Industry* (New York: Harper & Row, 1931), p. 143.

52. Erickson, *op. cit.*, pp. 113-114.

53. *Ibid.*, p. 114.

54. Brody, *op. cit.*, pp. 136-137.

55. Frank J. Sheridan, "Italian, Slavic, and Hungarian Unskilled Immigrant Laborers in the United States," *Bulletin of the Bureau of Labor*, Vol. 15 (September 1907), pp. 470-471.

56. U.S. Immigration Commission, *Abstract*, p. 499.

57. U.S. Immigration Commission, *Report of the Immigration Commission*, Vol. 37, *Immigrant Banks* (Washington, D.C.: Government Printing Office, 1911), p. 261.

58. *Ibid.*, p. 275.

59. Sheridan, *op. cit.*, p. 480.

60. John R. Commons, *Races and Immigrants in America* (New York: The Macmillan Co., 1907), p. 126.

61. *Ibid.*, p. 127.

62. Herman R. Lantz, *People of Coal Town* (New York: Columbia University Press, 1958), p. 37.

63. *Ibid.*, p. 67. For corroborating material drawn from a contemporary setting see John B. Knox, "Absenteeism and Turnover in an Argentine Factory" *American Sociological Review*, Vol. 26 (June 1961), pp. 424-428.

64. Lantz, *op. cit.*, pp. 49-51.

65. *Ibid.*, p. 52.

66. W. Lloyd Warner and J. O. Low, *The Social System of the Modern Factory* (New Haven: Yale University Press, 1947), p. 97.

67. Peter Roberts, *The New Immigration: A Study of the Industrial and Social Life of Southeastern Europeans in America* (New York: The Macmillan Co., 1912), p. 76.

68. Brody, *op. cit.*, p. 108.

69. *Ibid.*, p. 111.

70. U.S. Industrial Commission, *Report* . . . , Vol. 15, p. 314.
71. Commons, *et al., The History* . . . , Vol. II, p. 423.
72. Higham, *op. cit.*, p. 45.
73. J. J. Spengler, "Effects Produced in Receiving Countries by Pre-1939 Immigration," in Brinley Thomas (ed.), *The Economics of International Migration* (London: McMillan & Co., Ltd., 1958), pp. 29-30.
74. *Ibid.*, p. 31.
75. U.S. Immigration Commission, *Abstract*, p. 502.
76. *Ibid.*, pp. 502-503. See Isaac A. Hourwich, *Immigration and Labor: The Economic Aspects of European Immigration to the United States* (New York: G. P. Putnam's Sons, 1912), pp. 169-171.
77. Thomas, *Migration* . . . , pp. 142-152.
78. *Ibid.*, p. 154.
79. W. Lloyd Warner and Leo Srole, *The Social Systems of American Ethnic Groups* (New Haven: Yale University Press, 1945), p. 66.

6

The Immigrant and Business Unionism

The following pages continue the implementation of the argument as set forth in Chapter 1. Here we will be concerned particularly with the type of "adjustment" the immigrants made to American society and the implications this had for their participation in unions. It will be maintained that the migrating generation was primarily oriented to the economic aspect of the society it entered. Thus, its focus was on the contexts from which goods and services were derived, namely, the work setting, while the formation of ethnic systems of action precluded a widening of orientation to encompass American society as a whole.

We begin with a discussion of urbanization in the United States and note the pronounced urban character of immigrant residential patterns. This, of course, was related to the newcomers' overwhelming participation in industry. From this we proceed to examine the formation of ethnic subsystems within American cities and the (negative) consequences for genuine societal membership. Finally, we relate this continuing feature of expedient societal membership to the character of the American labor movement.

Urbanization and Modernization

Since modernization may be expected to involve the growth of a nonagricultural labor force, there is ample reason to posit urbanization as a concomitant of the process. In fact, a direct, and positive, relationship has been observed between industrialization and urbanization.[1]

As Kuznets points out, one could imagine an agricultural labor force being housed in large cities or an industrial labor force living in dwellings scattered throughout the countryside. In both cases, however, the concomitant costs of transport and other services, even in a relatively well-to-do society, would be prohibitively high.

It is because modern industry enjoys the enormous economies of the increasing size of the optimum unit, and because the cities provide such an effective way of exploiting the technological potentials of economies of scale, that industrialization and urbanization go together. In the less developed countries, it is the relative absence of modern industry and of economies of scale that limits urbanization.[2]

IMMIGRANT WORKERS

The history of urbanism in the United States typifies these remarks. "The growth of American cities shows the effects of the industrial revolution with its impetus to trade and shipping, as well as the division of labor that provides the basis of modern city growth."[3] The urban (persons in places of 2500 or more) proportion of the population increased almost without interruption from the first census in 1790 through 1930, "and by 1920 the census found that 51 percent of the total were living in urban places."[4] The figures in Table 6-1 reveal this trend.

TABLE 6-1
U.S. Urban Growth: 1790-1940

Year	Percent Urban
1790	5.1
1800	6.1
1810	7.3
1820	7.2
1830	8.8
1840	10.8
1850	15.3
1860	19.8
1870	25.7
1880	28.2
1890	35.1
1900	39.7
1910	45.7
1920	51.2
1930	56.2
1940	56.5

Source: Abridged from Conrad Taeuber and Irene Taeuber, *The Changing Population of the United States* (New York: John Wiley & Sons, Inc., 1958), Table 34, p. 118. Used with permission of the authors.

If urbanism is a corollary of industrialization, and if immigrants increasingly entered the industrial sector of the American economy, then their rather high concentration in cities occasions little surprise. In 1900, 66.3 percent of the foreign born resided in cities of 2,500 or more as compared with 36.1 of the native born.[5] The former accounted for 13.6 percent of the total population in the United States, while they made up 22.4 percent of those living in urban places.[6] Further:

By class of city, the percentage of foreign-born decreases regularly with the size of city. In cities of at least 100,000 population the percentage of foreign-born is 28.2; in cities of 25,000 to 100,000 it is 20.4; in cities of 8,000 to 25,000, 18.1; in cities of 4,000 to 8,000, 14.2; and in cities of 2,500 to 4,000, 13.3.[7]

It appears that the foreign-born segment of city residents represented a substantial proportion of the total from the 1860's onward.[8] Their gradual *decrease* as a proportion of the urban population was, ironically, at least partly due to:

> ... an increase in the proportion of sons and daughters of immigrants in the total population as a result of the accumulated effects of the birth rate imputable to successive groups of immigrants. It seems probable that the tendency of the immigrants to congregate in larger cities has thus led to an undue accentuation of the effect of these second generation foreigners in such cities.[9]

Viewed as a group, however, the foreign born settled increasingly in cities after mid-century. Seen in this manner, the urbanization of the foreign born not only paralleled, but considerably exceeded, the urbanization of the native population, as Table 6-2 indicates.

TABLE 6-2
Proportion Urban: White, Native White, and Foreign-Born White

Year	White	Native White	Foreign-Born White
1940	57.5%	55.1%	80.0%
1930	57.6	54.5	79.2
1920	53.4	49.6	75.5
1910	48.2	43.6	71.4
1900	42.4	38.1	66.0
1890	37.5	32.9	60.7
1870	28.0	23.1	53.4

Source: Donald J. Bogue, *The Population of the United States* (New York: The Free Press, 1959), Table 7-5, p. 127. © 1959 by The Free Press. Reprinted with permission of The Macmillan Company.

Thus, the foreign born were an overwhelmingly urban population by the turn of the century. They accounted, further, for a substantial proportion of the total population of American urban centers, particularly in the East. This made for a rather distinctive urban structure in comparison with the European urban experience.

Ethnic Systems and Societal Membership

The fact that immigrant settlement was not random and that it was highly sensitive to economic fluctuations indicates that some mediating process was at work in allocating foreign-born labor in the United States. The movement was not a mindless influx of individuals but rather a cumulative transfer made up of several streams coming from different areas in Europe to prespecified points within the United States.

The mediating process whereby this was accomplished has been referred to as chain migration[10] which involves aid and advice of previously arrived migrants to prospective colleagues in the home country. Thus, in its survey of European countries of emigration, the Immigration Commission provided the following account of "contributory or immediate causes" of emigration:

Chief of these causes is the advice and assistance of relatives or friends who have previously emigrated. Through the medium of letters from those already in the United States and the visits of former emigrants, the emigrating classes of Europe are kept constantly, if not always reliably, informed as to labor conditions here, and these agencies are by far the most potent promoters of the present movement of population.[11]

The Commission found ample evidence of this fact in every country of southern and eastern Europe. Of the two agencies mentioned, however, letters are by far the most important. In fact, it is entirely safe to assert that letters from persons who have emigrated to friends at home have been the immediate cause of by far the greater part of the remarkable movement from southern and eastern Europe to the United States during the past twenty-five years. There is hardly a village or community in southern Italy and Sicily but what has contributed a portion of its population to swell the tide of emigration to the United States, and the same is true of large areas of Austria, Hungary, Greece, Turkey, and the Balkans. There is a tendency on the part of emigrants from these countries to retain an interest in the homeland, and in consequence a great amount of correspondence passes back and forth. It was frequently stated to members of the Commission that letters from persons who had emigrated to America were passed from hand to hand until most of the emigrant's friends and neighbors were acquainted with the contents. In periods of industrial activity, as a rule, the letters so circulated contain optimistic references to wages and opportunities for employment in the United States, and when comparison in this regard is made with conditions at home it is inevitable that whole communities should be inoculated with a desire to emigrate. The reverse is true during seasons of industrial depression in the United States. At such times intending emigrants are quickly informed by their friends in the United States relative to conditions of employment and a great falling off in the tide of emigration is the immediate result.[12]

During a two-year interval (1908-1909), no less than 94.7 percent of the total number of European immigrants admitted to the United States expected to join friends or relatives who had preceded them.[13] Evidence further indicates that many of these later arrivals had been advised and given financial assistance by those who had come earlier.[14] Thus, the Immigration Commission could state that:

Immigration to the United States was not an indefinite movement westward on the part of the people studied. They came to a particular street in a particular city because relatives or acquaintances who had come earlier were living in that locality; or lacking personal connections they came to the city of their residence because it was the place to which the migration from their sections of the home country had been directed. There was no choice of location, they came to the only spot in America with which they were familiar by report. They knew nothing of opportunities elsewhere in the United States, and in many cases they still know nothing of the possibilities outside of the section of the city where they live.[15]

That this ignorance, to the extent that it existed, was not the major job-finding handicap that it may have seemed is indicated by Sheridan who points out that the vast majority of Italian, Slavic, and Hungarian immigrants (73.2 percent in 1900, 86.55 percent in 1906) moved into seven states, namely Massachusetts, Connecticut, New Jersey, New York, Pennsylvania, Ohio, and Illinois.[16]

That the movement of these immigrants to these particular States was not unintelligent or an evidence of a desire for a shiftless drift toward slum concentration, but has proceeded on rational lines, is shown by the extraordinary industrial activity, progress, and wealth of these States over all others, and by the fact that in these States the demand for labor was greatest and the wage rates the highest in the United States.[17]

The initial basis for chain migration was laid by the *padrone* system, already discussed. By recruiting an ethnically homogeneous work force, the *padrone* created the basis for the inception of ethnic systems in America. But the *padrone* system itself was self-liquidating.

As the immigrants who had been dependent on them became better acquainted with American conditions and learned English, they were able to fend for themselves and also help later immigrants. Thus the *padroni* gradually lost their monopolistic powers as the cluster of roles with which they had been vested were taken over by the close relatives and friends of prospective immigrants.[18]

Thus, although economic "push-pull" factors help explain the migration movement as a whole, they cannot explain the often minute American neighborhood breakdowns by European sector and even village of birth.[19] Of further striking importance with regard to chain migration is that it

... not only led to the growth of "Little Italies," but also produced "chain occupations," particular niches in the American employment structure to which successive immigrants directed their fellows on the basis of their own experience. The evolution of ethnic succession in this country is a reflection of this "chain occupation" process.[20]

Thus, the often-noted dominance of certain ethnic groups in particular occupations finds its origin in the migration process.

The MacDonalds state that: "The rapid peopling of America's Northern cities by migration from rural Europe between 1848 and 1924 resulted in social segmentation that differed strikingly from that of Western and Eastern Europe."[21] They go on to note that this social segmentation prevented the development of a "common working-class structure as in Western Europe."[22] We have previously considered the argument that ethnic diversity precluded a more radical labor movement in America. It is the contention here, given the radicalism expressed by some groups, that ethnic diversity in itself only partly accounts for this outcome. Given both the spatial and social concentration of ethnic groups, their failure to exhibit the radicalism evidenced by their compatriots who had remained at home must be laid to additional factors beyond the multiplicity of such groupings. The contention here is that the immigrants' orientation to the new society was of crucial significance.

The inception of ethnic subsystems within the larger American context, it is argued here, provided conditions conducive to business unionism, by making for the persistence of expedient societal membership among the migrating generation. The sojourner qualities which many immigrants exhibited was taken up in the first and fifth chapters. Most immigrants, however, ultimately chose to remain in the United States. Warner and Srole contrast the "permanent" immigrant with the "sojourner," as we have termed him.

The Jews, Armenians, and Russians, in the act of migration, "burned their bridges behind them." Arriving with the design of establishing themselves in this country permanently, they were anxious from the first to strike roots to adapt themselves to the basic demands of the American society.

On the other hand, substantial portions of the Italian (those from South Italy and Sicily), Greek and Polish groups migrated with the original plan to settle only temporarily. Generally, their aspiration was not to rise in status in this country but to secure sufficient funds with which to increase their landholdings and therefore their economic status in the homeland. The number of those among these groups who have actually repatriated themselves according to this original plan is comparatively small, but the decision to remain was reached only after about a decade or more of residence here; until the decision was made, there was little impetus to meet any but the minimum terms of the society. Therefore, although many of the P generation [i.e., migrating generation] members of these groups were as quick as any in accepting better jobs, they were somewhat late in selecting better places of residence, and they were especially slow in adapting to the opportunities and demands of class assent.[23]

Although ethnic systems were not exclusively a sojourner manifestation, this quality appears to have had a major effect on immigrant behavior.

Hawley notes that a group may voluntarily segregate itself from other groups. "Cultural enclaves are formed by immigrants because of their inability to effect an immediate transition to the mode of life in new areas, and by religious sectarians who wish to foster a peculiar pattern of living."[24] He goes on to assert that:

Segregation, whether voluntary or involuntary is a restriction of opportunity; it hampers the flow of knowledge and experience and thus impedes diversification of interests and occupations. Migrants settling in a new and strange community are for the most part fitted for only the least specialized functions. And to the extent that they establish a segregated existence in the new community the alien individuals tend to retain their uniformity within the group. Thus the group is exposed to categorical definitions of one kind or another. But spatial segregation also imposes a certain limitation of opportunity which interferes with the differentiation of individuals composing the group.[25]

The Immigrant and Business Unionism

This pattern appears to have been general, as Francis notes in referring to the majority who came to America from Europe around the turn of the century:

While the host society was in each case the same, the migrants themselves spoke quite different languages, were affiliated with different religious bodies, and belonged to different national culture societies. Nevertheless, irrespective of whether they were Irish, Italians, Poles, Czechs, Ruthenians, or what not, their behavior shows striking similarities; they ultimately formed segregated ethnic communities which went through a typical life-cycle, characterized, with few local modifications, first by the boardinghouse complex, then by ecological segregation, endogamy, associations of mutual aid, national parishes; later by nation-wide organizations, a foreign-language press, typical tensions in the second generation; and, finally, by gradual secularization, acculturation, and partial assimilation with retention of a differential class position.[26]

Thus, Duncan and Lieberson, examining residential distribution in Chicago for 1930, state: "The situation revealed by these data, therefore, is one of a multiplicity of ethnic colonies scattered among the residential areas occupied by the native population rather than of a single 'ghetto' for all foreign groups."[27]

Within these ethnic communities, distinctive social structures, derivative of the European origins of the inhabitants, were formed. As Oscar Handlin puts it:

Virtually all immigrants made valiant efforts to reconstruct the old communities on the soil of the New World. True, the setting was different; but group after group expressed the longing to perpetuate the forms and to preserve the values which seemed to extend far back into the past.[28]

Handlin goes on to point out that the old community could not be replicated in the new setting. Therefore, each group brought into being numerous "functional equivalents" adapted to the American environment.

... the different immigrant groups have formed spontaneously in America, organizations that reproduce to some extent the home society or replace it with forms more adapted to the needs of the immigrant here. These organizations are not, in fact, pure heritages, but the products of the immigrants' efforts to adapt their heritages to American conditions. The immigrant, therefore, comes to a society of his own people, and this society, not native American society, is the matrix which gives him his first impression.[29]

Thus, the immigrant did not confront American society directly but rather, as Park and Miller noted, from a distinctive ethnic matrix within which much of his life space was contained in the company of fellow migrants.

The importance of these associations for sustaining immigrant solidarity is affirmed by the author of a recent study who notes that the presence of formal organizations in an ethnic community tends to minimize contacts with the outgroup.[30]

Though virtually all immigrant groups formed such associations, they had no precise counterpart in the societies of origin. It might be pointed out that the ethnic systems we are considering very much eased transitional strains inherent in the migration process for the individuals involved. While recognizing this important point, our concern here is to assess the consequences for the labor movement that these systems presented. It is suggested here that these systems served to insulate the immigrant from the society he was entering, thereby preserving his orientation to his home society or, conversely, making for a persisting expediency with respect to American society.

In this regard it is interesting to note that peasant migrants, whose orientation had been highly localistic, came to have their conceptions widened with respect to their *home society* as a consequence of migration. Thus Handlin writes that

Sometimes a common language united the newcomers from the start. At other times, as the press and schools developed, the numerous dialects that shaded off into each other in their spoken forms were formalized for the mass of immigrants into separate languages. And ultimately all would establish connections with movements back in Europe which would seem to root them in the Old World.

Ultimately, the immigrants would describe themselves as Portuguese, Greeks, Albanians, Syrians, Armenians, Poles, and Lithuanians. But these were not clearcut designations in existence from the start. Rather they described affiliations worked out in the course of settlement.[31]

According to Park and Miller, the Polish peasant seldom defined himself as a Pole.

The lord was a Pole; he was a peasant. We have records showing that members of other immigrant groups realize first in America that they are members of a nationality: "I had never realized I was an Albanian until my brother came from America in 1909. He belonged to an Albanian society over here."[32]

That this altered definition of the situation was "real in its consequences" is illustrated by Wittke's remarks:

In a very real sense, Czechoslovakia was "made in America." The Czechs and Slovaks in this country provided much of the agitation and a large portion of the funds at the time of the World War to disrupt the old Austro-Hungarian Empire and to create a Czechoslovak national state.[33]

In 1918, the first national convention of Poles in the United States assembled at Detroit. A Polish Central Relief Committee, with Paderewski as honorary president has carried on propaganda for an independent Poland since 1915, and Polish-Americans contributed hundreds of thousands of dollars to the cause of liberation.[34]

Thus, a continuing, even an expanded, orientation to the parent society was exhibited by many immigrant groups involved in ethnic subsystems in the United States.

As indicated earlier, spatial proximity appears to be a condition for the inception of such systems. Lieberson's recent work, utilizing census materials dealing with the foreign born, is quite relevant here. He states that, for his data in 1930:

The Immigrant and Business Unionism

...although we are not in a position to attribute causal priority to either variable — the proportion of immigrants knowing English and the segregation of ethnic groups from each other — there does appear to at least be some connection between the two. That is, groups highly segregated from other groups are less likely to have as a common language of discourse the dominant tongue of the host society, i.e., English.[35]

Although citizenship cannot be taken as evidence of membership in a society,[36] those undergoing naturalization frequently exhibit a different attitude toward the new country from those who remain alien[37] and the process may therefore be seen as at least a movement along a continuum toward societal membership when dealing with aggregates. Lieberson finds that:

The correlations indicate that naturalization goes up with lower segregation ... and with longer length of residence.... Once again the partial correlations between segregation and naturalization ... indicate that segregation is consistently related to citizenship status in the direction hypothesized, that is, in this case segregation and naturalization are inversely related.[38]

It is suggested, then, that spatial separation made for social separation from American society and a persisting orientation to the parent society. As Lieberson says elsewhere of his data, "the magnitude of an immigrant group's isolation from the native white population appears to play a role in influencing the extent to which members of the group are prone to give up ties with their country of birth."[39] Park and Miller's striking observation points up the outcome of social insularity from the point of view of American society:

The immigrants here tend to reproduce spontaneously the home community and to live in it. Letters show that they frequently reply to inquiries from home for a description of America, "I have not yet been able to see America." There are immigrants on the lower East Side of New York who have been here for twenty years and have never been up town.[40]

The consequences of these conditions will be considered below.

The Myth of Immigrant Radicalism

Radicalism in America in the decades surrounding the turn of the century was frequently attributed to the massive influx of immigrants. Those who promulgated this charge argued that radicalism was alien to the fabric of American society and was borne by immigrants whose prospects for assimilation were small and who therefore undermined American ideals.[41]

Something close to the opposite has been contended here. We argue that the early periods of industrialism are generative of radicalism by those workers most intimately associated with the changes occurring. Thus radicalism in America was more to be expected from native Americans and those immigrants coming from backgrounds bearing a closer structural identity to American society than those deriving from strikingly dissimilar social origins.

It was primarily those immigrants with industrial backgrounds who added to the radical cohorts in this country. Germans were conspicuous in this regard, as Fine points out:

> Until 1914 the Germans held a position of prestige and power in the international socialist movement second to none. The theoretical literature of socialism, from the day that the *Communist Manifesto* was written down to the outbreak of the World War, was mainly of German origin. The spirit of a disciplined, intelligent, and aggressive socialist army was typified by the organized working class movement of Germany. The leaders of this mighty force were deeply respected at home and abroad. It was men trained in such a movement who tried to build up a duplicate in the United States.[42]

Fine points out that "It was not until capitalism had matured at the end of the nineteenth century and a native socialist movement began to develop that the Germans slipped into the background."[43]

Some immigrants, however, continued to add to the radical movement during this time. Most notable among these later recruits were the eastern European Jews. Shannon notes:

> The rank and file of the New York movement were immigrants, largely Jewish needle trade workers from eastern Europe. To these hard-working people Socialism was more than just a political movement; it was a way of life. In some neighborhoods one grew up to be a Socialist, a reader of Abraham Cahan's *Jewish Daily Forward*, in Yiddish, or the *Call*, in English, and a member of one of the needle trade unions just as naturally as in some other parts of the country one grew up to be a Republican and a reader of the *Saturday Evening Post*.[44]

Yet Jewish immigrants possessed social characteristics quite in tune with an industrializing America.

> Unlike the other "new" immigrants, the newcomers of the great Jewish immigration almost from the start had the making of a variegated middle class. Over the years their range of talents and skills mounted steadily. Yet despite a remarkable rate of economic and social mobility the successful in great numbers continued to respect, if not always to identify themselves with, the world of Jewish labor.[45]

On the other hand, those immigrants who could least impose an industrial definition of the situation in their new surroundings were the least likely recruits to radicalism. These were mainly from rural backgrounds, unaccustomed to non-agricultural employment. And they constituted the bulk of the new arrivals.[46] Hansen remarks that:

> Probably more immigrant Socialists were lost to the cause in the United States than were won from the ranks of the newcomers. Those who did not join the Republican party as the protector of the industries that employed them, found a home in the more liberal atmosphere of the Democratic party. Neither group, of course, questioned the fundamentals of capitalism. So in this respect also the voters of immigrant stock threw their weight into the scales for conservative progress.[47]

The Immigrant and Business Unionism

The charge of radicalism that was leveled against the immigrant frequently masked, as Preston suggests, an underlying nativism. Accusations of rampant anarchism among immigrants failed to be confirmed even after the most intense efforts.

Circularizing every major immigration station and working with the Secret Service and local chiefs of police, the Immigration Bureau sought to uncover deportable resident radicals. The response was overwhelmingly negative. Twenty-three areas reported no cases at all, and some four districts discovered a handful of anarchists who had lived in the country longer than three years.[48]

The law under which such proceedings could be carried out, the Immigration Act of 1903, was promulgated, Preston points out, to penalize "an alien population that had never been radical."[49]

It has more than once been indicated here that the increments to the radical ranks provided by some immigrant groups and not others suggest that an explanation for the failure of a militant left-wing movement to develop in America lies beyond mere ethnic diversity. Most immigrants were simply not attracted to left-wing movements in the first place. This was so despite the fact that they occupied positions in the labor force from which such movements often draw adherents.

The evidence strongly contradicts the notion that a leftist orientation was more repugnant to native Americans than foreign born. In 1908 fully 71 percent of the membership of the American Socialist Party were native Americans. Another 19½ percent were "old" immigrants while but 9½ percent were foreign born from other areas.[50]

Of the foreign born members, many, if not most, were from lands with advanced labor and socialist movements. From 1909 to 1917 also, the Socialist Party was a party of natives and assimilated immigrants. The delegates to its conventions in 1901, 1904, 1908, 1910, 1912, and 1917 were not of the foreign quarters of the United States. In appearance, language, tradition and outlook they were Americans of at least several generations.[51]

And this was during and immediately after the highest tide of immigration in American history.

With the advent of language federations in 1910, the foreign membership in the Socialist Party began to increase. Nevertheless, in 1912, when a high-water mark of 118,045 members were in the party, under 16,000 were foreign-language federation members.[52]

The foreign-language federations were shortly to gain a remarkable prominence. "In 1919 the Socialist Party of the United States had about 110,000 members, over half of whom, however, belonged to non-English-speaking bodies, to the autonomous and practically independent language federations."[53] This phenomenal surge in foreign-born membership is even more impressive when it is noted that the language federations came to comprise the left wing of the party. Ultimately a split was precipitated and the emergence of the new Communist organizations drew predominantly on these federations.[54]

This phenomenon may be accounted for by recalling that immigrants broadened the scope of their national identity with their homelands after coming to the United States. The rapid rise of a Communist movement among foreign born in this country appears to have been an exemplification of this process in that it was closely related with Communist upheavals in Europe, most notably the Russian Revolution. "Between December, 1918 and April, 1919 the membership of the Russian federation [of the American Socialist Party] jumped from 2,373 to 7,824, the South Slavic, from 1,200 to 3,115."[55]

After the split from the Socialists, the composition of the new Communist Party was quite revealing. "One of the interesting points . . . is the fact that almost two-thirds of the members of the Workers' (Communist) Party were born in countries which were either part of the old Russian empire or which are inhabited by Slavs."[56] As Shannon points out in considering this evidence, "Immigrants from eastern Europe were naturally more sensitive to events in their home countries than older-stock Americans, and in the months just after the end of the war the various Slavic federations grew tremendously."[57] This vast increase in immigrant radicalism was not primarily oriented to, nor the outgrowth of, operations in American society. It indicated an orientation to the home society and was a response to events taking place outside of America.

But prior to World War I and the Russian Revolution, immigrant adherence to radical activities was, as noted, quite limited. It is of further interest to review the regional differences in Socialist Party militancy. The New Yorkers, dominated by Jewish immigrants, constituted a conservative wing of the party. "Their leadership was evolutionist, strongly opposed to class violence, prone to emphasize reform rather than Socialism in order to attract votes, and quite sensitive to the opinions of the AFL trade unionists."[58] Similarly, "the majority of the Pennsylvania Socialists were in the conservative wing of the party."[59] On the other hand, the party in Ohio, Indiana, and Michigan, "was considerably more radical than in either Pennsylvania or New York . . ."[60] The Chicago membership, residing in the city of the national headquarters of the Socialist Party, reflected the differences in party constituency and was not united in one wing or another. Shannon characterizes it as somewhat to the left of the eastern Socialists.[61] In Milwaukee, however, Socialists "were cautious evolutionary social democrats."[62] But, "West of the Mississippi River, in Missouri, Kansas, Arkansas, Texas and especially Oklahoma, was a kind of emotional and radical Socialism that caused Berger, Hillquit, and most moderate Eastern Social democrats to shudder."[63] And finally,

In the Rocky Mountains and the Pacific Northwest the Socialist movement was dominated by revolutionaries who regarded the Oklahoma movement as effeminately mild. Here was the stronghold of Bill Haywood and the IWW. Here was clearly the most radical section of the Socialist Party.[64]

It appears that the deeper into the heartland of America one went, the more radical the left-wing movement became. It was not in the East, with its large immigrant population, but in the West that the radical Industrial Workers of the World was conceived. This union was ultimately to become entangled in immigrant labor strife and publicly identified with the foreign born. We turn, then, to a closer consideration of immigrant labor activities during the era of the IWW.

Labor Unions

In this section we will look at several aspects of immigrant participation in labor unions, some of which, on their face, appear to raise questions about the argument concerning immigrant indifference to radical unionism. Thus, we will scrutinize the social contexts in which immigrants did, in fact, ally themselves with radical union organizations in a pair of well-known instances. We begin by examining notions relating business cycles and union membership and see what part immigrant labor played in this process. We then go on to a more detailed view of the qualities of immigrant participation in unions. Throughout this discussion we will continue to rely on a central contention of this work which states that the immigrant's adjustment to American society centered around limited focuses of commitment. His initial reasons for coming had to do with job opportunities and his major context of commitment was the workplace. Living within an ethnic subsystem, his commitment to other features of American society was attenuated. For this reason, we argue, permanent residence made him an excellent prospect for conservative, "job conscious" industrial unionism that eschewed revolution and political activity. As will be developed below, the instances of immigrant alliances with the radical Industrial Workers of the World in no way contradicts their "job conscious" orientation to union activity nor their pattern of relating to unions through the ethnic matrices discussed above.

Commons has argued that labor activity during prosperous times is directed toward trade unionism, while "politics" is the outgrowth of depression.[65] With regard to political agitation during depressions, it is of interest to recall the close association between immigration and business cycles. Since immigration tended to decline and emigration tended to rise during downswings in the business cycle, we have yet another reason to claim that migration tended to mute the "politicization" of the labor movement. A substantial number of the unemployed did not become engaged in political agitation during depressions. They simply left the country. Thus, a countercyclical process was in motion that served not only to mitigate the political repercussions of depressive economic conditions but to lessen the severity of those conditions by a complete withdrawal of large numbers of workers from the labor market.

But it is also asserted that trade unionism is positively related to upswings in the business cycle. Bernstein finds the relationship to be a weak one. He does not, however, reject the importance of business cycles in union growth but indicates that they must be considered in combination with other factors.[66] The same author asserts that an upswing in the business cycle having been preceded by depressive economic conditions creating social unrest carries greater predictive power. These combined influences, Bernstein argues, help explain the rapid surge of union growth between 1897 and 1904 (from under half a million to over two million). "The coupling of deep-seated social discontent with wartime prosperity provided a field of immense fertility for seedling unionism."[67]

If it has frequently been argued that immigration fostered political radicalism in this country, it has at least as often been argued that it retarded unionization. Though Bernstein does not rely on upswings in the business cycle exclusively for his explanation of union growth, they nevertheless assume some prominence in his argument. The present point is that if prosperous economic conditions were a major factor (even if only one among several) in fostering union growth, they were also a major factor in fostering immigration.

Immigration was at a low point in 1897 with some 230,832 arrivals. This rose to over 800,000 in 1903 and 1904 and exceeded 1 million in the years 1905, 1906, 1907, 1910, 1913, 1914.[68] Yet, although immigration was rising to unprecedented heights, trade union membership was at its highest levels in American history. In 1897 the total membership in American unions was 447,000, by 1914 the figure was 2.7 million, and it reached 3.6 million by 1923. Between 1901 and 1910 trade union membership nearly doubled, jumping from 1.1 million to 2.2 million.[69]

Though this great surge in union membership cannot be credited to immigration, it is important to at least point out that one of the most rapid periods of union growth was accompanied by a similarly rapid rise in immigration, both being, in part, a consequence of the same phenomenon, a favorable economic climate. The routine assumption of immigrant subversion of unionization must at least be questioned in the light of these data.

It would be erroneous to relate this new high in union membership to the previous one in the eighties, dominated by the Knights of Labor. The new upswing was overwhelmingly accounted for by AFL gains.

> In fact, in 1897, independents accounted for roughly 40 per cent of the total union membership, while in 1901 they constituted only 24 per cent. This latter proportion has obtained practically throughout this whole period, 1901-1923 . . .[70]

The AFL was the direct descendent of the Federation of Organized Trades and Labor Unions which split from the Knights over severely divergent fundamental policies. Whereas the Knights sought the solidarity of all labor (including the unskilled), the AFL operated on the principle of "trade autonomy," with each union within the federation organized to achieve what was thought best for its own members. Samuel Gompers, president and one of the founders of the AFL, enunciated this philosophy in 1914 by castigating the "one big union" approach as then practiced in the IWW.

> There is not anything that could be more disastrous to the interests of labor than the establishment, if it could be established, of a so-called one big union. There are differentiations in all human activities. Perhaps no better example

might be cited than the Army on the battlefield and in preparation for battles, and the organized labor movement on the industrial field . . . You can imagine what would occur if the infantrymen, the cavalrymen — the men and the horses were all thrown together. The worst thing which could occur to such an army would be to order a movement of any kind — to advance or to retreat. The only safety for them would be to stand still forever and anon. And so it is with the labor movement.

The labor movement is organized in a trade, in a calling, in an industry with its departments such as have already been established, the coalition of each with the other, hoping that the other is to do the best thing that can be done for the one specific purpose of best protecting the men and women of labor, the children of our time, to promote, to help their best interests now and for the future, neither treading upon the other . . .[71]

Further, the AFL strategy was not revolutionary. Its members sought to operate within the framework of modern capitalist economic institutions. According to Commons, there

. . . developed a recognition of partnership with the employers — not the partnership of the individual employee with his employer, as preached by the "social harmony" advocates — but the partnership of the wage-earning class, organized in a national trade or industrial union, with the employing class, organized in a national employers' association. This recognition of partnership took full cognizance of the existing antagonism between the two classes but prepared to bridge it by a trade agreement.[72]

Thus, whereas the Knights protested the undermining of previous institutions resulting from modern capitalism and its attendant "wages system," the AFL people were content to seek worker improvement within such a context. The famous "more, more, here and now" philosophy that eschewed politics is expressed by Gompers in his testimony before the Industrial Relations Commission:

It is the effort of the Socialist Party to divert the attention of the American working people from the immediate need and from the immediate struggle to something remote. If the working people of America can be made to believe that they can secure the relief that they need, the improvement which is justly theirs, the freedom which they ought to have, by casting a vote once every year, wherefore join in the unions engaged in the everyday struggle to improve material conditions now? It is the difference between the man who preaches from the pulpit that the working people are in the positions God ordained and that they will have a better time in the sweet by-and-by. And on the same hand the Socialists who paint a beautiful picture of a future, alluring the workmen from the immediate struggles to the hopes for the future. It is the idea of men being diverted from the immediate struggle and immediate needs for the natural, rational development of the human race; and securing day by day and week by week and month by month and year by year, a little to-day, a little to-morrow adding, adding, gaining, gaining, moving forward, every step in advance, and never taking one receding step except to plant the foot forward firmer than ever before.[73]

Thus, the AFL was a labor organization oriented not toward revolution but to operating within the framework of industrial capitalism, securing material gains for its constituents via collective agreements with employers. A radically altered social structure was not part of its goal system and, according to its leadership, such aims were a vain effort that sapped worker energies from securing immediate improvements within the system. The argument put forward here is that the immigrant worker was particularly receptive to such unionism rather than to revolutionary aims.

One reason why it may be argued that unions could expand unimpeded during a period of rapid immigration has to do with the previously mentioned principle of noncompeting groups. Many of the major gains during this period of rapid unionization were made among the more skilled craft segments of the labor force,[74] while recent immigrants were predominantly unskilled. Thus, the almost virulent anti-immigrant attitudes of skilled American and "older" immigrant trade unionists were toward a worker element whose threat to their organizations was minimal if not nonexistent. "Labor leaders castigated unskilled workers for competing with American labor by taking jobs which the craftsmen who formed the bulk of the A.F. of L. membership would have scorned."[75] Despite this, members of the AFL were often outspoken advocates of immigration restriction.[76]

The growing nativism among AFL members, as much as the presumed immigrant indifference to unions, may help to explain the failure of the unskilled to enter such organizations in greater numbers. Leiserson, while noting that recent immigrants, due to their initial helplessness, may have weakened labor organizations, also indicates that "older" immigrants and native recruits to industry initially created similar difficulties.[77] The same author goes on to point out the failure or neglect of member AFL unions in organizing recent immigrants while the national headquarters of that body "have not stepped in to do the work which the constituent unions have left undone or failed in attempting."[78] Similarly, Pelling asserts that it "became apparent in this period that the conservative craft unions were more of a hindrance than a help to the new immigrants in their struggle for self improvement,"[79] while Commons remarks that

> Though the Federation was not unmindful of the unskilled, still, during this period it brought into its fold principally the upper strata of semi-skilled labour. In 1905 it did not comprise to any extent, either the totally unskilled, or the partially skilled foreign-speaking workmen, with the exception of the miners.[80]

This exception of the miners is a major and instructive one. The United Mine Workers represented an outstanding example of industrial unionism within the framework of the AFL. It was a singularly successful organizing victory among a substantially unskilled and foreign-born group of workers. Indeed, the UMW constituted a sizable proportion of the overall growth of the AFL during the interval we are considering. In 1897, the union numbered under 10,000 members; by 1901 membership had jumped to 198,000; it was over 250,000 in 1904, and reached 339,000 in 1914.[81]

The Immigrant and Business Unionism

Although Hughes claims that the immigrant was not eager to join a union, he notes that:

The transplanted peasants seemed to want nothing from their jobs but the money. Their children often wanted a lot of other things — the good opinion of their companions, prestige, a white collar job, a higher standard of living.[82]

This "job consciousness" of the foreign born was quite consistent with the unionism practiced in the AFL. Balch notes that Slavic workmen (who comprised the major immigrant group in mining) "came here to get money; their hearts are set on saving money, either to send home or to use here, and their main object is to secure the best possible wages."[83] Balch also asserts that Slavs "have proved surprisingly available union material . . ."[84]

In comparing mine workers and steelworkers in the Pittsburgh area in the beginning of the twentieth century, Commons and Leiserson found that "The Nationalities of the two sets of men are similar, with a large proportion of unskilled and semi-skilled Slavs in each industry."[85] They note, however, that:

Taking everything into account — wages, hours, leisure, cost of living, conditions of work — it appears that common laborers employed by the steel companies in their mines were 50 to 90 per cent better off than the same grade of laborers employed at their mills and furnaces; that semi-skilled laborers employed at piece rates were 40 to 50 per cent better off in the mines; and that the highest paid laborers, the steel roller and the mine worker, were on about the same footing.[86]

Commons and Leiserson make it quite clear that the superior conditions in mining were largely the result of union activity. Since Slavic immigrants were employed in both mining and steelmaking, the failure of the latter to unionize the less skilled cannot be attributed to the character of the workers. Rather, these authors suggest, the multiplicity of mine operators made it feasible for each to accept union contract agreements, thereby insuring a degree of predictability in their operations while, on the other hand, "since the consolidation of the United States Steel Corporation, employers have been secure in fixing labor costs in other ways than by agreements with their employees."[87] Further, the not uncommon neglect of the unskilled by the craft-exclusive Amalgamated Association of Iron, Steel, and Tin Workers must be compared with the policies of the UMW which, in "taking into its membership the entire body of workers, has been a greater benefit to the mass of unskilled labor than the few who are highly skilled."[88]

Though immigrants have, as noted, often weakened unions, they have also often taken the lead in unionization while native workers have demurred.[89] The willingness to become engaged in union activities is at least partially contingent on commitment to industrial labor. Carrol Wright, in an early article that is practically a model for reference group theory, states that:

. . . the union begins by teaching the immigrant that his wages are not so good as another man's, doing practically the same kind of work, while it neglects to tell him he is not doing it so well, so intelligently, nor so much of it perhaps; but the union gets him to compare himself not with what he was in Lithuania, but with some German or Irish family, and then "sting him with the assertion that he has as much right to live that way as anybody." The union attempts to show the immigrant that he can live better only by getting more money, and that by joining the union he will get it.[90]

Thus, for the standard of reference of the immigrant to shift, he must contemplate continued industrial employment and not returning to "what he was in Lithuania." But industrial labor commitment perforce meant commitment to *American* industry and hence permanent residence.

As we have had occasion to indicate of immigrants generally, and as Balch notes of the Slavic immigrant in particular, "They came here for high pay, the highest obtainable; if they do not get what they want in one place, they will go to another, or, if it seems best, they will go home."[91] The sojourner, whose initial intention was to return, would find it economically disadvantageous to engage in union activities, including strikes, if his goals in this country were short-term. But the majority of immigrants remained despite their initial intentions. Thus, when the great mass of unskilled workers in the steel industry ultimately acted in the famous steel strike of 1919, it was primarily those immigrants who had their homes and families in this country who struck, while the ones who worked during the strike "were those who expected to return to the old country in the following spring or summer."[92]

The argument advanced here is that permanent residence did not necessarily indicate genuine societal membership, but rather that it gave rise to separate ethnic subsystems within American society. Thus, in the steel strike,

A second element among immigrants who did not strike was from races with few representatives in this country or with so few workers in the iron and steel industry that it was either financially or otherwise impossible to secure organizers who spoke their language. Such nationalities have very few papers in their own language and no previous knowledge of trade unionism.[93]

The mass effort, then, of a major strike (involving some 365,000 workers at its peak) was mediated through the separate "ethnic matrices" we have spoken of earlier. As one writer puts it:

It is obvious that immigrants who become members of large social structures like factories or territorial communities make their decisions and concert their actions within those structures, not by the direct focus of attention on the central authority but, rather, by identification with some individual or individuals with whom they have primary group relationships and who serve to transmit to them ideas from and concerning the larger structure.[94]

The steel strike failed and industrial unionism did not reappear in this field until the thirties. But, the steel companies' complaints of radicalism notwithstanding, this massive effort was primarily oriented toward collective bargaining on a business union basis in affiliation with the AFL.[95] As suggested, the narrow

The Immigrant and Business Unionism

focus of the immigrant on the work context within American society limited the arena of conflict and precluded efforts for "larger" changes in basic institutions governing the operations of that context. In Leiserson's words:

If all immigrants, representing as they do no less than one seventh of the population of the United States, were distributed evenly among the native population, the chances would be excellent that the common contacts of American life might in a reasonable time teach them to think and act in unison with Americans. Actually, however, this even distribution has not taken place. And when we find immigrants spending their lives in industrial occupations where they form more than a third and often half and two thirds of all the employees, and living in communities where a majority of the population is of foreign stock, then the problem of uniting native with foreign born takes on quite a different character.[96]

That this made for a rather limited focus with regard to American society is affirmed by the MacDonalds, who note the following of recent immigrant arrivals:

They had little desire to learn English and become acquainted with the American scene. Remaining in great ignorance of the larger economy and society around them, they were able to find work through better established, more knowledgable compatriots who functioned as middlemen between new arrivals and American employers.[97]

Once committed to industrial labor, however, the immigrant was quite hospitable to union activity and the sacrifices, as in a strike, that it entailed. But while immigrant aims lay within the scope of industrial capitalism, a rather strong radical movement appeared to be the province of native workers. Thus, Commons, writing in 1908, noted that "The bitterest class struggle now going on in America is that of the Western Federation of Miners, the most purely American of trade unions." Commons argued that "class solidarity" was undermined by immigration, thereby weakening the class struggle. Our argument is that immigration indeed muted radicalism, but not necessarily conflict, as indicated by the steel strike. Thus Commons' remark that "To prohibit or greatly restrict immigration would bring forth class conflict within a generation,"[98] was, to some extent, consistent with the argument presented here which claims that the arena of conflict would be wider among workers who were genuine members of American society and narrower among expedient members.

The militant Western Federation of Miners which had once been affiliated with the AFL broke with the latter and became engaged in some of the most violent strikes in American labor history. Brissenden makes a revealing contrast with the UMW in discussing the Western Federation of Miners:

During the twelve years of the Western Federation's existence before the birth of the I.W.W., it figured in the most dramatic series of strike disturbances in the history of the American labor movement. Swift on each other's heels came the terrors of Coeur d'Alene in 1893, Cripple Creek in 1894, Leadville in 1896-7, Salt Lake and the Coeur d'Alene again in 1899, Telluride in 1901, Idaho Springs in 1903, and Cripple Creek again in 1903-4. The Federation was — in its first decade particularly — as militantly radical as the coal miners' union was conservative. The strikes in which it engaged have been usually marked by much disorder and violence.[99]

The WFM came to form the initial nucleus of the radical Industrial Workers of the World (IWW or "Wobblies").

The primary importance of the Western Federation of Miners in these beginnings cannot be too much emphasized. In a quite real sense the I.W.W. was born out of the Western Federation. It was from this militant miners' union that most of the financial bone and sinew came for sitting [sic] in motion the machinery of the new union. The Federation constituted probably one third of the membership of the organization which had in its mining department (while it did have it!) by all odds the most vigorously militant of all American unions. The Federation's bitter fights with the mine operators, especially in Colorado, Montana, and Idaho, prepared the ground and spread the sentiment for the extension of revolutionary industrialism beyond the relatively narrow limits of the metalliferous mining industry.[100]

Whereas the AFL was the descendant of the Federation of Organized Trades and Labor Unions, the IWW was the descendent of the Knights of Labor.[101] The "one big union" approach was adamantly hostile to the notion of "trade autonomy," the advocates of the former referring to the AFL as the "American Separation of Labor."

In nearly all respects the I.W.W. was the exact antithesis of the A.F. of L., as indeed it was designed to be. Centralization contrasted with the national-union autonomy of the older body; industrial organization cut across the craft basis of the A.F. of L. unions; and the policy of low dues differed markedly from the high contribution systems which Gompers and his colleagues favored.[102]

From its inception, the IWW's goals were quite different from those of the AFL. In the former's first convention,

... it was quite evident that an ideal labor union was conceived to be something more than an institution for improving the immediate conditions of labor. Through it immediate interests must be advanced, of course, but its primary object must be to make an end of labor as a slave function and to establish in place of the wage or capitalist system an industrial commonwealth of co-operators. The convention was convinced that the craft union was not only comparatively helpless in the matter of advancing immediate interests but was absolutely useless as a fulcrum for removing the capitalist system.[103]

There were, however, several factions within the IWW which ranged from some moderate eastern socialists who saw the union as the economic counterpart of a "political socialist movement," to those "who deprecated or wholly rejected political action, and who saw the only hope of the working class in united class action in the economic field."[104]

With the WFM, the IWW in 1906 may have had a peak membership of as much as 100,000.[105] The splits in ideology, however, together with conflict

The Immigrant and Business Unionism

over finances resulted in important defections, including that of the WFM. "After 1908, what was left of the IWW turned its attention mainly, if not exclusively, to the industries in which unskilled labor predominates."[106] Brissenden notes that these defections were not necessarily an unmixed calamity. The IWW "continued to exist, and finally to do more than exist . . . " Indeed, after these defections the organization was directed to pursue an "emphatic impulse toward a more revolutionary policy."[107]

Perhaps the most outstanding spokesman for this policy was William Haywood, a former WFM member, who presented his views in testimony before the Industrial Relations Commission:

We say that this struggle will go on in spite of anything that this commission can do or anything that you may recommend to Congress; that the struggle between the working class and the capitalistic class is an inevitable battle; that it is a fight for what the capitalistic class has control of — the means of life, the tools and machinery of production. These, we contend, should be in the hands of and controlled by the working class alone, independent of anything that capitalists and their shareholders may say to the contrary.[108]

Ironically politics was as much anathema to Haywood as it was to Gompers.[109] Both men sought their ends through direct confrontation with employers. But whereas Gompers sought gradual day-by-day improvement within the capitalist system via these confrontations, Haywood saw the strike as a revolutionary weapon which, when accomplished on a national level, might overthrow capitalism.

Although the IWW was born in the West, its national notoriety was in large measure due to several spectacular Eastern strikes among a largely immigrant labor force. One of the earliest of these was the conflict at the Pressed Steel Car Company of McKees Rocks, Pennsylvania. A number of grievances centering around a new system of wage payments resulted in a walkout in July, 1909.[110] The IWW entered the dispute fully one month after the walkout and after some considerable violence had occurred. Due to substantial public pressure resulting from exposure of worker conditions, management yielded entirely and the men returned to work.

In this struggle the role of the leaders of the Industrial Workers of the World was as yet a subordinate one. They offered advice and direction where no other established organization cared to step in.[111]

It was in the textile industry disputes that the IWW rose to national prominence. The most spectacular of these disputes was the Lawrence, Massachusetts, strike. Following a legislative reduction in maximum working hours, from fifty-six to fifty-four, for women and for minors under eighteen, the mills cut pay proportionately.

Since the owners had previously kept wages at the same weekly level when reducing hours and since the loss of twenty or thirty cents a week meant a great deal to the workers, they were worried and angry. The absence of adequate advance notice made them even more ugly.[112]

The strike began in mid-January, 1912. This was primarily a strike of "new" immigrants, particularly Italians, while native Americans and earlier immigrants were opposed to it.[113] Once again the "ethnic matrices" proved important.

The strike showed dramatically the importance of immigrant organizations in the life of the city. The meetings held at Chabis Hall, at the Portuguese center, at the Franco-Belgian Cooperative, and beneath the Syrian Church demonstrated the part played by national groups. So did the relief work of immigrant societies, the presence of the Syrian band at the head of a parade, and the contributions of the Franco-Belgian Cooperative. Local 20, which started the strike, divided itself along ethnic lines as did the strike and relief committees. No one was really on his own; all depended upon some group. As the strikers discussed their problems, French, German, Italian, Polish, Hebrew, and other languages were used. The outcome of the strike, just as the whole history of the city before it, depended upon ethnic considerations.[114]

These numerous ethnic groups came together under the direction of IWW leaders, including William Haywood and other national officials, who came to Lawrence to direct strike activities. They displayed remarkable solidarity, with more than 25,000 workers on strike within three days. Though the IWW had been active in the textile industry for more than six years, they had but a few hundred members prior to the strike. This rose to somewhere between ten and fourteen thousand immediately after the strike.[115]

Despite cries of rebellion from opponents, the evidence indicates that the IWW leadership prevented, rather than abetted, violence.[116] Indeed, the issues in this strike, as at McKees Rocks, were clearly wages and hours. In fact, the IWW top leadership not only failed to preach revolution but conducted themselves along fairly narrow business union lines. In doing this they reflected the wishes of the strikers as it was IWW policy that demands should originate with them.[117]

The strikers won this contest substantially after two months and returned to the mills. The consequences of their effort were widespread.

The effect of the Lawrence strike was felt beyond the confines of the city. Several days before a final settlement, an announcement was made of a raise in wages throughout the textile mills of New England. It was estimated that more than 250,000 benefited.[118]

Once the strike was settled, however, IWW membership dropped as dramatically as it had risen. By late 1913 the organization had, once again, but a few hundred members.[119]

A second major textile strike occurred in the silk mills of Paterson, New Jersey. It originated in late January 1913 with 800 workers walking out of one mill in protest against the instituting of the multiple-loom system.

During the following weeks, the rest of the broad-silk weavers, and the dyehouse laborers joined the strike. By the end of the first week in March, some 13,000 silk operatives had quit their jobs. Apparently these workers left spontaneously.

They did not receive the support of the local AFL, and the local IWW (Chicago branch) possessed only 100 scattered numbers. Not more than 5 per cent of those striking belonged to an organization.[120]

During the strike, however, the IWW membership expanded enormously and its leaders assumed direction of strike activities.[121] Shortly, "onto the scene came its dramatic national leaders – Big Bill Haywood, Elizabeth Gurley Flynn and Carlo Tresca."[122]

As in the Lawrence strike, the demands of the workers were of a business union nature.[123] Though violence erupted on a larger scale than in Lawrence, it partly had to be attributed to the incredibly repressive tactics of city officials. Indeed, many charges brought against IWW leadership either failed to be sustained on appeal or were subsequently dropped.[124]

The Paterson strike lasted twenty-two weeks but, unlike in Lawrence, it was lost.[125] However, as in Lawrence, the IWW membership dropped precipitously once the hostilities had subsided. During the course of the strike the IWW claimed about 9000 members in Paterson. This figure dropped, shortly afterward, to 1300.[126]

One interpretation of the rapid rise and fall in immigrant membership in the IWW suggests that:

Under great stress, produced as in Lawrence and at McKees Rocks by a reduction of an already miserable wage, these grievously treated workers are capable of revolting and of acting with the heroism of despair. It was then that the I.W.W. entered and by furnishing leadership and technical knowledge, converted a sudden revolt into a prolonged and disciplined campaign. However, the campaign once ended, whether in victory or defeat, the normal attitude of apathy towards the conditions of the job and the equally normal distrust of one nationality towards another, returned. Permanent labor organizations could hardly be expected in such an environment and from human material thus conditioned. Those who followed the I.W.W., confident of the superiority of their own ideology, learned the same bitter lesson.[127]

Our discussion indicates a contrary view. It is suggested here that a strike lasting upward of five months indicates anything but "apathy towards the conditions of the job." The rapid falling off of IWW membership, regardless of the outcome of a strike, suggests rather that the union served as a useful instrument in securing the limited ends of its constituency, but that the latter was not inclined to pursue the larger ends advocated by the body's leadership.

It was these larger ends which failed to sustain immigrant adherents after a strike and explain the lack of success of IWW agitators prior to such conflicts. Thus, according to Saposs, the IWW filled a leadership vacuum when spontaneous strikes erupted, while failing to organize during periods of relative calm.

From the standpoint of trade union action the chief accomplishments of the I.W.W. consisted in the providing of expert strike leadership to unorganized workers, and in the raising of funds for relief and litigation. Successful or unsuccessful termination of a strike would find the I.W.W. leaders and organizers withdrawing to other "class war" battlefields (free speech fights or strikes) or the agitational trail. In unorganized industries where spontaneous strikes did not occur they confined themselves to their usual propaganda and agitational activities. The two outstanding instances are the packing and the steel industries, in both of which recent immigrants predominate. During the height of the I.W.W.'s career no spontaneous strikes occurred in either the packing or the steel industry proper and the organization, consequently, never passed out of its routine propaganda stage in these industries.[128]

The small membership in the IWW before and after strikes in such large immigrant centers as Lawrence and Paterson indicates the minimal appeal such agitational activities bore.

But, as the coal industry indicates, the immigrant was not indifferent to becoming a part of a permanent labor organization. Writing in 1919, the chronicler of the IWW notes of the UMW:

It is unquestionably the strongest *industrial* union in the world. Since 1905 the revolutionary industrial I.W.W.'s have looked with admiration upon the structural form of the Mine Workers' Union – and with impatient scorn upon their conservative tactics.[129]

And Saposs writes:

From the outset it became evident that, in common with native workers, immigrants in successful unions were generally unresponsive to I.W.W. appeals. The most obvious example is the United Mine Workers of America with over 80 per cent recent immigrant membership. Indeed, the history of this union reveals the fact that the coal industry has been more highly and successfully organized since the advent of the recent immigration than at any other period. With the possible exception of the building industry it is the best organized industry. And the many attempts of the Industrial Workers of the World, through its ablest organizers, to win over the immigrant workers from this union have proved barren.[130]

It is of importance to note that though radicalism was not absent from the UMW, its center of strength was in the western reaches of the industry, particularly in Illinois, where English-speaking miners were concentrated. Such radicalism, Laslett writes, was definitely not a significant element among the foreign-born Italians, Slavs, or other Eastern Europeans.[131]

Once again, if American workers in successful unions failed to be won over, it was primarily because they formed the bulk of the more skilled and more conservative craft associations. The interesting point here is that the predominantly American WFM, made up of the less skilled, was the initial driving force of the IWW, while the predominantly immigrant UMW failed to be moved. Leiserson notes why:

The one big union as advocated by the I.W.W. is designed as an organization to accomplish social revolution. Industrial unions like the United Mine Workers and the unions of the clothing trades are organized for economic improvement.

The Immigrant and Business Unionism

It is the latter which gains a permanent hold on the masses of immigrant workers.[132]

It is of further interest to add:

As a result of the failure of the I.W.W. to function as an economic organization, the immigrant workers of the Eastern industrial centers who followed it formerly began to abandon it shortly after the war. So strong was their disappointment that at the I.W.W. convention of 1919 out of fifty-four delegates only five were from the East and six were from the Mid-West, the remainder coming from the Far West.[133]

Conclusion

The claim here has been that immigrant orientations to American society were confined to a limited segment of it. Their focus, both in coming and after arrival, had to do with economic conditions surrounding the job. Operating, as they did, within the boundaries of an ethnic subsystem, the scope of their orientations remained narrowly trained on these issues while broader societal attachments were sustained to their area of origin. It is on this basis that it is argued that the immigrant was a far more ready recruit for conservative business unions than for revolutionary unionism and/or political activity.

But within these confines, the immigrant's union solidarity was as great as any. It is not without significance that the largest industrial union in the United States, prior to World War I, was in an industry which is generally notorious for radicalism but which was, nevertheless, business union oriented and predominantly immigrant.

NOTES

1. Kingsley Davis and Hilda H. Golden, "Urbanization and the Development of Pre-Industrial Areas," *Economic Development and Cultural Change*, Vol. 3 (October 1954), p. 7.

2. Simon Kuznets, "Consumption, Industrialization and Urbanization," in Bert F. Hoselitz and Wilbert E. Moore (eds.), *Industrialization and Society* (Paris and The Hague: UNESCO and Mouton, 1963), p. 102.

3. Conrad Taeuber and Irene Taeuber, *The Changing Population of the United States* (New York: John Wiley & Sons, Inc., 1958), p. 112.

4. *Ibid.*, p. 117.

5. U.S. Immigration Commission, *Report of the Immigration Commission*, Vol. 1, *Abstract* (Washington, D.C.: Government Printing Office, 1911), Table 14, p. 139.

6. *Ibid.*, Table 15, p. 140.

7. *Ibid.*, p. 140.

8. See U.S. Bureau of the Census, *Immigrants and Their Children*, "1920 Census Monographs VII," by Niles Carpenter (Washington, D.C.: Government Printing Office, 1927), Table 18, p. 26.

9. *Ibid.*, p. 28.

10. John S. MacDonald and Leatrice D. MacDonald, "Chain Migration, Ethnic

Neighborhood Formation, and Social Networks," *Milbank Memorial Fund Quarterly*, Vol. 52 (January 1964), pp. 82-97.

11. U.S. Immigration Commission, *Report of the Immigration Commission*, Vol. 4, *Emigration Conditions in Europe* (Washington, D.C.: U.S. Government Printing Office, 1911), p. 56.

12. *Ibid.*, p. 57.

13. *Ibid.*, p. 59.

14. *Ibid.*, p. 61.

15. U.S. Immigration Commission, *Report of the Immigration Commission*, Vol. 26, *Immigrants in Cities* (Washington, D.C.: Government Printing Office, 1911), pp. 145-146.

16. Frank J. Sheridan, "Italian, Slavic, and Hungarian Unskilled Immigrant Laborers in the United States," *Bulletin of the Bureau of Labor*, Vol. 15 (September 1907), p. 409.

17. *Ibid.*, p. 411.

18. MacDonald and MacDonald, *op. cit.*, p. 87.

19. See *ibid.*, Appendix II, pp. 92-93, for a review of materials on Italian neighborhood formations.

20. *Ibid.*, p. 90.

21. John S. MacDonald and Leatrice D. MacDonald, "Urbanization, Ethnic Groups, and Social Segmentation," *Social Research*, Vol. 29 (Winter 1962), p. 434.

22. *Ibid.*

23. W. Lloyd Warner and Leo Srole, *The Social Systems of American Ethnic Groups* (New Haven: Yale University Press, 1945), p. 99. The reference to Russians is apparently to post-Revolutionary political émigrés.

24. Amos H. Hawley, "Dispersion Versus Segregation: Apropos of a Solution of Race Problems," *Papers of the Michigan Academy of Science, Arts and Letters*, Vol. 30 (1944), p. 668.

25. *Ibid.*, p. 672.

26. E. K. Francis, "Variables in the Formation of So-Called 'Minority Groups,'" *American Journal of Sociology*, Vol. 60 (July 1954), p. 9.

27. Otis D. Duncan and Stanley Lieberson, "Ethnic Segregation and Assimilation," *American Journal of Sociology*, Vol. 64 (January 1959), p. 367.

28. Oscar Handlin, "Immigration in American Life: A Reappraisal," in Henry S. Commager (ed.), *Immigration in American History: Essays in Honor of Theodore C. Blegen* (Minneapolis: University of Minnesota Press, 1961), p. 13.

29. Robert E. Park and Herbert A. Miller, *Old World Traits Transplanted* (New York: Harper & Row, 1921), p. 120.

30. Raymond Breton, "Institutional Completeness of Ethnic Communities and the Personal Relations of Immigrants," *American Journal of Sociology*, Vol. 70 (September 1964), pp. 196-197.

31. Oscar Handlin, *The American People in the Twentieth Century* (Cambridge: Harvard University Press, 1954), pp. 62-63.

32. Park and Miller, *op. cit.*, pp. 145-146.

33. Carl Wittke, *We Who Built America* (Englewood Cliffs, N.J.: Prentice-Hall, 1939), p. 417.

34. *Ibid.*, p. 424.

35. Stanley Lieberson, *Ethnic Patterns in American Cities* (New York: The Free Press, 1963), p. 137.

36. Marion J. Levy, Jr., *The Structure of Society* (Princeton: Princeton University Press, 1952), p. 126.

37. Lieberson, *op. cit.*, p. 139.

38. *Ibid.*, pp. 151-153.

39. Stanley Lieberson, "The Impact of Residential Segregation on Ethnic Assimilation," *Social Forces*, Vol. 40 (October 1961), p. 54.

40. Park and Miller, *op. cit.*, p. 146.
41. William Preston, Jr., *Aliens and Dissenters: Federal Suppression of Radicals*, 1903-1933 (Cambridge: Harvard University Press, 1963), pp. 22-23.
42. Nathan Fine, *Labor and Farmer Parties in the United States: 1828-1928* (New York: Rand School of Social Science, 1928), p. 89.
43. *Ibid.*, p. 90.
44. David A. Shannon, *The Socialist Party of America* (Chicago: Quadrangle Books, Inc., 1967), p. 8.
45. Moses Rischin, "The Jewish Labor Movement in America: A Social Interpretation," *Labor History*, Vol. 4 (Fall 1963), p. 243.
46. See Fine, *op. cit.*, pp. 324-325.
47. Marcus L. Hansen, *The Immigrant in American History* (New York: Harper & Row, 1964), p. 95.
48. Preston, *op. cit.*, p. 33.
49. *Ibid.*, p. 24.
50. Fine, *op. cit.*, p. 324.
51. *Ibid.*
52. *Ibid.*, p. 326.
53. *Ibid.*
54. *Ibid.*, p. 329.
55. *Ibid.*
56. *Ibid.*
57. Shannon, *op. cit.*, p. 128.
58. *Ibid.*, p. 13.
59. *Ibid.*, p. 16.
60. *Ibid.*
61. *Ibid.*, pp. 18-20.
62. *Ibid.*, p. 23.
63. *Ibid.*, p. 25.
64. *Ibid.*, pp. 37-38.
65. John R. Commons and Assocs., *History of Labor in the United States* (New York: The Macmillan Co., 1918-1935), Vol. I, pp. 10-11.
66. Irving Bernstein, "The Growth of American Unions," *American Economic Review*, Vol. 44 (June 1954), pp. 315-317.
67. Irving Bernstein, "Union Growth and Structural Cycles," in Industrial Relations Research Association, *Proceedings From the Seventh Annual Meeting*, Detroit (December 1954), p. 206.
68. U.S. Bureau of the Census, *Historical Statistics of the United States: Colonial Times to 1957* (Washington, D.C.: Government Printing Office, 1960), p. 56.
69. Bernstein, "The Growth . . . ," Table 1, p. 303.
70. Leo Wolman, *The Growth of American Trade Unions: 1880-1923* (New York: National Bureau of Economic Research, Inc., 1924), p. 63.
71. U.S. Industrial Relations Commission, *Final Report and Testimony* (Washington, D.C.: Government Printing Office, 1916), Vol. 2, p. 1578.
72. Commons, *et al., op. cit.*, Vol. II, pp. 519-520.
73. U.S. Industrial Relations Commission, *op. cit.*, p. 1576.
74. Leo Wolman, "The Extent of Labor Organization in the United States in 1910," *Quarterly Journal of Economics*, Vol. 30 (May 1916), p. 516.
75. Charlotte Erickson, *American Industry and the European Immigrant: 1860-1885* (Cambridge: Harvard University Press, 1957), p. 185.
76. John Higham, *Strangers in the Land: Patterns of American Nativism, 1860-1895* (New York: Atheneum Publishers, 1963), pp. 71-72, 163-164, 305-306. For a particularly severe point of view see Arthur Mann, "Gompers and the Irony of Racism,"

Antioch Review, Vol. 13 (June 1953), pp. 203-204.

77. William M. Leiserson, *Adjusting Immigrant and Industry* (New York: Harper & Row, 1924), p. 174.

78. *Ibid.*, p. 178.

79. Henry Pelling, *American Labor* (Chicago: University of Chicago Press, 1960), p. 121.

80. Commons, *et al., op. cit.*, pp. 522-523.

81. Wolman, *Growth . . .* , Table 1, pp. 110-111.

82. Everett C. Hughes and Helen M. Hughes, *Where Peoples Meet* (New York: The Free Press, 1952), p. 85.

83. Emily G. Balch, *Our Slavic Fellow Citizens* (New York: Charities Publication Committee, 1910), p. 293.

84. *Ibid.*, p. 290.

85. John R. Commons and William M. Leiserson, "Wage-Earners of Pittsburgh," in Paul U. Kellogg (ed.), *Wage-Earning in Pittsburgh* (New York: Russell Sage Foundation, 1914), p. 178.

86. *Ibid.*, p. 179.

87. *Ibid.*, pp. 179-180.

88. *Ibid.*, p. 180.

89. Leiserson, *op. cit.*, p. 186.

90. Carrol D. Wright, "Influence of Trade Unions on Immigrants," *Bulletin of the Bureau of Labor,* Vol. 10 (January 1905), p. 7.

91. Balch, *op. cit.*, p. 294.

92. David Saposs, "The Mind of Immigrant Communities in the Pittsburgh District," in Interchurch World Movement, *Public Opinion and the Steel Strike* (New York: Harcourt Brace Jovanovich, 1921), p. 235.

93. *Ibid.*

94. Jerzy Zubrzycki, "Sociological Methods for the Study of Immigrant Adjustment," *Migration*, Vol. 1 (October-December 1961), p. 60.

95. For a thorough account of this strike see David Brody, *Labor in Crisis: The Steel Strike of 1919* (Philadelphia: J. B. Lippincott Co., 1965).

96. Leiserson, *op. cit.*, p. 14.

97. MacDonald and MacDonald, "Urbanization . . . ," p. 442.

98. John R. Commons, "Is Class Conflict in America Growing and Is It Inevitable?" *American Journal of Sociology*, Vol. 13 (May 1908), p. 762. On the largely American-born character of the Western Federation of Miners see Melvyn Dubofsky, *We Shall Be All: A History of the Industrial Workers of the World* (Chicago: Quadrangle Books, Inc., 1969), p. 24.

99. Paul F. Brissenden, *The I.W.W.: A Study of American Syndicalism* (2d ed.; New York: Russell & Russell, Inc., 1957), p. 41. For a detailed account of WFM strikes see Vernon H. Jensen, *Heritage of Conflict: Labor Relations in the Nonferrous Metals Industry up to 1930* (Ithaca: Cornell University Press, 1950), esp. pp. 19-159.

100. Brissenden, *op. cit.*, pp. 105-106.

101. *Ibid.*, p. 30.

102. Pelling, *op. cit.*, p. 112.

103. Brissenden, *op. cit.*, pp. 84-85.

104. Louis Levine, "The Development of Syndicalism in America," *Political Science Quarterly*, Vol. 28 (September 1913), pp. 464-465.

105. *Ibid.*, p. 468.

106. *Ibid.*, pp. 470-471.

107. Brissenden, *op. cit.*, p. 177.

108. U.S. Industrial Relations Commission, *op. cit.*, Vol. 11, p. 10,574.

109. For a discussion of parallels between the IWW and the AFL see Will Herberg, "American Marxist Political Theory," in Donald D. Egbert and Stow Persons (eds.), *Social-*

ism in American Life (Princeton: Princeton University Press, 1952), Vol. I, pp. 491-492.

110. Commons, *et al., op. cit.*, Vol. IV, p. 263.

111. *Ibid.,* p. 265.

112. Donald B. Cole, *Immigrant City: Lawrence, Massachusetts, 1845-1921* (Chapel Hill: University of North Carolina Press, 1963), p. 179.

113. *Ibid.*, p. 184.

114. *Ibid.*, p. 193.

115. Edwin Fenton, "Immigrants and Unions, A Case Study: Italians and American Labor: 1870-1920" (unpublished Ph.D. dissertation, Department of History, Harvard University, 1957), p. 320. Brissenden, *op. cit.*, pp. 286, 294.

116. *Ibid.*, pp. 287-288. Commons, *et al., op. cit.,* Vol. IV, p. 270. Fenton, *op. cit.,* p. 334.

117. *Ibid.*, pp. 336-337.

118. Commons, *et al., op. cit.*, Vol. IV, p. 272.

119. Brissenden, *op. cit.*, p. 292. Fenton, *op. cit.*, p. 366.

120. Graham Adams, Jr., *Age of Industrial Violence: 1910-1915* (New York: Columbia University Press, 1966), p. 77.

121. *Ibid.*, U.S. Industrial Relations Commission, *op. cit.*, Vol. 3, pp. 2353-2354.

122. Adams, *op. cit.*, p. 79.

123. "The demands were the re-establishment of the two-loom system, the eight-hour day and a minimum wage of $12 a week for all dye workers." Commons, *et al., op. cit.,* Vol. IV, pp. 274-275. See also Adams, *op. cit.*, p. 78.

124. U.S. Industrial Relations Commission, *op. cit.*, Vol. 3, pp. 2529-2544.

125. Commons, *et al., op. cit.*, Vol. IV, p. 277.

126. U.S. Industrial Relations Commission, *op. cit.*, Vol. 3, p. 2457.

127. Commons, *et al., op. cit.*, Vol. IV, p. 281.

128. David J. Saposs, *Left Wing Unionism: A Study of Radical Policies and Tactics* (New York: International Publishers, 1926), p. 143.

129. Brissenden, *op. cit.*, pp. 38-39.

130. Saposs, *op. cit.*, pp. 132-133.

131. John Laslett, *Labor and the Left: A Study of Socialist and Radical Influences in the American Labor Movement, 1881-1924* (New York: Basic Books, Inc., 1970), p. 230.

132. Leiserson, *op. cit.*, p. 183.

133. *Ibid.*, p. 184.

7
Summary and Conclusions

American sociology, in an earlier day, could be depicted as social-problem oriented, contrasting with the highly macroscopic investigations of its European counterparts.[1] In recent years, however, sociologists in the United States have been increasingly addressing themselves to problems pertaining to the "broad outline" of society. This shift in concern has partially been quickened by a growing emphasis on problems of modernization. The present study may, to some extent, be identified with this evolving emphasis in the sociological literature. It has been concerned with the large-scale transformation the United States underwent in the post-Civil War era, when it became relatively modernized. We have attempted to account for the conservatism of the American labor movement when contrasted with those in Europe as an outcome of a distinctive pattern and sequence of events occurring during this period.

The implications of thoroughgoing changes, such as those related to modernization, are so stressful that they have frequently been taken as problematic to a society's stability and persistence, insofar as such changes are likely to threaten consensus as to values. It has become generally accepted in American social thought that substantial consensus concerning values is a requisite feature of a society's viability. Concerning this canon, the present study raises important questions which may point the way toward theoretically rewarding further research. Specifically, it has been suggested here that, where large portions of a population that is experiencing the process of modernization have *not* been basically socialized in terms of the society in which this process is taking place (and therefore lack adherence to the values of that society), potential cleavages and disruptive conflict during the onset of rapid change may be diminished rather than increased due to the presence of these "outsiders."

The emphasis here on the factor of social discontinuity during the initial stages of modernization has led us to analyze what have often been referred to by social theorists as the "strains" associated with rapid change. These strains are further identified in this work as the divergences from previously institutionalized practices *to which members of the society undergoing change have been socialized.* It has also been emphasized in the present study that an initial outcome of rapid and unmediated social change (with particular reference to production) is a *mobilization* of those who find that previously institutionalized practices no longer obtain and thus protest the "illegitimate" divergences from them.

The thinking involved in proposing this mobilizing function of severely discontinuous change is informed most especially by the work of Marx. The present study, however, places a much larger burden on these initial changes. The manner in which these strains are first confronted, it is argued, will condition the future character of the labor movement — which will become more moderate over time in any event. The present analysis has gone back to this initial period as a means of accounting for the observed contemporary differences between the labor movement in the United States and other modern ones.

Though Marx correctly perceived the structural alterations and class polarization involved in modern industrialism, he failed to envision the ultimate institutionalization of the economic practices he decried. He wrongly projected increasing class polarization instead of its lessening, the latter appearing to characterize highly modernized societies. Mobilization is here seen as Marx saw it, namely, as a collective response on the part of workers to inequalities in the allocation of scarce rewards. The present study, then, examines why this early mobilization of workers was less protracted in the United States than elsewhere, giving rise, correspondingly, to a more moderate labor movement.

By addressing the initial stages of American modernization, the present work examines evidence for the empirical generalization that it is this period in which the greatest labor radicalism is engendered. We attach major significance to the discontinuity aspects of the process which are most felt by the generation exposed to the onset of these changes. We have noted that severe inequality based on "unjust" practices is quite hospitable to radicalism.

Mobilization is here seen, as it has been by scholars for some time, as a necessary condition for labor radicalism. Thus it is suggested in this work that the failure of the American labor movement to exhibit the radical tendencies of its European counterparts is partially accounted for by the failure of the labor force to experience sustained mobilization during a period of extreme discontinuity and class polarization.[2]

In attempting to explain the failure of the American labor force to coalesce due to grievances associated with social discontinuity, the paired concepts of basic and intermediate socialization, and genuine and expedient societal membership, were utilized. Basic socialization, it will be recalled, has to do with the inculcation of the generalized norms of a society, while intermediate socialization refers to the inculcation of specialized patterns of action taking place in differentiated subsystems of the society that individuals variously enter. Genuine members of a society are those who have undergone basic socialization within it. Expedient members of a society are those who have transferred participation from another society to the one in question but who maintain primary orientation to the former.

Where large segments of the labor force are expedient societal members during the early phases of modernization, it is argued, the mobilizing function of

Summary and Conclusions

severe structural discontinuity is muted. An examination of the composition of the labor force during America's transition to a relatively modernized society reveals increasingly higher rates of immigration. It was proposed here that large foreign-born proportions in the labor force, particularly at the less-skilled levels, made for a relatively moderate labor movement and for the institutionalization of business unionism at the industrial as well as the craft union level.

The significance of large proportions of immigrants in the American labor force lay in the fact that they were "strangers" to American society; they had no prior acquaintance with the system they were entering. Further, immigrants during this period may be appropriately characterized as "sojourners" (a subtype of stranger) insofar as their goals were short-term, narrowly economic, and oriented toward ultimate return to their home society.

The mobilizing function of structural discontinuity during the early phases of modernization is accounted for by the disparities arising between basic and intermediate socialization. A virulent reaction is seen as most likely from those who have been basically socialized in the "preindustrial" social order. It is asserted that immigrants failed to take part in such a response because they could not legitimately protest the divergence from previously institutionalized practices *that they had never experienced.*

A major instance of the reaction of native labor to the disequilibrium brought about by early modernization is provided by the Knights of Labor. The Knights were indicative of an incipient mobilization of the labor force during the interval of severe structural strains in American society. The members of this organization protested the contracting of opportunity for independent proprietorship and the spread of the "wages system," which signaled the demise of economic individualism. We can attribute the precipitous decline of the Knights partly to the fact that immigrant entry into the American labor force was on the rise during the Knights' peak of activity. Immigrants were not sympathetic to reform unionism whose leaders decried the passing of conditions that they (the immigrants) had scant awareness of. Indeed, given his sojourner qualities, the immigrant was quite amenable to a narrow cash-nexus relationship with his employer. The "wages system," which the Knights bitterly protested, was the sine qua non of late nineteenth-century immigration.

In most social situations basic socialization gives way, over time, to intermediate socialization for any given age group. Thus, those moving into specialized structures of action within a society are normally genuine members of that society. The immigrant, however, *reversed* this process (with American society, of course, being taken as the point of reference). Typically, he first experienced intermediate socialization with the slight prospect of undergoing basic socialization. Though most immigrants remained in the United States despite their original intentions, permanent residence did not necessarily imply genuine societal membership. The formation of minority or ethnic systems functioned to perpetuate expedient societal membership among the migrating generation if not their children.

For the immigrant who remained, commitment tended to center on the one context of American society that he was constantly exposed to: the work setting. Following from this, we argue that immigrants were particularly congenial to business unionism, which pursues benefits derived from the employment situation, rather than inclining toward larger revolutionary aims.

The organizing success of the radical International Workers of the World among immigrants in the East appears, on its face, to belie this contention. But the transitory nature of immigrant membership, confined largely to periods of strike activity, suggests that the IWW provided an instrument in obtaining goals which were, in effect, of a business union character. After these strikes were concluded, whether in success (Lawrence) or in failure (Paterson), the membership decline in the IWW was almost as rapid as its rise.

In contrast, the well-organized, AFL-affiliated United Mine Workers was, in its time, a singularly successful example of industrial unionism, adhering to business union objectives, with a large immigrant constituency. Not only did immigration fail to undermine this union, but its great initial membership expansion took place at a time when immigration was rising to unprecedented heights. It was, furthermore, acknowledged to be one of the strongest industrial unions in the country. Thus, immigrant acceptance of unions that were oriented toward immediate gains in wages, hours, and conditions, as well as their willingness to endure lengthy strikes in achieving those ends, appeared to be somewhat more than their detractors of the period would acknowledge.

On the other hand, the Western Federation of Miners, possessing a largely native-born constituency in the metal-mining regions of the West, was the radical opposite number of the UMW. The WFM was a party to some of the most violent strikes in American labor history and ultimately became the major force in the establishment of the IWW.

This comparison of two mining unions is quite instructive, for, according to Lipset:

Wherever the social structure operates so as to isolate *naturally* individuals or groups with the same political outlook from contact with those who hold different views, the isolated individuals or groups tend to back political extremists. It has been repeatedly noted, for example, that workers in so called "isolated" industries — miners, sailors, fishermen, lumbermen, sheep shearers, and longshoremen — who live in communities predominantly inhabited by others in the same occupation usually give overwhelming support to the more left-wing platforms.[3]

Following from the argument advanced in the present study, social isolation among immigrants would produce the reverse (i.e., a more conservative posture) of the same conditions among native-born workers by making for a persistence of expedient societal membership among the former. It might also be noted that, although geographic isolation may be closely related to social isolation, it is not a necessary condition of the latter. The formation of ethnic subsystems insulating the immigrant from the larger society has been discussed earlier in this work.

Summary and Conclusions

The preceding comparison of the WFM with the UMW dramatizes a situation that was operative throughout areas of high immigrant concentration: their *social isolation*, whether in close geographic proximity to natives or not.

We may return now to the issue raised earlier concerning consensus and societal stability. We have found that the arena of conflict which workers engaged in was limited precisely by the scope of commitment. Men are not likely to engage in protracted struggles over areas of social life that they are indifferent to or minimally cognizant of.[4] We suggest that the failure of a major working-class challenge to capitalist economic institutions to mature in the United States is partially attributable to the fact that a large portion of those in the lower reaches of the occupational hierarchy, at the time mobilization was most likely to occur, simply did not identify themselves with the society in which they carried out their work lives. They did, however, become committed to their work setting, and it was in this context that conflict was most likely to — and did — occur.

This argument suggests, then, that the problems of consensus and conflict assume a more complex texture than has normally been recognized. The consequences of social isolation are variable and depend on predisposing orientations. It seems that such orientations become enriched when nurtured in a fairly sealed off social environment. Whether those who are cut off will challenge or acquiesce to the system which promotes their relative disadvantage depends not on isolation itself but on the orientations which are isolated.

The massive immigration which the United States experienced in the late nineteenth and early twentieth centuries was certainly an enormous asset when viewed in strictly economic terms:

> Immigration provides the receiving country with a supply of labor, the cost of whose upbringing has been borne elsewhere. It is a free gift of human capital, and the smaller the proportion of dependents among the new settlers, the greater the economic advantage.[5]

Nowhere was this free gift more appreciated than by the American "captains of industry" who "built" their railways, steel and textile mills, and mining enterprises with the assistance of millions of foreign hands. The incredible conditions under which immigrants initially subsisted were frequently cited by natives bent on restriction as evidence of foreign undermining of American standards. It is ironic that the full burden of guilt was laid on the victims of a ruthless exploitation rather than on its American-born perpetrators.

The immigrant, once committed to industrial labor, was quite as able as the native American to present a solidary front in lengthy strikes to stubborn employers. The manner in which he came to organize into unions, however, suggests that the fact that his upbringing was borne elsewhere had other consequences somewhat less amenable to cost analysis.

NOTES

1. Talcott Parsons, "Some Problems Confronting Sociology as a Profession," *American Sociological Review*, Vol. 24 (August 1959), p. 550.
2. We have placed the American period of this social discontinuity in the decades surrounding the turn of the century. In suggesting this interval we are not unmindful that important gains toward relatively modernized industrial production had been accomplished earlier in the nineteenth century. We argue, rather, that these initial innovations had reached a "buildup" point by our period, such that they were being applied to a multiplicity of productive enterprises resulting, generally speaking, in radical changes in the conditions of labor throughout industrial employment.
3. Seymour M. Lipset, *Political Man: The Social Bases of Politics* (Garden City: Doubleday & Co., Inc., 1960), p. 87. See also, Clark Kerr and Abraham Siegal, "The Interindustry Propensity to Strike," in A. Kornhauser, R. Dubin, and A. M. Ross (eds.), *Industrial Conflict* (New York: McGraw-Hill Book Co., 1954), pp. 189-212.
4. Wilbert E. Moore and Melvin M. Tumin, "Some Social Functions of Ignorance," *American Sociological Review*, Vol. 14 (December 1949), pp. 787-795.
5. Brinley Thomas, "The Economic Aspect," *The Positive Contribution by Immigrants* (Paris: UNESCO, 1955), p. 169.

INDEX

INDEX

ABEGGLEN, JAMES C., 42
absenteeism, 133
action patterns, 27-28, 37-38, 81, 87, 135
Adams, Graham, Jr., 171
agricultural-nonagricultural pursuits, gainfully employed in, 1820-1930 (table), 66
agricultural proletariat, 19
agricultural revolution, 57, 59
agriculture, modernization of, 58-60, 63, 64, 65, 67-68
Albanians, in U.S., 150
Amalgamated Association of Iron, Steel, and Tin Workers, 159
American Federation of Labor (AFL), 112, 154, 160, 161, 162, 165, 176; nativism, 158; trade autonomy, 156-157
American Federation of Labor-Congress of Industrial Organizations (AFL-CIO), 5
"American Separation of Labor," 162
anarchists, 153
anti-Semitism, 49
aristocracy, of business, 103
Armenians, emigration to U.S., 49; in U.S., 126, 148, 150
Australia, class conflict, 18-19
Austria-Hungary, emigration to U.S., 47, 50, 51, 71, 127, 146; labor radicalism, 22
Austrians, in U.S., 127

BACKWARD-LOOKING PROTEST, 13-14, 107-108, 115; *see also* renovating type of unionism
Balch, Emily G., 159, 160, 170
Balkans, emigration to U.S., 146
Barton, Glen T., 83
Belgium, coal and steel production, 66
Bendix, Reinhard, 13, 14, 17, 26, 36, 37, 41, 42, 43, 44, 117
Bernstein, Irving, 155-156, 169
Bers, Melvin K., 3, 21, 22, 34, 40, 42, 44
Berthoff, Rowland T., 43, 84
Bidwell, Percy W., 83
Bloch, Louis, 85
boarding-boss system, 132
boardinghouse mills, 98, 99
Bogue, Donald J., 145
bossism, 127-128
Bowler, Alida C., 43
Breton, Raymond, 168
Bridenbaugh, Carl, 97, 117, 118
Brim, Orville G., Jr., 90, 116
Brissenden, Paul F., 161-162, 163, 170, 171
Brodell, Albert P., 83
Brody, David, 124, 134, 139, 140, 170
Brown, E. H. Phelps, 22, 42
Bruchey, Stuart, 83
Bulgarians, in U.S., 127
Bull, Edward, 23, 24
bureaucracy, 8-9, 19
Burn, D. L., 62, 84
business cycles, and immigration, 47, 71-72, 125, 155-156; and unionism,

181

Index

business cycles (*cont'd*) 155-156
business unionism, 1, 2-5, 6, 21, 30, 36, 38, 135, 148, 160, 165, 175, 176

CAHAN, ABRAHAM, 152
Call (newspaper), 152
Canada, class conflict, 18-19
capital formation, 91
capitalism, 2, 5, 9, 10, 18, 24, 25, 30, 35, 61, 91, 101, 104, 107, 110, 111, 113, 130, 152, 157, 158, 161, 162, 177; resistance power, 21
Carpenter, Niles, 74, 85
Carr-Saunders, A. M., 46, 52
Catholic Church, and secret societies, 110
chain migration, 145-148
Citroen, H. A., 53
Clark, Colin, 67, 84
Clark, Victor S., 61, 63-64, 83, 84, 106, 117, 119, 122, 139
class, and political parties, 16
class conflict, and feudal heritage, 18-19, 20, 24, 25, 103
class consciousness, 5, 19
class struggle, 16-18; *see also* social stratification
Cochran, Thomas C., 83, 99, 117
Cole, Donald B., 122, 139, 171
collective bargaining, 4, 5, 6, 21, 112, 158, 160-161
Commons, John R., 20-21, 26, 42, 43, 103-104, 105, 106, 108, 112, 113, 114-115, 118, 119, 120, 133, 134, 135, 140, 141, 155, 157, 158, 159, 161, 169, 170, 171
communal action, 11, 14
Communist Manifesto, 152
Communist Party, 153, 154
conservatism, of union, 173, 175
contract labor, 127, 131
Cooper, Martin R., 83
Corey, Lewis, 102, 117, 118, 120
Coser, Lewis A., 35, 44
craft unions, 3-4, 6, 21, 39, 108, 109, 110, 112, 114, 115, 175
crime, and poverty, 11
criminality, of native vs. foreign born, 31-32
Cyriax, George, 5, 40
Czechs, in U.S., 149, 150

DAHRENDORF, RALF, 39, 40, 44
Danhoff, Clarence H., 83
Davie, Maurice R., 52, 53
Davis, Kingsley, 167
Davis, Lance E., 84
decentralization, vs. centralization, 90-91
democracy, 94, 103
Democratic Party, 5, 152
Denmark, modernization and unionism, 5-6, 19, 23
deviant behavior, 11, 12, 14
discontinuities, 7-8, 17, 23-24, 25, 27, 29, 37, 38, 79, 81, 89, 90, 91, 121, 134, 135, 173
Douglas, Paul, 85, 86
Dubin, Robert, 15, 16, 41
Duncan, Otis D., 149, 168
Dunlop, John T., 40

ECKLER, ROSS, 75
economic development: agriculture, 57, 59; industrialization, 23, 55-56, 57, 66, 80, 107; modernization, 56, 57; productivity, 55, 56, 57; stages of, 103-107, 113
economic motivation, of immigrants, 48-49, 50, 55, 72
Edwards, Everett E., 67-68, 83
eight-hour day, 108, 111, 114
Eisenstadt, S. S., 34-35, 44
employer-employee relationships, 96-101, 102
Engels, Friedrich, 25, 40, 42, 43, 117
England, *see* United Kingdom
Erickson, Charlotte, 127, 128, 130, 131, 139, 140, 169
ethnic specialty, 34
ethnic subsystems, 26-27, 32-33, 145-151, 155, 164, 167, 175, 176
European origin, of immigrants, 47, 49, 70, 71, 72, 78-79, 126, 132, 137, 166; areas of, 1820-1919 (table), 71
European population growth, and emigration, 48
Evans, George Henry, 111
expedient membership, in society, 29-30, 34, 35, 38, 39, 125, 126, 148, 174-175, 176

182

Index

FAULKNER, HAROLD U., 69
"Farmers" Alliance, 135
farm machinery, in U.S., 59-60
Federation of Organized Trades and Labor Unions, 112, 156, 162
Feldman, Arnold S., 7, 24, 35-36, 38, 39, 40, 44, 116
Feldman, Herman, 140
Fenton, Edwin, 139, 171
feudal heritage, and class conflict, 18-19, 20, 24, 25, 103
Fine, Nathan, 152, 169
Finland, emigration to U.S., 47
Flynn, Elizabeth Gurley, 165
Foerster, Robert F., 53
Foran Act, 127
Foster, Frank K., 120
France, coal and steel production, 66; real wage-rates, 1860-1939 (table), 22
Francis, E. K., 32-33, 44, 149, 168
free immigration period, U.S., 45
French, emigration to U.S., 47; in U.S., 126
Freudianism, 89

GALENSON, WALTER, 1-2, 5-6, 19, 23, 27, 29, 39, 41, 42, 43
Gallman, Robert E., 64, 84
Garment Cutters Union, 111
Gates, Paul W., 83
Germans, emigration to U.S., 47, 72, 79, 127, 146; in U.S., 121, 128, 152, 160
Germany, coal and steel production, 66; labor radicalism, 21, 26-27; real wage-rates, 1860-1939 (table), 22
Glazer, Nathan, 44
Golden, Hilda H., 167
Goldsmith, Raymond W., 58, 83
Gompers, Samuel, 156-157, 163
government, and modernization, 17-18, 91
Greeks, in U.S., 123-124, 127, 148, 150
Green, Constance McL., 99, 118
greenbackism, 108
Grob, Gerald N., 109, 110, 111, 114, 119, 120, 128, 140
Gulick, Charles A., 2, 21, 22, 34, 40, 42, 44
Gurley, J. G., 83

HABAKUK, H. J., 62, 76, 81, 84, 86, 129
Hacker, Louis, 83, 119
Handlin, Mary F., 52
Handlin, Oscar, 27, 43, 52, 53, 85, 129, 138, 140, 149, 150, 168
Hansen, Marcus Lee, 43, 52, 152, 169
Hartz, Louis, 41, 43
Hawley, Amos H., 148, 168
Haymarket riot, 114, 130
Haywood, William, 154, 163, 164, 165
Herberg, Will, 170
Hersch, Liebmann, 49, 53
Higham, John, 131, 136, 140, 141, 169
Hillquit, Morris, 154
Hourwich, Isaac A., 141
Holyoke, employer-employee relations, 98, 99
Hopkins, Sheila V., 22, 42
Horowitz, Irving, 44
horsepower per wage-earner, in manufacturing, 1869-1919 (table), 65
Hoxie, Robert F., 3, 4, 40
Hughes, Everett C., and Helen M., 159, 170
Hughes, R. T. Jonathan, 84
humanitarian period, in unionism, 108, 114
Hungarians, in U.S., 132, 147
Hutchinson, E. P., 77

IMMIGRANTS, IN U.S.: absenteeism, 133; age distribution, 1880-1920 (table), 73; age and sex distribution, 72-73, 78; Albanian, 150; anarchists, 153; antagonism toward, 136; Armenian, 126, 148, 150; Austrian, 127; average annual immigration, 1851-1910 (table), 46; boarding-boss system, 132; bossism, 127-128; Bulgarians, 127; chain migration, 145-148; contract labor, 127, 131; Czechs, 149, 150; earnings, comparative, 78-79; economic motives, 48-49, 50, 55, 72; ethnic subsystems, 26-27, 32-33, 145-151, 155, 164, 167, 175, 176; European areas of origin, 1820-1919 (table), 71; and European industrialization, 48; European northwestern vs. southeastern origin of, 47, 49, 70,

183

Index

Immigrants (*cont'd*) 72, 75, 78-79, 126, 132, 137, 166; and European population growth, 48; expedient membership, in U.S. society, 29-30, 34, 35, 38, 39, 125, 126, 148, 174-175, 176; foreign born vs. native workers, by occupation, 1910 (tables), 74-75, 77; free immigration period, 45; French, 126; German, 121, 128, 152, 160; Greek, 123-124, 127, 148, 150; Hungarian, 132, 147; industrial discipline, 133-134; industrial experience, 75-76, 78-79; industrial relations, 1, 2, 25-28, 30; in Industrial Workers of the World (IWW), 163-167; instrumentalism of, 35; vs. internal migrants, 134-135; Irish, 121, 122, 123, 129, 149, 160; Italian, 123, 127, 128, 132, 147, 148, 149, 164, 166; Jewish, 49-50, 75, 126, 148, 152, 154; job consciousness, 159; Lithuanian, 150, 160; Macedonian, 127; Mexican, 127; money transfers overseas, 132-133; naturalization, 151; new vs. old, 75-76, 78-79, 125-126, 137-138, 152, 153, 158, 164; numbers of, 45-46; numbers of, by periods, 1820-1940 (table), 70; occupational distribution, 73-75, 77, 81; in occupational hierarchy, 77-79, 81-82; *padrone* system, 128, 131, 147; peasant origin, 49, 50, 92, 150; Polish, 148, 149, 150; political motives, 49; Portuguese, 150; radicalism, 138, 151-155, 156; return movements, 46, 125, 126; Russian, 148, 154; Ruthenian, 149; Scandinavian, 121, 128; Slavs, 132, 147, 150, 154, 159, 160, 166; as sojourners, 33-36, 123-125, 126, 132, 148, 160, 175; and steamship companies, 126-127; as strangers, 28-29, 33, 82, 175; as strikebreakers, 130-132; Swedish, 128; Syrian, 150; transport facilities, 51-52; Turks, 127; and U.S. business cycles, 47, 71-72, 125, 155-156; wage rates and profits, 76, 79, 80-81, 121, 122, 124
income inequalities, and modernization, 79-81

individualism, 31, 36, 90-91, 94, 95, 99, 102, 110, 115, 128, 175
individuals, vs. action patterns, 27-28, 37-38, 81, 87, 135
industrial discipline, of immigrants, 133-134
industrial experience, of immigrants, 75-76, 78-79
industrialization, 1, 2, 23, 48, 55-56, 57, 66, 80, 93, 94-96, 107, 123, 143-145
industrial revolution, 56, 57, 113
industrial unionism, 4-5, 6, 21, 39, 158, 160, 166, 175, 176
Industrial Workers of the World (IWW), 19, 154, 155, 156, 161-167, 176
innovation, in modernization, 15, 106, 129-130
institutional invention, 15
instrumentalism, of immigrants, 35
internal migration, U.S., 72, 79, 80-81, 134-135
Irish, emigration, 72, 75; in U.S., 121, 122, 123, 129, 149, 160
Italians, emigration, 47, 51, 71, 72, 79, 127, 146; in U.S., 26, 123, 127, 128, 132, 147, 148, 149, 164, 166

JAFFE, A. J., 69, 85
Japan, labor radicalism, 24-25, 26-27, 33; modernization, 7, 8; peasant revolts, 12
Jefferson, Thomas, 93, 95
Jerome, Harry, 47, 51, 65, 71, 85, 125, 139
Jewish Daily Forward, 152
Jews, emigration, 49, 79; in U.S., 49-50, 75, 126, 148, 152, 154
job consciousness, 3, 22, 36, 159
Jones, Allen M., 139
Jones, Maldwyn A., 43

KERR, CLARK, 178
Kirk, Dudley, 52, 53
Klezl, Felix, 53
Knights of Labor, 110-116, 121, 127, 128, 130, 131, 134, 135, 136, 156, 157, 162, 175
Knox, John B., 140
Koren, John, 139

Index

Kuznets, Simon, 2, 39, 59, 64, 65, 66, 72, 78, 79-80, 82, 83, 84, 85, 86, 139, 143, 167

LABOR FORCE: employment status, 1800-1957 (table), 69
Labor Party, Norway, 19
Labor Party, U.K., 5
labor-saving techniques, 62-63, 65
Lane, Frederick C., 82
Lantz, Herman R., 133, 140
Laslett, John, 166, 171
Lawrence, Massachusetts, strike, 26, 163-164, 165, 170; immigrant labor, 122
Lebergott, Stanley, 69, 79, 86
Leiserson, William M., 158, 159, 161, 166, 170, 171
Letschinsky, Jacob, 53
Levine, Louis, 170
Levy, Marion J., Jr., 6-7, 12, 23, 24, 27, 29, 40, 41, 42, 43, 82, 116, 117, 118, 168
Lieberson, Stanley, 43, 149, 150-151, 168
Lincoln, Abraham, 107
Lipset, Seymour M., 16, 18-19, 26, 30, 36, 37, 40, 41, 42, 43, 44, 178
Lithuanians, in U.S., 150, 160
Low, J. O., 134, 140

MACDONALD, JOHN S., AND LEATRICE D., 123, 128, 139, 140, 147, 161, 167, 168, 170
McDougall, Duncan M., 84
Macedonians, in U.S., 127
McKees Rocks, Pennsylvania, strike, 163, 164, 165, 166
McKelvey, Blake, 119
Malthusian push, 71
Mann, Arthur, 169
Mannari, Hiroshi, 42
market, extension of, 104, 105-106, 107, 115, 121-122
Marsh, Robert M., 42
Marshall, T. H., 35, 44
Marx, Karl, 9, 10, 16, 17, 18, 40, 41, 95, 117, 174
Marxism, 6, 12, 18, 38, 130
master-journeyman-apprentice system, 94, 97, 98, 99, 100, 103-104, 107, 109, 110, 113
Mayer, Kurt, 18, 41, 117
membership, in U.S. unions, 21, 155-156, 158
merchant-capitalist, 104-105
Merton, Robert K., 11, 12, 14, 15, 16, 41
Mexicans, in U.S., 127
Miller, Herbert A., 149, 150, 151, 168, 169
Mills, C. Wright, 92, 117
mobilization, of labor, 8, 12, 89, 134-135, 173-175
modernization: of agriculture, 58-60, 63, 64, 65, 67-68; bureaucracy, 8-9, 19; capital formation, 91; class and political parties, 16; communal action, 11, 14; decentralization vs. centralization, 90-91; discontinuities, 7-8, 17, 23-24, 25, 27, 29, 37, 38, 79, 81, 89, 90, 91, 121, 134, 135, 173; extension of market, 104, 105-106, 107, 115, 121-122; feudal heritage, 24; forward-backward looking protest, 13-14; government, 17-18, 91; ideal vs. actual patterns, 11-13, 14, 16, 17, 35, 90, 92-96, 107-108, 110, 135; income inequalities, 79-81; individuals vs. action patterns, 27-28, 37-38, 81, 87, 135; innovation, 15, 106, 129-130; labor mobilization, 8, 12, 89, 134-135, 173-175; merchant-capitalist, 104-105; rationalization of production, 96-97, 101-102, 106, 110, 123; rebellion, 15, 16; as revolutionary, 88; socialization, basic vs. intermediate, 29-30, 36, 37, 38, 89-90, 173, 174, 175; social mobility, 14, 67; social stratification, 8, 9-12, 14-16, 16-18, 38, 79, 80-81, 103-104, 138, 174; specialization, 58-59; transitional stage, 13, 55; transport systems, 106-107; values and norms, 38-39, 87-88, 89, 173, 177; voting rights, 19-20
Molly Maguires (secret organization), 110
monetary reform, and unions, 108, 109
money supply, per capita, U.S., 59-60
money transfers, by immigrants, 132-133

Index

Moore, Wilbert E., 7, 11, 17, 24, 27, 35-36, 38, 39, 40, 41, 44, 48, 53, 82, 84, 85, 86, 116, 120, 140, 178
myth, 15

NATIONAL BUREAU OF ECONOMIC RESEARCH, 45
National Labor Union, 108-110, 111
naturalization, of immigrants, 151
natural rights, 5
Nelli, Herbert S., 139
new, vs. old immigrants, 75-76, 78-79, 125-126, 137-138, 152, 153, 158, 164
Newburyport, employer-employee relations, 98, 100
New Deal, 21
New England, boardinghouse mills, 98, 99; textile industry, 96, 103, 106, 121-123
New York State Mechanics' Association, 107-108
New Zealand, class conflict, 18-19
Norway, labor radicalism, 19, 20, 23, 24, 25, 31, 92; modernization and unionism, 5, 6

OAKSHOTT, ROBERT, 5, 40
Obolensky-Ossinsky, V. V., 53
occupational distribution, of immigrants, 73-75, 77, 81
occupational hierarchy, immigrants in, 77-79, 81-82
Oliver, John W., 83
"one big union," 112, 130, 156, 162, 166
open-class ideology, 14, 17

PADRONE SYSTEM, 128, 131, 147
Park, Robert E., 149, 150, 151, 168, 169
Parsons, Talcott, 116, 118, 178
paternalism, 24, 98, 99
Paterson, New Jersey, strike, 164-165, 176
patterns of action, ideal vs. actual, 11-13, 14, 16, 17, 35, 90, 92-96, 107-108, 110, 135
peasants, 18, 19, 25, 27, 32; origin of immigrants, 49, 50, 92, 150; revolts of, 12, 13
Peck, Morton, 84
Pelling, Henry, 43, 158, 170
Pennsylvania iron works, employer-employee relations, 100
Perlman, Selig, 20, 21, 42, 131, 140
Pessen, Edward, 105, 118
Philadelphia textile mills, 100, 103
Poles, emigration, 47, 49, 50-51, 79; in U.S., 148, 149, 150
political motives, for emigration, 49
political parties, and class, 16
Portuguese, emigration, 47; in U.S., 150
poverty, and crime, 11
Preston, William, Jr., 153, 169
productivity, 55, 56, 57, 58
protest, forward-backward looking, 13-14
Protestant Reformation, 93
public schools, 21
Puritan ethic, 30, 93, 95

RADICALISM, IN LABOR UNIONS, 19, 20, 23-24, 25, 26-27, 33, 38, 135, 138, 151-155, 156, 163, 174
railroads, U.S., 58, 59, 63, 106, 108
rationalization, of production, 96-97, 101-102, 106, 110, 123
Ratti, Anna Maria, 53
Ravnholt, H., 53
rebellion, 15, 16
Rees, Albert, 86
Reich, Charles A., 117
renovating type of unionism, 107-108, 109, 110, 111, 114, 115, 136, 175
Republican Party, 152
return movements, of immigrants, 46, 125, 126
revolution, 88
revolution from the top, 24-25
Rezneck, Samuel, 61, 84, 117
Rischin, Moses, 169
Robbins, Richard, 53, 139
Roberts, Peter, 140
Rogin, Leo, 83
Rokkan, Stein, 42
Ross, Arthur M., 4, 40
Rostow, W. W., 32, 44, 82
Rubin, Ernest, 2, 39, 85, 86, 139
Russia, Jewish emigration, 49, 50
Russian Revolution, 14, 159

186

Index

Russians, emigration, 47, 51, 71, 72, 79; in U.S., 148, 154
Ruthenians, in U.S., 149

SALOUTOS, THEODORE, 123-124, 139
Sanford, Charles L., 117
Saposs, David J., 165, 166, 170, 171
Sawyer, John, 61, 62, 84
Scalapino, Robert A., 24, 42
Scandinavians, emigration, 47, 72, 127; in U.S., 121, 128
Schlesinger, Arthur M., 2, 40
Schmoller, Gustav, 105
Schuetz, Alfred, 29, 43
Schumpeter, Joseph A., 25, 42, 117
Sellin, Thorsten, 44
Shannon, Fred A., 60, 83, 152, 154, 169
Shaw, E. E., 83
Sheridan, Frank J., 140, 168
Shlakman, Vera, 118
Sicily, emigration, 146
Siegal, Abraham J., 13, 41, 178
Simmel, Georg, 28, 29, 33, 43
Siu, Paul C. P., 33, 34, 44
Sklare, Marshall, 44
Slater, Samuel, 84
Slavs, in U.S., 132, 147, 150, 154, 159, 160, 166
Slovaks, emigration, 79
Smith, Adam, 60, 83, 105
socialism, 1, 5, 9, 152, 154
Socialist Party, U.S., 153-155, 157
socialization: basic vs. intermediate, 29-30, 36, 37, 38, 89-90, 173, 174, 175
social mobility, 14, 67
social stratification, 8, 9-12, 14-16, 16-18, 38, 79, 80-81, 103-104, 138, 174
sojourner immigrants, 33-36, 123-125, 126, 132, 148, 160, 171
Sorge, Friedrich, A., 43
Sorokin, Pitirim A., 43
Spain, emigration, 47
specialization, in modernization, 58-59
Spengler, J. J., 136, 137, 141
Srole, Leo, 141, 148, 168
steamship companies, and immigration, 126-127
Stepanek, Joseph, 117
Stephens, Uriah Smith, 110, 111

Stewart, Charles D., 69, 85
strangers, immigrants as, 28-29, 33, 82, 175
strikebreakers, immigrants as, 130-132
success ideal, U.S., 30-31, 90, 91-92, 94-95
Sullivan, William, 118
surplus, economic, 56, 57
surplus value, 20
Sutherland, Edwin H., 41
sweatshop, 105
Sweden, labor radicalism, 19, 20, 23; real wage-rates, 1860-1939 (table), 22, 23
Swedes, emigration, 79; in U.S., 128
Switzerland, emigration, 47
Sylvis, William H., 109
symbiotic class, 25
syndicalism, 19
Syrians, emigration, 49; in U.S., 150

TAEUBER, CONRAD AND IRENE, 144, 167
Taft, Donald R., 53, 139
textile industry, 93, 103, 106, 121-123
Third International, 19
Thomas, Brinley, 71, 79, 80, 84, 85, 86, 125, 129, 138, 139, 140, 141, 178
Thomas, William I., 123, 124, 139
Thorp, Willard L., 85
Thurnstrom, Stephen, 117, 118
Tocqueville, Alexis de, 103, 118
Torgerson, Ulf, 42
transitional stage, in modernization, 13, 55
transport systems, 51-52, 106-107; see also railroads
Tresca, Carlo, 165
Tumin, Melvin M., 178
Turks, emigration, 146; in U.S., 127

ULMAN, LLOYD, 21, 42, 105, 115, 119, 120
unionism: Amalgamated Association of Iron, Steel, and Tin Workers, 159; American Federation of Labor (AFL), 5, 112, 154, 156-157, 158, 160, 161, 162, 165, 176; backward-looking, 107-108, 115; and business cycles, 155-156; business unionism,

Index

unionism (*cont'd*) 1, 2-5, 6, 21, 30, 36, 38, 135, 148, 160, 165, 175, 176; collective bargaining, 5, 112, 158, 160-161; Communist Party, 153, 154; conservatism of, 173, 175; craft unions, 3-4, 6, 21, 39, 108, 109, 110, 112, 114, 115, 175; 1827-1837 period, 105; eight-hour day, 108, 111, 114; Federation of Organized Trades and Labor Unions, 112, 156, 162; Garment Cutters Union, 111; growth of, 155-156, 158; humanitarian period, 108, 114; industrial, 4-5, 6, 21, 39, 158, 160, 166, 175, 176; Industrial Workers of the World (IWW), 19, 154, 155, 156, 161-167, 176; Knights of Labor, 110-116, 121, 127, 128, 130, 131, 134, 135, 136, 156, 157, 162, 175; Lawrence strike, 26, 163-164, 165, 170; McKees Rocks strike, 163, 164, 165, 166; membership, 21, 155-156, 158; Molly Maguires (secret organization), 110; monetary reform, 108, 109; nationalization of, 108; National Labor Union, 108-110, 111; Newburyport, 98, 100; new trade unionism, 1840-1860, 108; New York State Mechanics' Association, 107-108; "one big union," 112, 130, 156, 162, 166; paternalism, 24, 98, 99; Paterson strike, 164-165, 176; radicalism, 1, 5, 6, 18, 19, 20, 21, 22, 23-24, 25, 26-27, 31, 38, 92, 135, 138, 151-155, 156, 163, 174; renovating type, 89, 92, 108, 109, 110, 111, 114, 136, 175; United Mine Workers, 158, 159, 161, 166, 176, 177; Western Federation of Miners, 161-162, 163, 166, 176, 177

United Kingdom, 14, 27, 48, 61, 88, 95, 106; backward-looking protest, 13-14; coal and iron production, 66; emigration, 47, 72, 79, 127, 137; historical legacies, 7, 8; labor unionism, 4, 5, 7, 8; real wage-rates, 1860-1939 (table), 22

United Mine Workers, 158, 159, 161, 166, 176, 177

United States: agrarian-based society, 93-94; agriculture, modernization of, 58-60, 63, 64, 65; aristocracy, of business, 103; business cycles and immigration, 47, 71-72, 125, 155-156; coal and iron production, 66; criminality, of native vs. foreign born, 31-32; early employer-employee relations, 96-101, 102; early opposition to industrialization, 93, 94-96; farmers and middle class, 92; farm machinery, 59-60; first labor party, 20; horsepower per wage earner in manufacturing, 1869-1919 (table), 65; individualism, 31, 36, 90-91, 92, 94, 95, 99, 102, 110, 115, 128, 175; industrial production, 61-63, 64; internal migration, 72, 79, 80-81; labor force, employment status, 1800-1957 (table), 69; labor force in agriculture, industry, and service, 67-68; labor-saving techniques, 62-63, 65; manufacturing establishments, growth in, 1859-1919 (table), 69; mass demand and internal markets, 61, 63, 68; master-journeyman-apprentice system, 94, 97, 98, 99, 100, 103-104, 107, 109, 110, 113; money supply, per capita, 59-60; nonfeudal history, 18-19, 20, 25, 103; pecuniary success ideal, 30-31, 90, 91-92, 94-95; percent of gainfully occupied in agricultural/nonagricultural pursuits, 1820-1930 (table), 66; productivity, per capita, 58; railroads, 58, 59, 63, 106, 108; rationalization of production, 96-97, 101-102, 106, 110, 123; real wage-rates, 1860-1939 (table), 22, 23; self-employment vs. employeeship, 92-96, 97, 102, 107, 175; South and slavery, 93; urbanization, 144-145; voting rights, 19-20; wage-rates, 1860-1939 (table), 22, 23

U.S. Immigration Bureau, 153

U.S. Immigration Commission, 31, 32, 43, 44, 51, 53, 75, 76, 78, 79, 85, 86, 124, 125, 126, 132, 137, 139, 140, 141, 146, 167, 168

U.S. Industrial Relations Commission, 157, 163, 169, 170, 171

United States Steel Corporation, 159

Index

urban growth, U.S., 1790-1940 (table), 144
urbanization, of foreign born, 144-145; and industrialization, 143-145; proportion urban, native vs. foreign born, 1870-1940 (table), 145
urban native vs. foreign born, 1870-1940 (table), 145

VALEN, HENRY, 42
values and norms, and modernization, 38-39, 87-88, 89, 173, 177
Van Vechten, L. L., 31-32, 44
voting rights, 19-20

WAGE RATES: and immigration, 76, 79, 80-81, 121, 122, 124; real, 1860-1939 (table), 22-23
Ware, Caroline F., 98, 117, 118, 138
Ware, Norman, 108, 113, 119, 138, 139
Warner, W. Lloyd, 134, 140, 141, 148, 168

Weber, Max, 8, 9, 10, 11, 12, 40, 61, 83, 101
Western Federation of Miners, 161-162, 163, 166
Wheeler, Stanton, 116
Whelpton, P. K., 83
Whitney, Eli, 62
Wiers, Paul, 52
Wilcox, Walter F., 46, 52, 53, 73, 85
Williams, James M., 117, 118
Wittke, Carl, 52, 150, 168
Wobblies, 162
Wolman, Leo, 169, 170
Wood, Arthur Lewis, 32, 44
Workers' Party, 154
Wright, Carrol, 119, 159-160, 170

YANKEE CITY, 134

ZLOTNICK, JACK, 75
Znaniecki, Florien, 123, 124, 139
Zubrzycki, Jerzy, 53, 170